JACK CARROLL

And the rise of Australian boxing

PAUL CUPITT

Australian Boxing Books

JACK CARROLL

Copyright © 2019 by Paul Cupitt

All rights reserved.

Published by Australian Boxing Books

ISBN 978-0-646-80130-8

No part of this book may be reproduced in any form or by any electronic or mechanical means, including information storage and retrieval systems nor otherwise circulated in any form of cover or binding, other than that in which it was published, without written permission from the author, except for the use of brief quotations in a book review or for instances of 'fair use'.

While the author has made every reasonable effort to determine copyright owners for any/all photographs/images used in this book, there may be some omissions of credits; for which we apologise. Any additions, amendments or corrections can be forwarded to the publisher.

To my parents;

for always encouraging me to use my brain and follow my dreams.

CONTENTS

Introduction	ix
1. Early Career	1
2. Sydney	11
3. Australian Champion	21
4. Ambrose Palmer	37
5. Jack Haines	43
6. Jack Haines vs Ambrose Palmer	61
7. The Title Claimants	75
8. Fred Henneberry	97
9. Ambrose Palmer vs Fred Henneberry	103
10. Jack Carroll vs Fred Henneberry	113
11. Ambrose Palmer vs Fred Henneberry II	119
12. Ambrose Palmer vs Young Stribling	125
13. Fred Henneberry vs Jack Carroll II	135
14. Ron Richards	143
15. Fred Henneberry vs Ron Richards	157
16. Jack Carroll vs Fred Henneberry III	175
17. The American Invasion	187
18. Jack Carroll vs Ron Richards	211
19. Climbing the World Rankings	225
20. Jack Carroll vs Bep van Klaveren	253
21. Fred Henneberry vs Ron Richards VII	273
22. #1 Contender	301
Aftermath	329
Acknowledgements	339
Bibliography	341
Notes	345

INTRODUCTION

On Boxing Day in 1935, Arthur Hardwick, better known by his ring alias "Jack Carroll," climbed through the ropes of the ring set up at the Sydney Sports Ground in front of 25,000 soaked Sydney fight fans to face Bep van Klaveren, the 1928 Olympic gold medallist and number two contender for the world welterweight title. An unexpected storm had hit Sydney shortly before the fight was due to begin, but the Sydney fight fans still braved the elements to see the long-time Australian welterweight champion in action, such was his popularity. For Carroll, who was in the 14th year of his professional boxing career, it was a chance to cement his place among the best welterweights in the world as well as finally earn some decent money after years of fighting in front of half-empty stadiums up and down Australia's east coast.

The popularity of Australian boxing had suffered a massive blow after the death of Les Darcy in 1917. Darcy, who was just 21 years old when he died in the United States, had defeated a series of world-rated fighters. These world-class contests that were staged predominantly at Sydney Stadium had given Australian fight fans

INTRODUCTION

high expectations when it came to boxing. While Australia produced some talented boxers in the next ten years, such as Billy Grime, Tommy Uren and Frank Burns, the lack of mouth-watering domestic battles, as well as the lack of world-class importations, left few interested in spending their hard-earned dollars on seeing second-rate boxing. This lead to a decline in attendances, leading many Australian fighters, including Grime and Burns, to leave Australia at the height of their popularity.

While boxing had stalled in Australia, in the United States it was entering its most popular period. With the passing of the Walker Law in 1920, which legalised boxing with a regulatory commission as well as unified the rules, and the popularity of heavyweight champion Jack Dempsey, boxing was one of the most popular sports in America. Unlike in the era of Les Darcy, top boxers from America did not need to travel overseas to prove themselves among the best in the world, and there was little incentive for a world ranked boxer to go to Australia, where attendances were low.

Boxing in Australia was controlled by Stadiums Ltd, who ran a combination of boxing and wrestling at their major stadiums in Sydney, Melbourne and Brisbane. With boxing shows held weekly for much of the year, boxers were able to earn a second living by fighting in preliminary contests on these shows, and trying to work their way up the rankings, where they could headline and earn a larger share of the takings. The chance to make a bit of extra money enticed many young men living in these major cities to try their luck with very little training.

One of these was 17-year-old Arthur Hardwick. Fighting under as alias so his mother wouldn't find out, the lanky teenager from the Melbourne suburb of Kensington turned professional in 1923, earning a draw in a six-round preliminary contest at West

INTRODUCTION

Melbourne Stadium. Carroll's physical appearance hid his incredible ability in the boxing ring:

"Carroll is different from any other boxer to be seen these times. His skin is snow-white, whereas most of those we see are sun-browned. His face in the ring suggests years greater in number than those which have passed over his fighting head. But Carroll differs most of all from his contemporaries in his craftiness and cleverness, in his elusiveness, in his shifty footwork and most of all in his uncanny gift of hitting with the left from any angle short, sharp, stinging punches. He is the last word in scientific cleverness and in speed. Exemplary in sporting attitude in the ring, he is a colourful boxer. To sting him with a punch is to make him still more colourful until he becomes a veritable wasp."[1]

Although labelled as "box office poison" in the first half of his career, due to his physical appearance and the often one-sided nature of his fights, Carroll's popularity would emerge on the coattails of a series of middleweight contests involving Jack Haines, Ambrose Palmer, Fred Henneberry and Ron Richards. The story of Jack Carroll would be under-appreciated without telling the story of these four men. Despite being smaller, Carroll fought two of these men and actively sought contests with the other two. The bouts involving these five would usher in a golden age of boxing in Australia.

In similar fashion to Darcy, Carroll would establish himself as Australia's most popular fighter and, also in a similar fashion to Les Darcy, Carroll would defeat a number of the top ranking boxers in the world. At a time when the welterweight division, in which Carroll competed, was at the peak of its competitiveness, Carroll proved himself as one of the top fighters by defeating many of the best boxers in the world. At the height of his popularity, Carroll was headlining shows in outdoor arenas in front of more than 30,000 fans. The Victorian's popularity was only second to cricket

INTRODUCTION

legend Don Bradman, who attended many of his big fights and even organised to meet with the Australian welterweight champion in the days before his rematch with Jimmy Leto.

Less than ten years after his retirement, however, Carroll had faded into obscurity. Happily married with three children, Carroll did not relish the spotlight. Unlike many Australian boxers, Carroll did not invest his money, but instead bought a house and a car and, at the end of his boxing career, he continued to work in the abattoir that he had worked in while he boxed. This quiet nature is another reason why many have forgotten Jack Carroll. While Carroll never won a world title, his list of victories rivals that of any other Australian boxer, including Darcy, and his name should be mentioned among Australia's greatest boxers.

EARLY CAREER

The seventh child of parents Thomas and Elizabeth, Arthur Ernest Hardwick, was born on 3 February, 1906. Arthur's grandparents, David and Jane, were farmers who immigrated from the United Kingdom, settling in the small regional town of Kyneton, approximately halfway between Melbourne and Bendigo in Victoria. Thomas became a truck driver and had moved to Smith Street, Kensington with his large family. The smallest of the male siblings, Arthur used to hide behind his mother during fight scenes when she took him to the pictures.

Arthur first attended the Boundary Road State School, where he was picked on repeatedly by a kid he referred to as 'Jonesy' for his tall and skinny build. The first fight he remembers having was with 'Jonesy' after his tormentor challenged him to a fight after school one day and Arthur gave him "a father of a hiding." After finding that he could whip the bully, Arthur decided to hand 'Jonesy' some payback, and he began to bully his former tormentor regularly. The mother of 'Jonesy' wrote so many letters to the school about her sons bully, whom she referred to as 'Red Hardwick' that the teachers suggested Arthur changed schools and soon after he began attending Kensington State School.

At the new school, Arthur began wrestling and athletics, which he said helped calm down a lot of the bullying tendencies he had started at the Boundary Road school. It was at this point that he first tried his hand with the boxing gloves, although he said he preferred wrestling as a child. 'Red' attended Billy McWilliams' gym in Carlton with a friend named John Woolley, where they boxed under instruction on Tuesday's and Thursdays. The two also complimented their guided instruction by sparring with a number of friends in a nearby stable:

> "We had a smelly old set of gloves and the four or five of us would paste each other unmercifully and how I loved it, I couldn't get enough of it." [1]

Arthur loved it so much that he decided to try it for real and spoke to McWilliams about fighting a preliminary bout. Worried that his parents would find out about his endeavour, Arthur chose the name "Jack Carroll," the birth name of the popular Melbourne middleweight who fought under the name Charlie Ring, as his alias and McWilliams matched him for an "emergency bout" at West Melbourne Stadium. Emergency bouts were a part of the undercard on the weekly Wednesday and Saturday night shows at West Melbourne Stadium, and these contests may or may not take place on the night they were matched for, depending on the length of the other bouts on the card. Arthur's first bout was with Fred O'Brien as an emergency bout for Saturday 17 March; however, the two men didn't fight until Wednesday 21 March.

Still living at home and working by day at a flour mill, Arthur had to get out of the house and to the fight without being noticed, and then return without a mark on his face from the contest in order not to arouse the suspicion of his mother. Coming home during his lunch break, Arthur packed his bag and stashed it in the laneway by the house before smuggling it to the shop where he worked. He returned home after his shift and then left for the fights, telling his mother that he was attending as a spectator. While getting ready for his pro debut in the dressing room, in walked Charlie Ring, who said to Arthur "Hey Red, if you disgrace my name tonight, I'll disgrace you."[2] While Arthur told reporters in a 1936 interview that he won his pro debut, the first newspaper account of his career stated that Jack Carroll and Fred O'Brien fought to a draw "in willing style" over six rounds.[3]

Arthur's mother, Elizabeth, would eventually find out about her son's second job after Arthur told his sister that he had been fighting preliminary bouts at West Melbourne Stadium. After his sister had sold him out to their mother, she checked the newspaper but could only find reports of a "Jack Carroll," although he confessed when she confronted him. Although Elizabeth worried about him being hurt, she consented to him fighting but would thoroughly check him over when he would come to see her after every fight. Elizabeth had a knack for finding bruises that no one else had seen during her post-fight examinations of her son.

A win over Norm Edwards and a points loss to Tasmanian southpaw Horrie Conley followed. "Carroll's" fourth recorded bout, a four-round slugfest in which he stopped fellow preliminary fighter Reg Brierly, earned him a bit of early newspaper exposure. Described by *The Sporting Globe* as a "ginger-headed wildcat who lacks skill but makes up for it by his fierce fighting instinct" and "a lad who would rather scrap than eat," Carroll's "unceremonious, vicious swings" wore Brierly down. After dropping him for an eight count in the fourth round, a follow-up assault by Carroll forced the referee to stop the contest.[4]

"Carroll" won eight of his next nine bouts over the following months before a six-round loss to Dave Palmer on 12 December in which Palmer outboxed Carroll, who was mistaken in thinking he could outslug Dave.

> "A week or so before we fought I saw Jack Cameron stop Dave and I reckoned I wouldn't have much difficulty in doing likewise; but Dave, as wily as they make 'em, had me fighting him all the time, and he adopted the correct defensive and counter tactics that outpointed me. Dave quickly found that I wanted him to join me in a slugging match, so he did just the opposite. I wasn't versatile enough to make him alter his successful tactics, and he took the decision."[5]

Some sources list a second fight between Carroll and Dave Palmer having occurred three days later with Palmer winning another six-round decision in a preliminary bout on the undercard of the Alf Stewart vs Les Kemp middleweight title fight; however, this is not backed up by any newspaper sources. *The Referee* reports the bout having taken place on the 12th as a preliminary bout on the Ben Martin vs Sid Shannon undercard with Palmer winning on points "after a solid slugging six rounds."[6] An article in *The Sporting Globe* in 1928, in which Dave talks about his wish to fight Carroll again, only refers to one bout having taken place between Dave Palmer and Jack Carroll.

After a six round draw with Jack Smith on 2 April, Carroll graduated to his first ten round bout three days later, also against Smith, in what was an "emergency bout" at West Melbourne Stadium. In their first bout, also held at West Melbourne Stadium, Carroll built an early lead but slowed down in the second half of the contest, and Smith rallied, almost scoring a knockout in the final round, but doing enough to overcome Carroll's lead and earn a draw. In the rematch, three days later, Carroll again started stronger but had to survive a torrid final two rounds in which Smith hurt him numerous times with body blows. Carroll switched to southpaw in the last round, which confused Smith enough for Carroll to get through to the final bell and his early lead held up, earning him the referee's decision.

The 18-year-old Carroll, who started out as a bantamweight, had now outgrown the lightweight division where he had most recently battled Palmer and Smith. Standing at 5' 10½" tall, Carroll had a height and reach similar to that of a middleweight or a light heavyweight and six months after his bouts with Smith he returned as a welterweight to take on "Young" Roy Stewart. The two would fight three times over the next six weeks, with all three won by Carroll.

The first, on 5 November, saw Carroll win on points in a "whirlwind ten rounds."[7] Two weeks later Carroll used "wild cat tactics" and "threw punches from all directions and kept on throwing them" to offset the better style of Williams to take the decision.[8] With the excitement of the previous two bouts between Carroll and Stewart, the newly formed Geelong Boxing Syndicate matched the pair a third time to headline their first show on 9 December at the West Park Theatre in the Victorian town of Geelong. The bout didn't disappoint with the two men again trading punches for ten rounds with Carroll's work rate once again earning him the decision.

Carroll closed out 1924 with a decision victory over Doug Hamilton at Melbourne Stadium a week after his Geelong bout with Stewart. He won similarly, with Melbourne newspaper *The Sporting Globe* reporting that Hamilton was the better boxer of the two and perhaps even the harder puncher, but the endless barrage of punches from Carroll was too much for Hamilton. After taking a break through January, Carroll wasn't matched until midway through 1925 and had to make do with his wages at the flour mill.[9] An emergency bout with Red M'Kay on 7 February was not needed, and while Carroll was in training, he only fought sporadically in the first half of 1925.

After a six round points win over touring American fighter Sailor

Ritchie on 1 August, Carroll accepted his first fifteen round bout against Geelong's Darcy Lee at the West Park Theatre three days later. Lee reportedly came into the fight undefeated in his previous 24 contests, and he would prove too slick for the ring rusty Carroll, scoring knockdowns in rounds nine and ten but having to overcome a strong finish to hand Carroll his first loss since the Dave Palmer fight in 1923. The initial reports of a Carroll hand injury were published in October when *The Sporting Globe* reported that on 7 October he had recovered from this injury. This injury would hamper Carroll throughout his career.

Carroll returned to training, but a back injury would keep him out of action until March 1926, where he recorded two wins in the main preliminary bouts at West Melbourne Stadium. The first fight with American born Jack Reid saw both men "commence aggressively" landing heavy blows on one another over the first half of the fight. Reid had a big sixth round but Carroll's fitness took over down the final stretch, and he was awarded the bout on points after "severely punishing" Reid in the late rounds.[10] Jack Smith, who had fought Carroll twice in 1924 and had also won a ten round preliminary earlier in the month, fought Carroll again over ten rounds on 20 March. While Smith had success in the late rounds against Carroll in their previous two meetings, Carroll showed his significant improvement in their third fight. He severely punished Smith until the referee stopped the contest in the seventh round due to Smith's right eye being swollen shut.

Previously trained by Billy McWilliams, an ex preliminary fighter out of Carlton whose last recorded bout was in 1921 in Melbourne, Carroll relocated to nearby Kensington and began to work with trainer Bill O'Brien. It was a move that would have long-term benefits to Carroll's career. O'Brien, a barber by trade, was a technician who drilled the basics into Carroll and most importantly developed a jab to complement Carroll's height and reach[11] and this weapon would be used to take Carroll from struggling preliminary fighter to become one of Australia's greatest boxers. O'Brien was also a very philosophical trainer, analysing even the smallest of mistakes to death until lessons were learned.

Bill O'Brien
(National Library of Australia, nla.obj-148582450*)*

Carroll's first bout under trainer O'Brien would be against former rival Roy Stewart in a 15x2 minute round contest which served as the main preliminary to an international wrestling match. Having outgrown the lightweight division, both men were now competing at welterweight and comfortably made the limit with Carroll holding a slight weight advantage. Carroll's previous bouts with Stewart were wild affairs, but under O'Brien, Carroll showed the improved left jab, which he used to keep Stewart off balance throughout the first half of the bout. In the late rounds, Carroll's superior work-rate and fitness was the difference, and he won comfortably on points.

After an emergency bout with Bert Jenkins on 3 July fell through, Carroll fought Snowy Christensen on 10 July in a ten round preliminary contest. Christensen was a hardened veteran with a big punch, who had previously battled over the 20 round distance. Carroll showed improved skills again in the opening rounds of the contest, building up a clear lead after the first four rounds with his left hand. Carroll opened well in the fifth before making a rookie mistake of backing away with his hands down after an exchange and Christensen caught the 20-year-old with a right cross that dropped Carroll. Carroll beat the count, but Christensen sensed that he was hurt and ended matters with another right cross moments later, giving Carroll the first knockout loss of his career.

Reporting from Bill O'Brien's gym later that week, *The Sporting Globe* wrote that Carroll had suffered "no ill-effects" from the knockout loss and had resumed training. O'Brien had Carroll analyse his mistake and drill the correct technique in order not to make the same mistake again, but the loss was a big stumbling block for the young fighter. Carroll had just begun to emerge as a main-event fighter in Melbourne, and the knockout loss relegated him back to "emergency bout" status. A fight with Stan Reid, scheduled for both 24 July and 29 July, did not go ahead. After this cancellation, a series of boils left Carroll unable to train until properly until November.

Carroll finally returned from his knockout loss, taking on Bert Jenkins over ten rounds at Melbourne stadium. Unlike Carroll, Jenkins had been very active having fought in the three previous weeks leading up to the ten round bout. Despite the ring rust and the activity of his opponent, Carroll showed his class and won every round of the contest, taking the referee's decision. The win propelled Carroll back into the mix, and he was booked the following week against experienced Doug Hamilton, whom he had defeated in 1924. Hamilton had been a regular at Melbourne Stadium since his debut in 1921 and was known for his dangerous right hand, but he had been absent from the ring since the end of 1925. Carroll dominated the fight with his left and almost ended it in both the 4th and 8th rounds, but Hamilton's power kept Carroll honest, and he boxed cautiously in the final rounds to win the referee's decision.

Despite the two wins in quick succession at Melbourne Stadium, Carroll was unable to secure another Melbourne bout in January. At the end of January Carroll travelled to the seaside town of Wonthaggi to face their local boxer Gordon Kiely on short notice after Kiely's original opponent Frank Allan from Western Australia dropped out at the last minute. Kiely was a veteran of the sport who had just returned from a successful stint in Sydney where he even headlined at the Rushcutter Bay Stadium. Kiely was a considerable step up for Carroll in terms of both experience and size, having fought many 15 and 20 round contests during his career and his more recent bouts were at the middleweight limit.

Carroll weighed in at 10st-7.5lb, slightly above the welterweight limit he had made comfortably for the last two years while Kiely weighed in at 10st-10lb. The bout drew a large crowd at the Union Theatre in Wonthaggi. Kiely put Carroll through the ropes in the opening round with a left hand to the body, but it wasn't ruled an official knockdown and Carroll fought back on even terms, taking the fight to the hometown fighter. Kiely put Carroll down for a second time in the fifth round with a right hand, but Carroll rose and fought back strongly once again. Carroll had the better of the next few rounds, and while Kiely was landing the harder blows, Carroll had taken a slight lead on points heading into the 11th round. Kiely showed his experience in the final two rounds, however, winning the 11th and dropping Carroll for an eight count in the final round to take a narrow decision.

Despite losing the decision, Carroll received a "splendid reception" from the Wonthaggi fans for his effort in the bout,[12] especially considering he had taken the bout on two days notice. He returned to the gym that week and declared to *The Sporting Globe* that he was ready at a minute's notice to take on any welterweight in his class. His next bout wasn't until 25 February, and it would be a third with Doug Hamilton. This bout would headline the first smaller show in the Melbourne suburb of Richmond, with these shows taking place on a Friday to rival West Melbourne Stadium's Wednesday and Saturday shows.

Hamilton had fought twice at the Stadium since the December loss to Carroll, scoring a knockout over local Dick Flint before succumbing in the fourth to Queensland fighter Billy Samuels. Both men weighed in at 10st for the bout in front of a "well-filled house" at the Richmond Town Hall.[13] Hamilton started better in his third contest with Carroll and fought on even terms throughout the first seven rounds. From the eighth round though it was all Carroll, who scored three knockdowns in the 8th and dominated rounds nine, ten and eleven. In the twelfth round of the fifteen round contest, Carroll backed Hamilton to the ropes where Hamilton slipped to the canvas and injured his leg, after which his corner threw in the towel.

The win paved the way for Carroll to return to the big shows Melbourne Stadium and he was scheduled for a rematch with Snowy Christensen on 30 March with a £25 side wager reportedly placed on the bet. Christensen, however, travelled to Broken Hill, New South Wales for a series of bouts and Carroll faced travelling Welsh fighter Bert Bartlett, who was having his last fight in Melbourne before returning to Wales. It was a mismatch which Carroll dominated from start to finish and the referee stopped the bout in the fifth round with Bartlett outclassed.

SYDNEY

Carroll continued to train but was unable to get matches. In May, Bill O'Brien told *The Sporting Globe* that Carroll had "been in training for eight months for three fights" and that he would like to fight Snowy Christensen in a rematch.[1] His next opponent was local Red Scott, who was grossly overmatched. Carroll knocked out several of his teeth on his way to an eighth-round technical knockout. After the bout, Carroll took most of July off but returned to the gym in the last week of the month. On 8 August, Carroll outpointed another visiting British fighter Sid Buxton at Melbourne Stadium, scoring a pair of knockdowns in the second and seeing off a late rally from the visiting fighter.

Following these bouts, Carroll again sat on the sidelines waiting to be matched. While he had won four contests in a row, he was proving difficult to match in Melbourne. Boxing writer Frank Brown wrote about Carroll in September of 1927 that:

"The boxing public would like to see more of Jack Carroll, the promising young welterweight. He has done all that has been asked of him in defeating two boxers from other states, and it is time he was tried against a ring man just one grade higher. Carroll has speed and a hefty punch. He is game and tough. He is just a little raw and awkward in some respects. Ring Experience will remedy that. If a young boxer lays off too long he fails to improve. He can progress only when given hit contests which draw the best out of him. A man can only go so far in the gymnasium."[2]

With nothing on the horizon in his home city, Carroll took a break and travelled to Sydney in September for a holiday. While at a horse racing carnival, Carroll reportedly met one of the matchmakers from Sydney Stadium, and they convinced him to take a fight that Wednesday. His opponent was a welterweight from the New South Wales town of Wagga Wagga named Gil McGrath, whose opponent had withdrawn the day before. McGrath had been a regular at Sydney Stadium during 1927 and reportedly had fought 35 professional contests, winning 30 of them. Carroll was described as "well-credentialed" but seemed to be there as an opponent to help build the career of the more promising McGrath. The bout would change the course of Carroll's career.

Sydney Stadium, on the corner of New South Head Road and Neild Avenue in Rushcutters Bay, was the premier boxing stadium in Australia. Hugh D. McIntosh had built the stadium in 1908 to stage a rematch between heavyweight champion Tommy Burns and Australian champion Bill Squires, whom Burns had knocked out in eight rounds in Paris in June. McIntosh saw an opportunity to make a significant amount of money as US President Theodore Roosevelt's Navy was in the midst of a round-the-world voyage to show the world their power at sea. The bout was set to take place on 24 August with the American fleet entering Sydney Harbour on 20 August.

Despite the lack of interest from the 12,000 American sailors in town, 15,000 Australian's filled the Stadium to see Tommy Burns again knock out Bill Squires, this time in the 13th round, in a one-sided bout. On Boxing Day of that year, McIntosh would then promote one of the most historically significant heavyweight title fights in boxing history at Sydney Stadium. In front of 20,000 fans, with a further 30,000 outside unable to get tickets, Jack Johnson became the first African American to win the world heavyweight championship with a 14th round stoppage over Burns. Since the Burns-Johnson title fight, the Rushcutters Bay stadium had been the home of boxing in Australia. Les Darcy had fought the majority of his contests at the Stadium while great African American heavyweights Sam Langford and Sam McVea fought four of their six Australian fights at Rushcutters Bay.

Carroll made the weight comfortably, tipping the scales at 10st-4lb while McGrath weighed in right on welterweight limit of 10st-7lb. From the opening bell, Carroll dominated McGrath with his left jab while McGrath's leads failed to land. McGrath was in the contest early on, but Carroll's left was the difference, and he sidestepped McGrath's rushes with ease as the bout progressed. By the fifth round, Carroll was hooking off his jab and had cut McGrath's nose and lips. McGrath's ability to absorb punishment allowed the contest to last into the eighth round, where he was knocked down twice, first with a left hook and then with a right cross. The bell saved McGrath on the second knockdown, but when Carroll put him down a third time, with another right hand, early in the ninth round, referee Joe Wallis stopped the fight.

Sydney Stadium immediately offered Carroll a contract with the 21-year-old set to earn £40 per fight for three fights over six weeks.

Carroll signed the contract but went back to Melbourne for two weeks of training at Bill O'Brien's gym before returning to Sydney. O'Brien, however, was unable to travel to Sydney with Carroll due to his work and gym commitments. Carroll's second opponent at Sydney Stadium was Bill Torrens from the Sydney suburb of Newtown. Torrens had been a regular around the smaller shows in New South Wales such as the Marrickville, Leichhardt and Newcastle Stadium but was unable to graduate to the larger shows at Rushcutters Bay.

While Carroll was viewed as "the opponent" in his opening bout in Sydney, his reputation had quickly grown after his one-sided win over McGrath. Torrens began the contest well, taking a small lead in the opening three rounds with his aggressive style but Carroll had him tamed in the fourth round, and from there it was one-way traffic. Carroll used his left jab to set up body blows on the inside, which slowed Torrens down, before punishing him with left hooks to the head. Torrens took the punishment "manfully" and somehow lasted into the twelfth round of the scheduled 15 before the referee mercifully stopped proceedings.

Matchmakers at Sydney Stadium decided to test Carroll against a more seasoned fighter for his next bout at Sydney Stadium, matching him with former Australian welterweight title challenger Billy Richards as the main event of their Wednesday show. Richards, who was born in New Zealand but fought his entire career in Australia, had been a regular at Sydney Stadium since 1925. In May of 1927, Richards had challenged for the Australian welterweight title, losing a fifteen round decision to Eddie Butcher in Brisbane.

Richards had also won his last three contests, scoring stoppages over Sid Buxton and Jimmy Pearce and outpointing Wally Hancock, all three bouts taking place on smaller shows in New South Wales. There were rumours that Richards would meet

Australian welterweight champion Al Bourke in December should he be victorious over Carroll. Compared with Torrens and McGrath, Richards also had a polar opposite style. Rather than the crowd-pleasing, aggressive style that Carroll's former Sydney opponents fought with, Richards was a renowned spoiler who often made other fighters look bad.

Carroll opened the contest the quicker of the two men and immediately established his jab. Richards offered little effort through the first four rounds and, in the fifth round, referee Joe Wallis warned him to fight back, or he wouldn't be paid, which prompted a short-lived rally in the sixth round. Carroll tamed Richards' onslaught and was back in command by the end of the round. He punished Richards for the remainder of the contest and almost had him out at the final bell, winning the referee's decision by a landslide.

The win catapulted Carroll into the elite welterweight ranks of Australia. Carroll had quickly moved from struggling preliminary fighter to top contender and a match for the Australian title was on the cards. Al Bourke, however, had surrendered the title on a foul to Gunnedah's Hughie Dwyer days before the Carroll-Richards contest. Bourke had overcome the early lead that Dwyer, who also held the Australian middleweight title but had often fought larger men during his career, had built in their Leichhardt Stadium bout, and was fighting on even terms when he landed a left below the belt in round thirteen that left Dwyer unable to continue. The title was returned to Bourke two weeks later when Dwyer announced his retirement from the ring due to health reasons. Due to the length of Dwyer's reign at middleweight, his middleweight title declared vacant but the welterweight title returned to the previous holder.

Following the Richards fight, Carroll had accepted an offer to fight at Brisbane Stadium on 2 December against powerful punching Frank Austin. Brisbane Stadium was "well-filled" for the bout, and many fans left believing they had witnessed Australia's next great welterweight as Carroll methodically took Austin apart. His trademark left was there from the opening bell and, apart from the occasional right hand that slipped through his defences on the inside, the bout was one-sided. Early in the seventh round, Austin indicated to his corner that he couldn't continue and they threw in the towel.[3]

A second fight at Brisbane Stadium occurred two weeks later on 16 December against local contender Les Robson, and a victory for Carroll would likely set the stage for him to face Bourke for the welterweight championship. Major bouts in Melbourne, Sydney and Brisbane had now made Carroll a nationally recognised star. His opponent Robson was an excellent boxer whose skills outweighed his toughness. A number of his losses came by knockout while he was well ahead on points, including his most recent fight, where he was knocked out by Frank Austin. The clever Robson showed his skills against Carroll, outboxing the Victorian in the opening round, but his inability to take Carroll's punch was his undoing. He was hurt in the second round by a Carroll left hook but boxed well after until another Carroll left hook dropped him at the end of the third. In the fourth round, Carroll put Robson down three times, each for the count of nine, before another three knockdowns in round five forced referee Fred Craig stopped the bout.

After his two bouts in Brisbane Carroll returned to Sydney, where his handlers Charlie Pilkington and Sammy Chapman looked to see him matched with Bourke for the national title. British born Bourke, who resided in Newcastle, NSW, had taken a break from training after his loss to Dwyer but returned to the gym just before Christmas. The handlers of both men agreed to the matchup, with reports that the bout would take place on either 21 January or 28 January at Sydney Stadium. Carroll set up his camp in Sydney, training at the Sydney Gymnasium on Oxford street with his workouts supervised

Chapman. The title challenger had the opportunity to spar with the Italian 70-fight veteran Bruno Frattini to prepare for the bout.

Bourke, who was yet to turn 18 years old (he turned 18 a few days after the rumoured date with Carroll), was known for his lanky frame and dangerous punching power. Before losing the title to Dwyer, Bourke had taken the title from Eddie Butcher, a southpaw from Western Australia. Bourke first stopped Butcher in an over the weight bout in Newcastle on 17 September in the twelfth round before they fought a rematch less than one month later, which Bourke also won by knockout, this time in the second. Despite the rumour of the January fixture, the Bourke-Carroll fight would not take place until 31 March. Bourke initially asked for more time to prepare for the contest, and the January bout was pushed back to 25 February. Carroll remained in Sydney to train, sparring rounds with Irish middleweight Johnny Sullivan at the Sydney Gymnasium. Bourke's trainer, Tom Maguire, stated that Bourke was showing excellent form in his workouts leading up to the February date. Bourke pulled out of the contest after injuring his back at work two days before the fight.

Bourke resumed training two weeks later, and the new date for the bout was 31 March. The constant postponements affected the crowd and the gate; there were pre-fight expectations that the contest would draw over £1000. However, the gate was estimated to be less £350, showing the fight game in Australia was yet to re-reach the heights that it had in the days of Darcy. Bourke held a slight weight advantage, but both men comfortably made the welterweight limit during the afternoon weigh-in. Upon entering the ring, Carroll brimmed with confidence while Bourke looked anxious and hesitant.

It did not take long for the action to begin as both men immediately tore into one another after the opening bell. Carroll established his jab early in the first round, and while he was landing more shots,

Bourke was exchanging with him and was scoring with his right hand from time to time, although most of his punches were missing wildly. One particular right hand landed flush, but Carroll took the shot well and was dishing out punishment in a neutral corner at the bell. Bourke started fast in the second and landed a solid right hand and a left hook shortly after that, but Carroll came straight back and hurt Bourke midway through the round with a left hook. The champion boxed defensively for the remainder of the round, but Carroll kept the pressure on him although he was unable to land any more heavy leather.

From midway through the third round onwards, the highly anticipated title match was one-sided. Bourke went back after Carroll to start the third, but the wiry Victorian outpunched him once again. Carroll began to focus on the body as Bourke retreated and landed a number of left rips to Bourke's rib cage to go with the jabs and left hooks to the champion's face. Bourke responded with a right to the body to open the fourth round but was met with Carroll's rapier-like jab and stung again with a right hand. In the fifth round, Bourke was in trouble, and Carroll put him down for the first of three knockdowns with a left to the body. Bourke rose at the count of eight and finished the round, landing a hard right hand after the bell. The Victorian's left hook couldn't miss in the sixth and, after a punishing round, a pair of left hooks followed by a right hand put Bourke through the ropes and out of the ring. Somehow Bourke climbed back through at the count of nine and made it to the seventh round. The third and final knockdown came early in the seventh, another body shot ended Bourke's title reign. He beat the count, but the referee had seen enough and crowned Carroll the new Australian champion.

Jack Carroll
(National Library of Australia, nla.obj-148582356)

AUSTRALIAN CHAMPION

With Carroll at the top of the fight game in Australia, it did not take long for the challenges to come in. His recent sparring partner Johnny Sullivan, an Irish middleweight who had been training at the same gym as Carroll, challenged the new champion after the bout to a fight above the welterweight class. The Carroll-Sullivan bout would never take place, with disagreements between from Carroll's Sydney trainer Sam Chapman and Sullivan's Australian handler Charles Lucas, regarding the weight limit and the wager proving too large of an obstacle to overcome. Lucas, who was known for his connections in Britain and bringing British boxers to Australia, would eventually have an enormous impact on Carroll's career. Sullivan instead fought a rematch with Scottish import Tommy McInnes, who had just defeated Billy Richards. In April, Sullivan had won the first bout with McInnes after the Scot was disqualified for a low blow.

With no matches on the horizon, Carroll returned to Melbourne to spend time with his family in his home city before returning to Sydney in the middle of May to reportedly meet some American boxers who were being imported to battle the local stars. Carroll went back to work in the gym with Bill O'Brien and was showing great form, despite six weeks without a contest.[1] On 28 May, McInnes defeated Sullivan by decision, despite weighing half a stone less than the Irishman, and issued a challenge to the Australian welterweight champion for a welterweight contest with a £100 side bet. The challenge was accepted, and Carroll would box McInnes over fifteen rounds at Rushcutters Bay on 9 June.

McInnes had been hit and miss during his time in Australia, which was now close to a year. Arriving in September 1928, McInnes fought many top middleweights before slowly making his way down to the welterweight division. He had defeated Gordon Kiely, who had beaten Carroll and had won five of his last seven, with both of the defeats avenged in his previous two bouts. Carroll easily outboxed McInnes in the early rounds, scoring a knockdown in the second and piling up a huge lead through the first six rounds. In the seventh Carroll switched his attack to the body and shortly after this McInnes' tactics turned sour. McInnes received his first warning for head-butting in round nine and then repeated in the infraction in the tenth. When McInnes' head hit Carroll on the point of the chin in the eleventh round and dropped him, the referee awarded the Australian the contest on a foul. In a 1934 interview, Carroll would label McInnes as the hardest opponent he had fought:

> "Not only a good boxer he (McInnes) had good ring sense, and a firm knowledge of tactics; he was always trying to find a way to get past me."[2]

Carroll was immediately booked to face American Danny Lewis two weeks after the McInnes bout. *The Australian Worker* stated that Lewis was 23 years old, from San Francisco and had scored 11 knockout wins in his 39 professional contests. Lewis had shown good form in his public workouts since his arrival in Australia, and his reputation may have caused Carroll to give him too much respect. The Australian took a few rounds to get going, but while Lewis was game, he was never in the contest. The Australian champion had him in trouble in the eighth round but cruised to a decision rather than force matters, trying to end it inside the distance. Lewis' reputation and public training sessions may have gotten inside Carroll's head, but they didn't help with the ticket sales as the bout drew a below average crowd.

With Lewis and McInnes showing that they weren't in the league of the Australian champion, Carroll was hopeful of a match with Harry Mason, the British and European lightweight champion, who arrived in Sydney in July. Mason briefly held the British welterweight title too and had been campaigning as a welterweight in recent contests. Mason's first opponent, however, would be lightweight Tommy Fairhall. Carroll bitterly complained that he had only agreed to meet Lewis and McInnes if he had the first date with Mason. After Fairhall got the first bout with Mason, Carroll began negotiations with the New Zealand Boxing Association for a tour across the Tasman. On 6 July, the day after boxing an exhibition bout with former Australian welterweight champion Ed Butcher for charity, Carroll left with Chapman, arriving in New Zealand four days later.

The voyage to New Zealand was "one of the roughest trips on record" with Carroll telling *The Sydney Sportsman* that he would rather go through half a dozen scraps than have the four-day journey over again. Carroll's first fight took place two weeks after he arrived and it would be against another Australian boxer Harry Casey. After struggling through preliminary bouts in Queensland during the first four years of his career, Casey had made a good career in New Zealand where he had plied his trade since November 1925. Casey had won and vacated the New Zealand middleweight title and was unbeaten in close to a year.

The visit of an Australian champion was massive news in New Zealand, and Carroll was now the one drawing the crowds to his public workouts. The Wellington Town Hall drew a large crowd for the bout, and Casey wasted no time after the opening bell, taking the fight straight to his opponent. Casey rushed across the ring and tore into Carroll, who attempted to establish his jab to fight off the crowd favourite. Carroll wasn't successful until the second round where he scored with hard jabs that left Casey's punches falling short of their mark. Carroll controlled round three and was in command in the fourth until a left hook drove him to the ropes. Casey jumped on Carroll and the two men traded until the bell.

Casey continued to attack Carroll in the fifth, and while his attacks were often wild, he landed a huge right hand near the bell to end the round that deposited the Australian champion onto the seat of his pants. Carroll beat the count but returned to his corner groggy and fought the sixth round on the defensive while Casey wildly tried to end it. Casey worked his way onto the inside more in the seventh round but Carroll had more success with his jab, and he was back in control in the eighth. Carroll landed the cleaner blows in round nine and ten, but Casey would roar back with a barrage every time Carroll began to take over. The Australian champion fought well down the stretch, but Casey appeared to be the fresher of the two and rushed after Carroll for the duration of the final rounds. Carroll's jab continued to land, but he couldn't find the target with his right hand. Casey attacked for the entirety of round 15, but Carroll was fighting back gamely as the final bell ended the bout.

At the end of the fight, the decision was awarded to Harry Casey, handing Carroll his first loss since January 1927. The decision was met with an uproar by one section of the crowd, who believed that Carroll had done enough to win the contest. *The Evening Post* reported that Casey was the rightful winner, reporting that his more forceful punches and aggression were the deciding factors, while Carroll's blows lacked "vigour or persistency."[3] A rematch was scheduled, with the Christchurch Sports Club securing the combatants for a fifteen round clash on 16 August. Carroll wanted to stay busy and improve his fitness, and he agreed to fight another Australian, Charlie Purdy, in between on 9 August.

Purdy, from Auckland in New Zealand's north island, had just returned from Sydney, where he had defeated Bluey Jones, the Australian lightweight champion. Purdy was rushed into the contest with Carroll, fought at Wellington Town Hall, squaring off just five days after arriving from the voyage. The Aucklander was an excellent defensive fighter and gave Carroll some trouble in the early rounds of the fight with his elusiveness. By the fifth round, Carroll had found his target and was landing with forceful shots although Purdy still defended with skill. Carroll had control by round six and, while Purdy showed signs of life, he was unable to mount a sustained attack and Carroll systematically outworked him, scoring more and more as the rounds progressed. The final three rounds were one-sided, and Purdy was visibly tired, and while he did well to last the distance, he lost a wide decision to Carroll.

The rematch with Casey, which would be the first professional contest held in Christchurch in almost two years, was fought just days later. A purse of £150 was on offer for the winner, and The Municipal Concert Hall had sold out for the highly anticipated rematch. Casey again started well in the Christchurch bout, and his early aggression confused the Australian welterweight champion, and he seemed to have an answer to Carroll's educated jab, side-stepping or crouching under the blow and answering with punches to Carroll's body. Casey took the first three rounds with ease and appeared to be continuing where he left off three and a half weeks prior.

Carroll's offence was better in rounds four and five, and Casey resorted to rough tactics which made the fight ugly, muscling Carroll into the ropes and pushing him over them on two occasions in round five. The mauling continued in rounds six and seven. Carroll landed more to the body but both men often ended up in clinches, and neither looked eager to break. Carroll's jab finally found the target at the halfway point of the fight, and it proved the difference in the second half of the contest. Although he still fought in spurts, he won the eighth round emphatically. The ninth round livened up, with Casey taking his first clear round since the opening three, but Carroll came back in round ten and outworked Casey on the inside.

The final five rounds were all Carroll's. He opened the eleventh with a left hook that forced Casey back and then drove him into the ropes with punches from both hands. Carroll had little trouble finding Casey with any punches in round twelve, and despite a Casey rally in rounds 13 and 14, Carroll continued to tattoo him with punches from both hands and never looked like losing either round. Casey fought desperately in the final round, sensing he was behind on the cards, but soon retreated after Carroll again fought vigorously, and Carroll's domination over the last five rounds gave him the victory.

While Carroll claimed to be still feeling the effect of his voyage during the first fight, Casey blamed a cold for his sluggish performance in the rematch. Casey fancied a third fight between the pair, but Carroll and Chapman decided to call an end to their trip and headed back to Sydney so Carroll could defend his title, or fight one of the international boxers who had been brought out to face the top Australians. Harry Mason had disappointed in his Australian debut, dropping a decision to Fairhall despite almost a 1st weight advantage. Carroll arrived back home on 5 September and his handlers stated he would be ready to return before the end of the year. Both Harry Casey and Charlie Purdy also returned from

New Zealand after boxing each other to a draw in Palmerston North in September.

The champion took a break for two weeks following his arrival back in Sydney, probably to shake off the effects of the voyage that hampered him throughout his trip to New Zealand. Carroll resumed training towards the end of September and was back in shape by the end of the month. On 13 October, Harry Mason showed a marked improvement in his second contest on Australian soil, knocking out Billy Richards in the seventh round with a right hand to the jaw. With Carroll already in shape, he was matched with Mason the following weekend at Sydney Stadium.

While Mason was only three years Carroll's senior, the 25-year-old from Leeds was vastly more experienced, with over 100 professional fights to his name. Mason would be the first truly world-class operator that the young man from Kensington would face. Carroll arrived at 1 pm on the day of the fight for the weigh-in, weighing in right on the welterweight limit of 10st-7lb. Mason showed up much later and refused to be weighed in front of Carroll, reportedly coming in almost 5lb over the weight limit. Despite the international flavour of the bout, the description of the crowd was "meagre," and while a large number of spectators were there for Mason, his extra weight was as a result of poor conditioning and he gave a dismal showing.[4]

The former European lightweight champion started well, stunning Carroll in the opening round and getting the better of the little action in the first three rounds. After an even fourth round, Carroll took the fight to Mason in round five and six, and despite eating the occasional counter punch from the experienced Englishman, Carroll's work rate gave him both rounds. Mason was breathing hard by round seven and couldn't match Carroll's pace over the next three rounds, allowing Carroll to build a lead on points. Mason landed well with the right hand in round ten and eleven, but Carroll dominated the final rounds, having too much left in the gas tank for Mason to overcome. Carroll took the decision comfortably at the end of fifteen rounds.

After a short break from training Carroll was back at the Sydney Gymnasium to prepare for a rematch with Al Bourke on 24 November at Rushcutters Bay. Bourke, who twice pulled out of fights with Carroll before losing his title to him in March, again pulled out of the original date with Carroll, re-injuring his back by lifting a heavy bag for his trainer Tom Maguire. Carroll did not need to wait for Bourke again and agreed to a match with the New Zealander Charlie Purdy, whom he had defeated in his trip across the Tasman but who had shown good form since.

Purdy had since defeated Tommy Fairhall, who had also been enticed to tour New Zealand after his win over Harry Mason in Mason's Australian debut. After his win over Fairhall, Purdy had followed Carroll and Casey back to Australia. Many believed that this was a more attractive bout down due to Purdy's performances on his last trip to Australia. His manager, Pat Connors, thought that he could defeat Carroll this time around. Despite coming in lighter than usual at 10st-3lb, Carroll weighed almost half a stone heavier than his opponent at the afternoon weigh-in.

Rather than fight in his usual defensive style, Purdy rushed across the ring at the opening bell and took the fight to Carroll and landed a number of his blows. His defensive skills were still evident, and he took the first three rounds easily, scoring with clean punches on the Australian champion while making Carroll miss with his counter punches. Carroll targeted the body in round four and five and had more success, but Purdy was still fighting on at least even terms. Although Purdy was landing his best punches, they had no impact on Carroll short of bloodying his nose and mouth, and he grinned at Purdy as he landed a number of one-twos flush in round seven.

Purdy was getting the better of the exchanges in round eight until a left-hand cut his right eye, which sent Purdy on the defensive. From here it was all Carroll, who stalked the import landing vicious body shots while walking through his punches. A low shot in round nine brought a warning, but the round was Carroll's. He received another warning in the tenth round for a low blow, but his punches seemed to have Purdy on his last legs. In round eleven a pair of right hands had Purdy on the retreat again. Carroll gave chase and missed some punches over Purdy's head before he sunk in a third blow in as many rounds that landed below the belt. After Purdy collapsed to the floor, referee Joe Wallis immediately ended the fight and ruled Purdy the winner by disqualification.

Because the bout was fought under the welterweight limit, over 15x3 minute rounds and because Purdy had previously spent twelve months on Australian soil, the Auckland native claimed the Australian welterweight title after his victory. Carroll and Sam Chapman disputed this as they had agreed pre-fight for the bout not to be for the title, as Al Bourke was promised the first shot at Carroll's belt. Purdy's manager Pat Connor wanted a rematch with the title on the line, but Carroll decided to wait for Al Bourke. Purdy agreed to fight the New Yorker Harry Stone, winning on points on 15 December. Carroll injured his right hand in training shortly after the bout with Purdy and returned to Melbourne for the Christmas period.

After resting his hand, Carroll returned to training with his old friend Bill O'Brien and decided to have his first bout in his home city since winning the title. His opponent would be Carlo Galbusera who, according to *The Sporting Globe*, held the Italian welterweight title. Galbursera was touring the world on his own and was not brought to Australia by any promoter, having first fought many times in South Africa in 1928, but Carroll would be his first opponent on Australian soil. Carroll's Sydney trainer Sammy Chapman left for Melbourne to assist Carroll for the bout.

Despite weighing in over the welterweight limit, Carroll's performance in the ring showed that he was indeed in fighting shape. The Italian's wild rushes were no match for the Australian champion's skills, and Carroll showed that his right hand had healed, timing Galbusera's rushes with a right uppercut that landed throughout the contest. Carroll used his feet to avoid the wild swings and by round three was backing Galbusera into the corners. The Italian showed incredible toughness but was "cut to ribbons" by Carroll's blows, and after rising from a sixth-round knockdown, Galbusera indicated to referee Val Quirk that he had enough.

Impressed by Galbusera's toughness, Carroll told *The Sporting Globe* after the bout that he believed the Italian could trouble other fighters during his time in Australia.

> "I hit him repeatedly and with considerable force and it was amazing to me the amount of punishment he took. The Italian is game if nothing else. He comes in for more all the time and his ability to take punishment should serve him in good stead against some boys who may find him very worrying."[5]

The Melbourne fans were also impressed, but with Carroll's improved boxing ability after his time in Sydney. He was quickly booked for another bout the following week against the American Jack Sparr, who had defeated Tommy Fairhall in Sydney on the same night.

The match between Carroll and Sparr marked the first attractive bout in Melbourne in months with a lot of Australia's top boxers travelling to Sydney to have a chance at a national title. Sparr, whose birth name was John Spaw, had been fighting professionally since 1920 in America and was in Australia with Olympic gold medallist and former flyweight world champion Fidel La Barba, serving as his sparring partner. Sparr claimed to have never been down in over 200 contests as a professional, and his bout with

Fairhall attracted a large crowd. The fight would be Carroll's toughest to date and a chance for him to erase the loss to Purdy in the fans eyes.

Both men made the welterweight limit, with Sparr holding a slight weight advantage, and the matchup produced an enthusiastic crowd at West Melbourne Stadium. Carroll had the height and reach advantage, and he used it early on, out-jabbing the American in the early rounds. Sparr had success with a right hand to the body under Carroll's jab in rounds two and three, but Carroll's range and speed gave him the edge, and he opened up on the inside in the fourth, tattooing Sparr with combinations to the head and body. Sparr made Carroll miss more in the fifth and began to land short right hands in return in a see-saw battle.

Carroll sat down on his punches more in round six and, after Sparr fell short with his jab, Carroll landed a right-hand counter on the jaw of the American. Sparr took the blow well, but it opened a severe laceration inside his mouth. The corner stopped the bleeding between rounds, but Carroll had the blood flowing again in the seventh round, and Sparr appeared to be slowing down. Round eight was all Carroll as the corner was having trouble stopping the blood between rounds. Sparr rallied in rounds nine and ten and fought Carroll on even terms. Carroll fought aggressively in the eleventh and was nearly down after a counter right-hand to the solar plexus from Sparr. Sparr attacked as Carroll held on, but Carroll boxed his way out of trouble and was in command towards the end of the round. Another right hand further damaged the American's mouth at the bell, and the blood was pouring from his mouth as he returned to the corner.

After first pleading with Sparr to give in and then consulting with Sparr's trainer, referee Val Quirk stopped the contest before the start of round 12. Sparr protested the stoppage, but the referee and his corner were worried about the amount of blood he was swallowing. Despite the blood, Sparr's mouth injury proved to be superficial, and he was booked against Harry Mason in Sydney just three weeks after the laceration caused an end to the bout with Carroll. Carroll also planned to return to Sydney, looking to defend his title against Al Bourke but Bourke's back injury continued to plague him, and his doctor ruled him out of training for at least six months. Sammy Chapman stated that Carroll was willing to meet the winner of the Mason-Sparr bout during the first week of March at Sydney Stadium. Mason continued his disappointing form against Sparr, holding more than fighting and losing the 15 round decision.

Sparr suffered a cut eye against Mason, delaying the rematch with Carroll would for one week, but the bout was agreed to and set for 9 March. Carroll left for Sydney on 24 February and returned to the Sydney Gymnasium, impressing reporters with his speed in his workout before the bout. Despite training at Sydney Gymnasium, moments before the rematch with Sparr was about to kick off Carroll's usual trainer Sam Chapman had a confrontation with 'Slam' Sullivan, another Sydney trainer, and after a verbal altercation involving referee Joe Wallis, Chapman walked out as Carroll had hired Sullivan to work his corner.

Sparr boxed better in the opening round as Carroll fought almost exclusively with the jab, which Sparr defended against well. The jab worked well for Carroll in the second, and he landed it with regularity to the head and body to take the round. The fight seesawed again, as it did in the third, with Sparr taking the third round on the back of a right hand that momentarily shook the Victorian, and Carroll fought back wildly. Carroll took round four, again drawing blood from Sparr's mouth with a left uppercut on the inside and Carroll dominated the round and round five. He was warned in the sixth for a backhand, but otherwise took the round, and he was winning the seventh as well until a clash of heads split his left eyebrow.

Sparr attempted to take advantage of the injury, but Carroll began to time him coming in and battered the American in rounds eight and nine. After the two men clashed heads for the second time, another cut was opened, this time on Carroll's forehead. Despite being covered in his own blood, Carroll administered a beating to the American over the final five rounds. His left uppercut, in particular, worked well and his footwork twice caused Sparr to fall through the ropes. Many were calling for the referee to stop the bout in the last two rounds, but Sparr stood up to the assault. Joe Wallis crowned the Australian champion the winner on points at the end of the fifteenth.

Sparr had nothing but praise for Carroll after the bout and told the Australian champion that he had what it takes to compete in the US. A lot of the talk post-fight turned to the confrontation between Sullivan and Chapman before the start of the first round. Chapman insisted he had Carroll under contract and he would take legal action if Carroll attempted to fight for anyone else. Carroll returned to Melbourne and was booked to take on the American Bobby La Salle on 13 April. La Salle, who had reportedly won 90 of his 187 contests by knockout, was yet to fight since arriving from San Francisco but his debut would have to wait after Carroll injured his ribs during training and had to withdraw. La Salle fought Charlie Purdy a week later, losing a fifteen round decision.

With any interest in Carroll-La Salle killed off by Charlie Purdy, who was still claiming the welterweight championship and was pursuing a rematch with the recognised champion, Carroll was matched with another American Meyer Grace upon his recovery. Grace, from Philadelphia, was one of the latest Americans to reach Australia and the bout with Carroll was to take place on 18 May in Melbourne. The American sparred with Snowy Christensen, the only man to stop Carroll, in preparation for the bout and their public workouts showed that he both moved well and packed a punch. Carroll continued to train with Bill O'Brien after permanently splitting with Sammy Chapman, who had decided to take legal action with Carroll to settle the dispute with him in court on 30 May.

Despite Carroll's strong showings in his previous bouts in Melbourne, it was a disappointing crowd who witnessed the battle. Grace, described as short and stocky but with long arms, showed his skill in the first round of the contest, nullifying Carroll's jab early by crouching underneath it. Carroll had trouble adjusting to the lack of openings the shorter man's crouching tactics presented, and only lead sporadically in the first two rounds.

Grace himself did little leading but punched Carroll's body whenever he got close. Carroll had more success in the third and fourth round by dropping his left to his waist and throwing an up-jab, and his punches seemed to be bothering Grace, who complained of a low blow in the fourth and a rabbit punch in round five.

It was Carroll's turn to claim a foul in round six as he went down from what he thought was a low blow but the referee Val Quirk told him to get up and box on. Grace boxed well in the seventh until he was stunned by a right hand over the top. Carroll outboxed Grace in rounds eight and nine, and a sideshow had developed after his frequent arguments with the referee after he again claimed to have been fouled in the eighth, and was warned himself for a head-butt in the ninth. The American rallied after the warning to even up the ninth, but Carroll proved too sharp for him in the tenth and had the lead on points heading into the final five rounds.

A left hook scored for Grace early in round eleven, landing behind the Australian champion's left ear and Carroll, who seemed to take it well at first, then staggered and ended up on the canvas. Carroll popped straight back up but was clearly hurt, and a barrage of punches that mostly missed the mark sent Carroll down again. Carroll took his time rising, letting referee Quirk reach the count of eight. Grace was more relaxed in his attempts to finish this time and landed a right-hand flush on Carroll's chin that dropped him for the third time. Carroll couldn't beat the count and Grace had scored a knockout in round eleven.

Both men were full of compliments of one another after the bout with Grace stating that Carroll was one of the very best men he had faced in his more than 100 career bouts whereas Carroll described Grace as "strong, tough and a capital mover."[6] The fight drew a gate of £250, which was good business in Melbourne, where the fight game had stagnated throughout 1928. Attempts to stage a rematch would repeatedly fall through, and the two men would never again face each other in the ring. Grace would only fight one more time in Australia, outpointing Australian middleweight champion Ted Monson, before he returned to America.

The bout was a massive blow for Carroll who was on the verge of moving onto the world stage after his wins over Sparr and Mason. Some good news for the champion came less than two weeks after the bout when a Sydney judge ruled that he was not under contract to Sammy Chapman and he did not owe him money from his contests in January in Melbourne as he had not used Chapman's gym or any of his boxers as sparring partners. Carroll returned to O'Brien full time after convincing his old trainer to travel with him interstate for his future fights in Sydney and Brisbane. O'Brien viewed the loss as nothing but a learning curve for his young star, and the two men went back to basics, drilling the correct technique to prevent the mistake from happening again.

Despite the loss, Carroll was just 23 years old and was forced to fight international opponents because of the lack of depth in

Australian boxing. Another boxer from Melbourne, who had turned professional in February, would play a significant role in bringing boxing back to the spotlight in Australia, and the excitement generated from his bouts would boost boxing in both Sydney and Melbourne, which Jack Carroll would take full advantage of in the years to come.

AMBROSE PALMER

Ambrose Harold Palmer was born in Footscray, Melbourne on 16 October 1910 to mother May and father William (Bill), a former Victorian lightweight champion who fought professionally from 1899 to 1909. Ambrose was the third son of four boys, and the father trained his sons as boxers from a young age. Ambrose's older brothers Billy and Dave, who defeated Jack Carroll early in his career, were both professionals before Ambrose. Ambrose was the runner up in the 1927 national amateur titles, losing to Doug Barling in the final after he had captured the Victorian title earlier that year.

Ambrose had no intention of following his older brothers into the professional game, but when he was laid off from his job as a blacksmith's striker, he turned professional. Boxing under the alias 'Young Palmer' he made his professional debut with a points victory over veteran Hughie Whitecross in the main-support bout of the card on 20 February at West Melbourne Stadium. Rather than fighting four and six round fights, a practice that is common among novice boxers, Palmer debuted in a ten-rounder. Palmer gave away a slight weight advantage, weighing in at 10st-13lb compared to Whitecross at 11st. While he slowed down in the later rounds of the contest, his more varied work and his right uppercut allowed him to score a comfortable win on points.

One month later Palmer, with almost half a stone extra on his frame, was back in the ring against Reg Johnson. Scheduled for ten rounds, Palmer boxed smarter in his second professional outing waiting for openings rather than trying to create them and easily defended against Johnson's wild swings. Early on in the contest, Johnson complained of a rib injury to his corner and Palmer began targeting it with right hands to the body. During the second round, one of the lights over the ring exploded, and some of the glass hit Johnson, and the fighters continued with glass on the canvas; however, neither boxer suffered an injury. Johnson retired on his stool after the fifth round due to the rib injury resulting in a stoppage win for Palmer.

Wasting no time in advancing his career, Palmer headlined at West Melbourne four days later meeting the more experienced "Snowy" Moss, this time over a scheduled 12 rounds. Moss was also headlining for the first time in his career but had much more experience than Palmer having competed in ten previous contests at the West Melbourne Stadium for seven wins. Palmer started aggressively but was having trouble connecting solidly with punches as Moss choose to fight his younger, stronger opponent on the back foot. Palmer was warned for a low blow in the fourth round but scored a knockdown later in the round with a body shot, and Moss barely survived the round.

Moss was down again in the sixth, round but his experience allowed him to survive and come back over the second half of the contest. Despite splitting Palmer's lip, Moss' late rally was too little, too late and Palmer won the contest on points. Palmer and Moss met in a return bout in May, with Palmer's split lip taking four stitches and six weeks to recover. The rematch wasn't as competitive, and Palmer ended matters quickly in the 2nd round with a right uppercut to Moss' chin.

Dave Palmer organised for a group of Victorian boxers to fight for Stadium Ltd in Perth in a series of bouts in June, July and August. Young Ambrose toured with Tiger Andrews and Fred Johnson and while Dave hadn't fought since August 1928 and was acting as manager he stated he was open to bouts during the tour, however, he did not return until later that year in Melbourne. Ambrose only fought once on the trip to Perth, a seventh-round stoppage over local Irish heavyweight Pat Magill. Magill weighed in a stone more than Palmer but had little answer to Palmer's onslaught and was knocked down ten times during the contest. Perth newspaper *The Daily News* reported that Palmer was "by far the most attractive importation to appear in Perth in years."[1] Ambrose and Dave left Perth to head back to Melbourne two weeks later when Dave's wife became seriously ill.

With willing opponents hard to come by, American born journeyman Johnny Priston travelled south from Sydney to meet young Palmer. Priston had fought a number of the top fighters in the country, including Wally Hancock and former Australian welterweight champion Al Bourke, the latter whom he had knocked out in seven rounds in July. He had also faced Billy Richards and former Australian title challenger Jimmy Pearce since relocating from the West Coast of America. The fifteen round contest was scheduled for 17 August but had to be postponed one week due to an illness suffered by Priston.

Fighting in what was billed as a "15 round Preliminary" on the undercard to a wrestling main-event,[2] Palmer had little trouble with his more experienced American opponent, winning an easy 15 round decision. Boxing from the southpaw stance, Priston tried and repeatedly failed to land his hard left hand while the Victorian scored from the outside and tied up the American when they got in close. Palmer again tired in the late rounds but was well ahead at the final bell, winning an easy decision.

Ambrose Palmer
(National Library of Australia, nla.obj-162673690)

Ambrose served as a sparring partner over the next month for older brother Dave, who had an itch to return to the ring following Ambrose's success. Dave originally wanted to come back to avenge one of his four stoppage losses in 1926, a tenth round stoppage to fellow Melbourne fighter Dave Ross. However, he agreed to fight Tasmanian middleweight Gordon Kieley the night before taking on Ross! The tactic worked for Dave, and despite losing the twelve rounder to Kieley on points on 20 September in Wonthaggi Victoria, the rounds proved to sharpen him up for, in Dave's mind, the more important contest with Ross. Travelling 100 miles back to Melbourne to appear on the undercard to a wrestling main-event at the West Melbourne Stadium the following day, Dave thoroughly thrashed Ross. Scoring with an accurate left jab and using it to set up his right hook, the older Palmer scored two knockdowns in the seventh round of a one-sided contest before Ross advised the referee he couldn't continue.

According to records, Dave Ross fought one more time in his career against Ambrose Palmer, losing again in the seventh round on the weekend after his contest with Dave Palmer. This record is apparently supported by an article in Melbourne newspaper *The Argus*, however, when searching that newspaper, I could find no record of the contest. The advertisement in *The Argus* on 28 September, the day of the fight, makes no mention of any boxing, and only lists wrestling was taking place that evening. Sydney newspaper *The Referee* makes no mention of the bout occurring. However, it does list the results of the preliminaries that took place on that date as being on the undercard of a wrestling contest at West Melbourne Stadium, but there is no mention of Ambrose Palmer fighting Dave Ross.

Palmer did return on Wednesday 30 October, headlining at West Melbourne Stadium against Sydney preliminary fighter Dave Jackson. Palmer worked Jackson's body over the fifteen round contest and won the bout on points. Palmer closed out 1929 with a tenth round stoppage over South Australian journeyman Pud Segar. Palmer overcame Segar's reach advantage and wore the taller man down, dropping him in the eighth round with a right uppercut before a pair of knockdowns in the tenth round forced the stoppage.

There were concerns for Segar's wellbeing following the knockout as Segar collapsed following the bout. The fight doctor was unable to revive Segar, who was rushed to the hospital. No operation was needed, and Segar regained consciousness the following day and made a full recovery. After the fight, an inquiry revealed that Segar had lost significant weight in the days leading up to the fight and hadn't undergone a strict training regime for the contest.

With nine wins in 1929 and no losses, Palmer had established himself as one of the top middleweights in the country and, along with Queenslander Norm Johnson and Frank Vann, were in line to meet popular new Australian champion, Jack Haines. Haines, from the small town of Hay near the Victorian border in New South Wales, had won the title and was beginning to establish himself as Australia's greatest middleweight champion since Hughie Dwyer had retired with the middleweight and welterweight titles in 1927.

JACK HAINES

Haines worked his way up fighting in small shows in the south-east of New South Wales in the towns of Wagga Wagga and Albury from 1922-1927. In 1928 he relocated to Sydney and fought preliminary bouts at Leichhardt and Sydney Stadium. After a series of victories in the early part of the year, Haines would headline against former champion Frank Burns at Sydney Stadium, on 9 May. Frank Burns had lost both of his contests since returning to Australia, a fifteen round decision loss to Hughie Dwyer for the Australian title and then a 10th round stoppage loss to former New Zealand middleweight, light heavyweight and heavyweight champion Eddie Parker. Burns had taken time off after the loss to Daniels to try and build up his strength before returning to the ring. The former champion was a solid test for 20-year-old Jack Haines.

Haines fought cautiously in his first main event fight and fought as if overawed by his opponent's reputation. In the fourth Haines got going and deposited the former champion on the canvas with a right hand. Burns was up at the count of 8 and fought back over the next few rounds. Burns cut Haines over his left eye in the tenth round which, according to *The Sporting Globe* reporter "stirred Haines into action and he came out for the 11th round with a wicked long right that caught Burns behind the ear."[1] Burns was hurt and a second knockdown in the round forced referee Joe Wallis to stop the fight.

Haines hadn't impressed in his first main event as many in the press felt that he took too much time to finish off Burns. However, *The Sydney Sportsman* reported that Haines was a prospect to watch out for and that given his relative inexperience compared to Frank Burns, he shouldn't be expected to fight like a main event fighter.

> "His fight before the Burns battle was merely a ten rounds preliminary affair. Why expect him to step from that position and exhibit startling main-event form? The bridge is too big to be covered at a bound, and Haines, like all other fighters before him will have to gain his experience in a tough and torrid apprenticeship."[2]

Haines continued this apprenticeship with a 15 round decision win over experienced Sydney fighter Denny O'Donnell in June at Sydney Stadium. Haines showed his inexperience at times, and despite scoring knockdowns in rounds two and eight was unable to put his opponent away. Haines' trainer Jack Dunleavy, a former fighter himself who had to retire due to hand injuries, sidelined his new star for almost the remainder of the year firstly due to a hand injury suffered in the bout with O'Donnell before a skin disease in August again forced him out of action.

Returning for two bouts in December, Jack Haines firstly fought to a draw before scoring a fifteen round decision over Newcastle's Jimmy Pearce on 5 December and 22 December respectively. Pearce was vastly more experienced than Haines, competing in his 50th recorded bout compared to Haines' 20th and having fought for state honours on two occasions as well as a 16th round knockout loss to Eddie Butcher for the Australian welterweight title.

Having been out of the ring for the last six months, Haines, who suffered a cut in the first round after an accidental clash of heads, showed typical ring rust in the first meeting with Pearce. In front of a reportedly "good gate," Pearce got out to an early lead before Haines got going in the middle rounds and did his best work of the fight, especially in the 8th round when he had Pearce hurt. Haines slowed in the final few rounds; however, Pearce was unable, or possibly unwilling, to press the advantage and seemed especially pleased with the verdict when the bout was ruled a draw. Sydney newspaper *The Referee* reported that Haines did enough to score a narrow victory on their scorecard.[3]

Headlining the show at Sydney Stadium three Saturday's later, the rematch was a much different contest than the first with both men not afraid to let their hands go. Pearce opened the contest scoring with a hard jab but by the third Haines was the stronger of the two and he dealt out most of the punishment over the next 13 rounds. Pearce attempted to fight back, but with his left eye leaking blood from a cut he suffered in the fourth round he was only able to fight back in spurts. Haines received a warning in the 11th and 12th rounds for kidney punches but other than those infractions he thoroughly dominated the final five rounds as Pearce could only hold on in return. After fifteen rounds Haines was declared the winner by a clear points decision.

At the beginning of 1929, Haines was one of the best young attractions that Stadiums Limited had and was also a target for some of the more experienced middleweights in Sydney. Both Tommy Cribb and Frank Vann had publicly issued challenges to Haines, with the former offering a side bet of £20. The pair headlined at The Stadium on 16 January with the winner possibly in line to fight Ted Monson for national honours. While Cribb showed confidence placing a wager on the bout, he was no match for the 21-year-old Haines, and Haines won an easy points decision. Haines once again was forced to sit out with an injury after dislocating his right thumb during the fourth round of the bout.

Haines was matched with South African born-American citizen 'Oakland' Billy Harms on his return in a fifteen round bout at the Stadium. Initially scheduled as the main event for 20 March, the fight was postponed one week after Jack Sparr wanted one more contest in Australia before departing back for the United States following his second loss to Jack Carroll, and he was scheduled to fight Wally Hancock on that date. Despite suffering a cut over his left eye in the seventh round from a head clash, Haines easily defeated Harms over fifteen rounds.

The cut left eye would cause another spell of inactivity for Haines as he did not return to the ring for three months. Australian champion Ted Monson, meanwhile, wasn't showing championship form. The referee stopped his title defence against former Queensland middleweight champion Merv Williams in February and ruled a no contest after determining that neither man was giving his best effort. While waiting for Haines, the logical top contender, to recover from the cut eye, Monson kept busy with a decision win over Harms in June, however, this time it was the champion who injured his right hand, delaying any potential of a title defence against Haines.

Haines finally returned to face former champion Lachie McDonald, who had bested Ted Monson 2-1 in three bouts in 1928. The last of their series, with the title not on the line, was fought at the middleweight limit and was won by McDonald. Haines had continued to improve rapidly during his layoff, and he was maturing as a fighter. Despite McDonald's experience, he was no match for Haines at Sydney Stadium on 26 June. If not for a broken right hand in the sixth round suffered by the injury-prone Haines, he likely would have stopped McDonald. McDonald took a nine-count after being decked by a combination of blows in the fourth round and another in the fifth courtesy of a right hook. Shouts of "Stop the fight!" were heard around the stadium between rounds five and six however a right hand to the head early in the sixth round caused the injury and Haines used his weapon sparingly after that.

McDonald continued to take punishment against his now one-handed opponent, but was brave and fought right to the end. Showing signs of maturity and cleverness to box with just one hand for the last nine rounds of the bout, Jack Haines continued to display why he was the top contender for the Australian middleweight title. Haines' injured right hand required a specialist, and another layoff further postponed his long-awaited title shot.

Ted Monson, by way of default, scored a fight with the American Meyer Grace. Headlining at Sydney Stadium on 13 July, Monson was brave but overmatched against Grace.

> "Monson took a hiding, but he battled through to the end without a murmur, and tried to the last second to land a knockout blow. Grace, however, was too experienced to be caught by any of Monson's' "sneak" punches, and, for that matter, seemed too tough even when caught."[4]

Monson shook off the loss, again defeating 'Oakland' Billy Harms on points in an August title defence while Haines was ruled out until at least October with his hand injury. While Haines had missed out on the chance to fight American import Meyer Grace, his chance to battle another import came with his return to the ring in November. Not wanting to go into the title fight with Monson on the back of almost six months of inactivity, Haines fought Welsh champion Ben Marshall on 19 October. Marshall was still in Australia following an August defeat to Jack Carroll, the first loss of his professional career, and was coming off a win over Jimmy Mollette in Sydney. Monson took a short notice bout with Frank Vann on the same date in Wollongong; however, the title was not on the line as Vann missed weight following the quick turnaround after a midweek draw with 'Oakland' Billy Harms.

Monson and Haines' fortunes were at opposites on 19 October. Haines disposed of Marshall in the second round while Monson lost his bout with Vann via close decision, however keeping his title as it was a non-title bout. After briefly dropping Marshall in the first with a right hand, Marshall was badly knocked out in the second round with a left hook to the chin. Described as "one of the most willing encounters witnessed at the South Coast town,"[5] Vann defeated Monson via close decision, punishing the champion in the later rounds after a slow start before punctuating the performance with a fourteenth round knockdown.

Rather than granting Vann a rematch with the title at stake, Haines' recent performance and run of victories finally earned him the shot against Ted Monson for the Australian middleweight title:

> "November 23 is the date set aside for the middleweight championship battle between holder Ted Monson and Jack Haines. There is an idea that it will be an easy victory for Haines, owing to the fact that Frank Van defeated Monson a short time ago. But, as I see it, the title is in Monson's keeping til he is beaten. A tigress defending her young is not a lot keener than a champion saving his title. Champions have a habit of bringing out everything they have in them when their crown is in danger."[6]

Haines was expected to walk through Monson, with newspapers

declaring that he is "likely to be the best middle this country has bred since the days of Les Darcy."[7]

While Monson had struggled throughout 1929, losing in non-title fights and against international opposition, and even though many had already given his title to Haines before the pair had fought for it, Monson gave it everything before the referee intervened in the 13th round. Injuring his right bicep in the sixth round, Monson showed his grit by taking the punishment that Haines delivered and never going down. Referee Joe Wallis asked Monson after both the 11th and 12th rounds if he wanted to continue, but early in the 13th, he stopped the contest due to the injured right arm, and the punishment that the champion was taking.

Frank Vann scored a stoppage over 'Oakland' Harms the week before the Monson-Haines title bout, which made him the favourite to get the first crack at Haines' new title. Queensland's Norm Johnson was another option, having not lost since March 1928, and was coming off an impressive win over Tommy Cribb. Ambrose Palmer was also in the mix after his knockout over Pud Segar, who had previously defeated Monson.[8] These challengers would have to wait as Haines was matched up with American import Andy 'Tiger' Anderson on 28 December. Little is known of 'Tiger' Anderson. *The Referee* reports that 'Tiger' had 150 fights including bouts with "Ace Hudkins, Meyer Sullivan and Al van Ryan" and that he claimed to have never been stopped in his career.[9] Whatever Anderson's background was, he was pulverised by Haines in front of a huge crowd, who were expecting a much better showing from the American. Anderson was counted out after a body shot in the fifth round.

With the emergence of Haines, Palmer and Johnson, the Australian middleweight scene was exciting again heading into 1930. The title picture became less confusing as a result of Haines' dominance, and there were quality domestic matchups to be made. Frank Vann was the logical choice to fight Haines as he was more experienced than both Palmer and Johnson and his win over Monson was better than any that either of those two had on their record. Palmer agreed to travel to Brisbane to face Johnson, with the winner to be in a strong position to face Haines. Frank Vann agreed to meet 'Tiger' Anderson in Sydney after a fight with Merv Williams in Brisbane. After those bouts, Vann was willing to put up a £100 side bet to get Haines in the ring.

Initially scheduled for 3 January, Norm Johnson requested an additional two weeks of training, delaying the contest until 17 January. Meanwhile, Frank Vann stopped Merv Williams in the eleventh round on 10 January and then headed back to Sydney to meet Anderson at Sydney Stadium over fifteen rounds on 18 January; one day after the Palmer-Johnson clash in Brisbane. The middleweight division of Australia was somewhat shaken up by the results of both of these fights.

Little is recorded about Norm Johnson apart from accounts of his fights in newspapers. *The Daily Standard* states that before his bout with Palmer that Johnson was 21 years old and had competed in 24 contests for 21 wins and was on a 15 fight winning streak. On 8 August 1928, Johnson even fought twice in one night, defeating Vince McCann by 4th round stoppage on a morning show and stopping Ron Richards in the first round of the evening show.

Johnson moved towards the top of the Australian middleweight rankings thanks to wins over Tommy Cribb and 'Oakland' Billy Harms at the end of 1929. These victories were Johnson's first headlining bouts, and both opponents were brought up from NSW to test the young Queenslander. Cribb, who would score a knockout win over retired Australian welterweight and middleweight champion Hughie Dwyer the week after the Palmer-Johnson clash, was far more experienced than Johnson and "thoroughly tested Johnson's stamina and gameness" but lost a close decision to the young

Queenslander.[10] Johnson's win over Harms was razor thin, and many at ringside felt that the South African born Harms should have got the decision.

Despite Johnson having over twice as many bouts as Ambrose Palmer, Palmer had fought his last five contests over the fifteen round championship distance, and he showed more confidence in the opening round, punishing Johnson with both hands. Johnson boxed on even terms in the second but was hurt early in the third with a left hook and Palmer also landed heavily to the body. In the fourth round, "only Johnson's amazing toughness kept him on his feet."[11] Johnson fought back in the fifth, taking his first round of the fight while Palmer began to focus his attack to Johnson's body. The battle began to get sloppy, and both men began to foul with Johnson scoring a blow to the back of Palmer's head in the fifth round and Palmer earning numerous warnings from the referee for hitting below the belt in the sixth and seventh rounds. Both fighters showed signs of heavy fatigue in the seventh round, and at one point Johnson pushed Palmer through the ropes.

Palmer won the eighth round dominantly as he punished Johnson for the duration and he began the ninth in the same way before the sudden end to the contest. Palmer's assault forced Johnson back to the ropes where he dug in several shots to the body. One of these blows landed below the belt and the referee Major Fred Craig was forced to disqualify Palmer. Despite the fight taking place in Johnson's hometown, the crowd were unhappy with the referee's decision to terminate the bout and award it to the local.

> "A big section of the crowd disagreed with the verdict, and gave Palmer a flattering reception as he left the ring. He was the superior boxer all through and was well ahead on points when he deprived himself of what seemed certain victory."[12]

Johnson's hometown reporters thought the disqualification was fair due to Palmer's earlier infractions:

> "One foul blow can sometimes be overlooked, but not several. Palmer was allowed too much latitude altogether by the referee (Mr. Fred Craig), who should have disqualified the Melbourne youth for delivering low punches in the fifth round. Cautions had no effect on Palmer, and he punched Johnson low again on several occasions in the following rounds, and in the ninth session was disqualified. I had a look at Johnson subsequently , and he bore the marks of numerous low punches."[13]

Palmer had lost the first contest of his professional career, and the bout with Haines would have to wait. Haines' next opponent was up in the air when Frank Vann was upset by Tiger Anderson in Sydney the following night by a 15th round technical knockout. Vann dominated the American early on, scoring numerous knockdowns in the first eight rounds but Anderson kept marching forward and slowly began to turn the tide in the ninth round after barely beating the count following a blow to the solar plexus in the eighth round. The crowd began to cheer the American's rally in the tenth and eleventh rounds, and he scored three knockdowns in the 13th as Vann began to fade fast. Following two more knockdowns in the 15th round, the referee stopped the contest and awarded Anderson an unlikely come from behind victory.

Anderson won the crowd over with his victory, and it also earned him a rematch with Haines the following week. Sydney Stadium lost big on Anderson's upset victory, however, as the highly publicised bout between Vann and Haines was almost a guaranteed full house. There were talks of a Haines giving Monson a rematch following this bout to keep Haines busy and allow for the next viable challenger to emerge. Despite the one-sided manner in which Haines dispatched of Anderson in the first bout, Anderson's showing against Vann had won him a large following among Sydney fans, and many were expecting a better contest in the return:

> "I don't expect Anderson to win or even to have much of a chance of winning. But it is probable that he will make a far better showing than in his first bout with the champion. Unacclimatised, undoubtedly also "short a gallop," he met Haines at a very great disadvantage."[14]

Anderson gave a much better showing in the rematch despite only lasting to the sixth round and visiting the canvas seven times. Anderson attacked from the opening bell, but Haines was in a different class, timing the American's rushes and punishing him with body shots and uppercuts. Anderson was down three times in the third round courtesy of left rips to the body and was out on his feet at the end of the fourth. The fifth round was better for 'Tiger' as Haines took his time more and was careful not to make the same mistake as Vann did the week before.[15] Haines dropped Anderson with a right to the body early in the sixth round. Three more knockdowns from lighter blows forced referee Joe Wallis to stop the bout.

Ambrose Palmer returned to Melbourne following his disqualification against Norm Johnson, however, despite the loss to Johnson, a match with Haines was scheduled for 15 February at Sydney Stadium. Palmer left for Sydney on 28 January to train for the bout. A few days out from the contest the fight fell through. Whether Palmer was injured or not is unknown. The newspapers reported on 11 February that Palmer's handlers withdrew him and Palmer didn't compete again until 11 April, when he stopped Dave Jackson in twelve rounds in Brisbane, so an unspecified injury is likely.

Former Australian champion Billy Edwards, who lost the title to Hughie Dwyer in 1927, re-established himself as a contender with a knockout over 'Oakland' Billy Harms in Newcastle on 1 February.

Norm Johnson couldn't capitalise on his victory over Palmer and earn a shot at Haines. In his next bout, he was knocked out in the first round by Merv Williams on 14 February. A match between Ted Monson and Billy Edwards was arranged on 22 February at Sydney Stadium with the winner set to meet Haines for the title. Monson stopped Edwards in the sixth round after Edwards turned his back during an exchange and surrendered. Haines signed to face Monson in defence of his Australian title with the bout taking place on 8 March.

Monson was in tremendous shape having trained through December and January for the bout with Edwards following the recovery of his right bicep injury. His fitness showed in the contest as he gave Haines one of the toughest fights of his career. The bout started slowly as Monson used a high guard and looked to crowd Haines, who boxed cautiously on the back foot. The fight came to life in the third, when Monson rushed Haines at the bell and cornered him and unleashed a barrage of punches that kept Haines cornered for a minute. Haines looked to get even after escaping the corner and the two traded blows in the centre of the ring until the bell.

Monson continued to crowd Haines in rounds four and five effectively, but Haines had his best round of the contest in the sixth. He began to let his punches flow and scored with clean jabs and rips to the body before a left hook-right uppercut almost dropped Monson towards the end of the round. Monson battled back in the seventh, eighth and ninth rounds, opening a cut over Haines' right eye, but Haines was landing the cleaner punches and was punishing Monson from range. Monson showed his incredible toughness to last the fifteenth round as Haines punished him in the final five rounds. Haines put Monson down twice in the fifteenth round, both for nine counts, to put the victory beyond doubt. The final knockdown came with just seconds to go in the contest with Monson rising at nine just before the final bell.

With no logical contender to his title, Haines fought a keep busy fight in Leeton, NSW, approximately 100 mile from his hometown of Hay, NSW, winning a decision over Tommy Cribb on 2 April. Meanwhile, Ambrose Palmer was meant to be booked to fight Norm Johnson in a rematch two weeks after his victory over Dave Jackson in April. This bout, however, did not take place and Johnson wouldn't return to the ring until June forcing Palmer to return to Melbourne. Palmer, however, found it difficult to fight in his home state after Richard 'Dick' Lean, general manager of Stadiums Ltd, ruled that the only fighters who would be allowed to compete at the West Melbourne Stadium, which he controlled, would be fighters who were from gyms specially licensed by him. Among the top Victorian trainers who were not licensed by Lean was Ambrose's brother (and trainer), Dave Palmer.

Lean, born in 1892 in Melbourne, became Treasurer at the West Melbourne Stadium in 1912 and became the Stadium manager in 1915 when Reginald 'Snowy' Baker was bought out by John Wren, owner of Stadiums Ltd. Lean managed the main stadium in Melbourne while Harry Keesing managed the Brisbane Stadium and Harry Miller ran the stadium in Rushcutters Bay. Lean was a hard man who had a reputation for his toughness in negotiating and for holding fighters to every last detail in their contracts, and this partly helped Stadiums Ltd build the monopoly they had in Australian boxing.

The move by Lean and Stadiums Ltd to exclude Palmer from their list of licensed trainers was a blow to Palmer and the highly anticipated Palmer-Haines bout. After having nine fights in his first 12 months as a pro, Palmer was unable to secure a contest in the first half of 1930 in Australia. Palmer, along with his brother Dave and another Victorian boxer Bert Osborne, set sail for New Zealand to fight a series of bouts there, away from the grasp of Stadiums Ltd.

Palmer's first, and only official matchup, while in New Zealand was against 1928 New Zealand Olympic representative Alf Cleverley. Despite his Olympic pedigree, Cleverley was no match for Palmer, who won a one-sided contest, dropping Cleverley three times before the referee stopped the fight in the tenth round. Palmer also engaged in a number of tent' fights where he would meet any and all comers from the crowd, with the challenge for them to last three rounds. A fight with Tommy McInnes fell through as well as an attempt to bring Frank Vann to New Zealand to battle Palmer in August, so Palmer returned to Australia to again try and lure Jack Haines into the ring.

Meanwhile, Haines was about to build himself into the biggest boxing star in Australia. With no logical domestic challenger available, Haines met a series of international boxers who were imported by Stadiums Ltd over the next few months. His first opponent, Louis Vauclard, arrived in Australia from his native France on 24 April and had over 100 professional fights on his record, winning more than half of them. While most of his opponents were obscure, Vauclard had fought Ted Moore, who challenged world middleweight champion Harry Greb, 'The Pittsburgh Windmill' in 1924.

Vauclard's experience allowed him to last the fifteen rounds with the Australian champion, but despite some success up close in the middle rounds, Haines hurt Vauclard early before battering him in the final rounds, winning a comfortable decision. The bout was a success, with 8,000 spectators paying to see the one-sided contest, and they were impressed with Vauclard's ability to stand up to Haines' assault with talks of a rematch at a later date. Haines, however, was back in the ring the following week for his third bout in April, this time against the Italian middleweight Orlando Leopardi, who had travelled to Australia with Vauclard.

Leopardi was not as experienced as Vauclard, but he had also shared the ring with Ted Moore, losing by fourth-round technical knockout in 1927 and he had twice battled future world title claimant Marcel Thil, losing on both occasions. Leopardi was reported to be more scientific in his approach than Vauclard and looked to be in tremendous shape for his first bout in Australia. The Italian used his speed well in the opening round, but Haines adjusted and trapped him repeatedly along the ropes in the ensuing rounds, hurting him with a left hook at the end of the second round and staggering him again in the third. Leopardi boxed well in the middle rounds when he stayed off the ropes, but Haines mounted a body attack that took the remaining fight out of him, reducing Leopardi to a punching bag. Leopardi held on for dear life in the ninth round, and the referee crowned Haines the winner in the tenth when the Italian continued to offer no resistance to the assault.

It was the second week in a row that Haines drew a crowd of approximately 8,000 and, despite the one-sided nature of the bouts, it appeared that Sydney had its best draw card in many years in the young Haines. Sydney Stadium was keen to keep Haines active, and booked him in for a rematch with Vauclard on 10 May, followed by a bout with American Larry Brignoli on 24 May. Brignolia, of Cambridge, Massachusetts, had arrived in Sydney on 14 April along with featherweight Billy Hindley and lightweight Billy Golden. Haines was forced to withdraw from the rematch with Vauclard due to a stomach illness. Newcastle's Jimmy Pearce took the bout with Vauclard on short notice and scored a decision win over the Frenchman, killing off any interest in a Vauclard rematch with Haines.

Haines' bout with Brignolia was also delayed until June due to the champion's illness. Brignolia was an experienced fighter on the American scene, but his reputation was somewhat overblown in the Australian newspapers, who incorrectly reported that he had defeated former world welterweight champion, Jack Britton. Brignolia had fought Britton, but he lost the ten round decision in 1928.

Despite the experience advantage held by the 50 fight veteran Brignolia, Haines had much more experience over the fifteen round distance than Brigonolia.

The stomach illness limited Haines' ability in the Brignolia bout, and many felt that Brignolia also would have performed better had he more time to train. Haines' skills were too much for the American, and he won the fifteen round decision. Brignolia showed incredible toughness and heart and did not stop trying for the knockout while Haines fought conservatively, cautious of expending his limited energy.

> "If Boston Larry Brignolia possessed the boxing ability of Jack Haines, or if Haines had Brignolia's fighting instinct, one feels certain that either would go close to winning the world's middleweight championship."[16]

The champion's jab proved the difference against the crouching Brignolia, but the game effort from the import led to a rematch one month later. Haines showed the difference in class in the rematch as well as how much his illness had played a part in his poor showing. Less than a minute into the round Haines put Brignolia down after a brief exchange. Brignolia's crouch gave Haines little trouble this time, and he found his mark repeatedly, bloodying the American's nose in the third and swelling his eyes in the fourth. Brignolia took a beating in rounds five and six and somehow made it out for the seventh, where he was dropped twice causing the corner to throw in the towel.

Haines defended his title two weeks later against the Bathurst middleweight Johnny Shields. Shields was dangerous but not considered on the level of Haines, and his walk-up punching style gave Haines little trouble. The challenger "failed to land a decent punch" in the 202 seconds that he lasted, being rocked by a left hook less than one minute into the contest before being pummelled until the referee stopped the bout 22 seconds into the second round. Shields never went down, but the fight was so one-sided that many were calling for Haines to fight a higher calibre of opponent.

It was announced days after the Shields match that Frank Vann would finally get his chance with Jack Haines after calling for the fight for over a year. The two were to headline at Sydney Stadium, although Haines' Australian title was not at stake. An Australian champion only had to defend his title once every six months, and because Haines had placed his title on the line in his July mismatch with Shields, it was not a requirement that he risk his title in the bout with Vann. If Vann was to win their non-title bout, he could claim the title and force Haines into a rematch, with the title on the line. Vann had performed solidly since losing to 'Tiger' Anderson, avenging the loss in April with a fourth-round knockout before stopping Louis Vauclard and Tasmania's Pat Appleton, both in the 11th round, in May and July respectively.

The 5,000 spectators in attendance were not disappointed as Haines, weighing in slightly over the middleweight limit (11st-6lb) at 11st-7lb, set a fast pace in the opening round while Vann was content to fight him off with his jab. Vann tried to force the fight more in the second round but walked into a right cross which put him down. Vann easily beat the count, but Haines punished him for the remainder of the round. Rounds three through six saw Vann fight on more even terms, but Haines again had him in trouble in the seventh with Vann forced to tie the Australian champion up to avoid tasting the canvas.

Vann showed his gameness in rounds eight and nine, landing several hard body punches in these rounds although Haines scored with his body shots of his own at the end of the ninth. The first two minutes of round ten saw Vann launch an all-out assault, "punching for all he was worth"[17] although at the end of the round Haines hurt him with a huge right uppercut as Vann leant in on him. Hard left hooks early in the eleventh had Vann on rubbery legs, and a right hand to the jaw put him down for a nine count. Vann barely survived the eleventh and was even helped back to his corner by Haines at the end, but bravely came out for round twelve. After further punishment, referee Joe Wallis crowned Haines at 1:20 of round twelve.

JACK HAINES VS AMBROSE PALMER

Jack Haines and Ambrose Palmer were finally scheduled to meet after over a year of speculation, on 4 October 1930 at Sydney Stadium. Rumours circulated that Haines would travel to New Zealand to meet Palmer but Haines' manager Jack Dunleavy rejected the offer. Palmer had returned from New Zealand in August, but due to inactivity and the hospitality in New Zealand, he had put on significant weight. Upon his return, a bout with Frank Van was proposed, with the winner to meet Haines, provided Palmer could shed the excess weight, however, Vann didn't return to the ring until the end of October, possibly due to injuries sustained in his bout with Haines.

Haines and Palmer were scheduled to headline at Sydney Stadium many times throughout September, but Palmer needed extra time to get his weight down and overcome the inactivity. Haines kept busy the week before, taking on New Zealand's welterweight, middleweight and light heavyweight champion Artie Hay. Haines scraped in under the middleweight limit, weighing 11st-6lb for the bout, advertised as being for the Australasian middleweight title.

Hay, giving away half a stone in weight, was no match for the Australian champion, suffering three knockdowns in the second round courtesy of Haines' body punching before he was mercifully saved by the referee early in the third round.

While Haines had been thrilling Sydney fans with his victories over international talent, the Sydney fans didn't know Palmer, and his bout with the champion would be his first in New South Wales. Sydney fans were hopeful that Palmer would be able to give Haines a more even fight than they had been experiencing him in.

> "It is to be hoped that he (Palmer) will be able to make a better showing than the champion's last opponent, Artie Hay, and maybe he will. He looks huskier and bigger, anyhow, and, though we know very little of him in this city, the Victorians think a whole heap of him."[1]

Jack Haines (left) and Ambrose Palmer
(National Library of Australia, nla.obj-148564454)

It was a battle between the future of Australian boxing. The 23-year-old Haines had essentially mopped up the mess that was the Australian middleweight division, defeating what was left of the old guard and restoring credibility to the sport by establishing himself as the clear champion. The 19-year-old Palmer, who, in just twelve professional bouts, had boxed in Victoria, Queensland, Western Australia and New Zealand, represented, to everyone outside Sydney, the first real challenge to the young Haines' crown. The likes of Vauclard, Leopardi and Brignolia were hyped up as top international opponents but were no better than the Monsons and Cribbs, and the public's patience with the imports lack of ability was growing thin. Haines' dominance over his recent opposition had even affected his popularity, with less than 4,000 turning out to see the champion battle the young Victorian. Both men weighed in at 11st-6.5lb, slightly over the middleweight limit of 11st-6lb, which meant the title would not be on the line.

Palmer boxed cautiously in the opening round with Haines also, uncharacteristically, on the defensive, but appearing the more confident of the two men. Haines opened up more in the second and third rounds, and it looked as though Palmer was another challenger who just wasn't on Haines' level. The champion feinted Palmer out of position, landing with many hard left hooks and made Palmer fall short with his counters. Palmer was cut late in the third over his left eye but showed he had the fighting spirit to be in with the champion. When Haines landed with clean punches, the 19-year-old fought straight back and never stopped coming forward. Haines had built up a slight lead through the first five rounds and his ability to make Palmer miss that was giving him the edge.

Palmer, though, was growing in confidence and, after an even sixth round, began finding a home for his left hook to take the seventh. In the eighth, the left hook continued to land, and Haines started to feel the effects of it. Palmer continued to march forward in round nine, opening a cut over Haines' right eye and punishing him on the ropes. The champion looked in trouble at the end of the round while Palmer showed no indication of slowing down. Haines, sensing he was falling behind, rallied in the tenth and threw a "barrage of blows from everywhere that, for the moment, stopped Palmer almost to a standstill."[2] However, the Victorian's blows in the previous rounds were beginning to take their toll and Palmer battled back in the final minute of the as Haines' rally finished.

The pace slowed in rounds eleven and twelve, but Palmer continued to be the aggressor and was getting the better of the action. If not for Haines' experience and defensive skills, Palmer may have put the champion down in these rounds. Haines dug deep in the thirteenth, and while Palmer continued to press the action, the champion was beginning to score with punches as he had in the early rounds. Palmer seemed to be in front heading into the fourteenth round, and while the championship wasn't at stake, Haines fought desperately to keep his undefeated streak alive. Haines scored with heavy punches, but his opponent showed a skill level far beyond his experience level and made Haines miss more than he landed. Haines continued to try for the knockout in the final round, but Palmer never looked in trouble and won many of the exchanges in the final round. The bout was close with many at ringside expected a draw; however, the referee awarded the decision to Palmer, and the crowd cheered the verdict.

The loss was Haines' first in 27 bouts at Sydney Stadium and his first loss in over three years. Palmer had more than made up for his disappointing year with the Haines victory, and not long after the bout, there were already talks of a rematch, this time with the Australian middleweight title on the line. Haines was due to meet American import Tony Tuzzolino on 25 October but cancelled the bout to focus on Ambrose Palmer, with the rematched scheduled for 1 November, less than four weeks after their first bout. Instead,

Tuzzolino met Frank Vann in his Australian debut, scoring a fourteenth round technical knockout at Sydney Stadium.

Thanks to the showing of Palmer in their first bout, a large crowd was expected in the return bout with the gate expected to exceed £1,000. Additional trams were organised to cope with the large crowds expected for what was the most anticipated domestic bout in Australia for years. Palmer enlisted Frank Vann and Aboriginal welterweight contender Alby Roberts as sparring partners for his training camp at Pat Kearon's Central Gymnasium near Sydney's Central Railway Station.

Many Sydney fans felt that Haines' poor conditioning was to blame for his loss to Palmer and were expecting him to make amends in the rematch. Haines regularly sparred with Russ Critcher and touring Welshman Billy Thomas at Jack Dunleavy's gym and was said to be showing his old form. Interviewed by Sydney newspaper *The Labor Daily* Haines described Palmer as a "tough youngster" and "one of the best punchers I've met" and further stated he would be disappointed if he didn't avenge the defeat.[3] Both men made the middleweight limit on the afternoon of the bout, Palmer at 11st-4.5lb with Haines weighing a quarter of a pound more, meaning the title would go home with the winner of the fight.

Haines opened the contest well behind his left lead, penetrating Palmer's defence repeatedly but Palmer rallied late in the round and was taking many of Haines' leads on his gloves by the end of the opener. The champion's timing was better in this fight, and he nailed Palmer with a right uppercut early in the second, but Palmer's better infighting skills again allowed him to finish the round strongly. Haines' cut from the first fight was reopened in the third round as Palmer poured on the pressure, scoring with his jab and landing his right hand inside Haines' vaunted left hook. Palmer's left eye began to swell in the fourth as Haines had his best round of the contest and he landed a hard right cross that briefly stunned Palmer. Palmer, however, was showing no ill effects from Haines' punches and a left hook from the challenger sent Haines to the ropes late in the round.

Ambrose Palmer was much more confident after the first fight, and the pace he set was beginning to take its toll on Haines, who was visibly tired at the end of round five. Despite an apparent lead on the scorecard, and opening a cut over Palmer's right eye, Palmer was beginning to force the fight on the inside where he had the advantage. The champion launched a minute long rally in the seventh, earning him the round, but Palmer landed a hard right hand-left hook combination to Haines' chin in the eighth that turned the tide in his favour. He focused an attack on Haines' body in the ninth round, and a hard right hand inside Haines' left hook hurt the champion in the tenth.

A left hook had the champion in trouble again in the eleventh, and began to hold at regular intervals while the crowd "hooted him for cuddling." Rounds twelve and thirteen were all Palmer as he landed hard left hands to the body and right hands to the chin. Haines fought back more in these rounds, although Palmer was landing the better punches at the end of the exchanges. A left hook in the thirteenth made Haines' knee dip, but he returned fire enough to keep Palmer from finishing him. A left hook at the end of the thirteenth from the champion started a rally in the fourteenth but Palmer was the stronger of the two men, and his punches still had more force.

The crowd, sensing the crowning of a new champion, began to chant Palmer's name heading into the final round as the two men shook hands. Haines threw everything at the Victorian in an attempt to keep his title, and the two men were engaged in a fierce exchange as the final bell sounded.. Referee Joe Wallis, however, ruled the fight a draw, meaning that Haines would retain his title. The crowd reportedly booed the decision for many minutes after the conclusion of the contest. The reaction to the decision seems to be in favour of Palmer, with newspapers *The Referee*, *The Australian Worker* and *The Sporting Globe* all agreeing that he should have won the contest. However, *The Labor Daily* reported that a draw was a good decision as Haines had the better of the early goings while Palmer finished the stronger:

> "Not for years has such a crowd witnessed so glorious a spectacle. Referee Wallis refused to split hairs and called it a draw. His summation, although in accordance with the rules - and writer's opinion - found little favour with the multitude. Fight crowds have the habit of favouring the "underdog." Certain prejudices against Haines, and the desire to see Palmer succeed, probably influenced some of the regulars in their opinion."[4]

Sydney newspaper *The Truth* also believed the decision was a correct one and spoke to both fighters after the contest, who, while comparing battle wounds backstage, both agreed that a draw was the correct decision. There was great mutual respect after the fight with Palmer stating that "I let go with everything and was content to get a draw out of it. But, lemme tell you, that fellow certainly makes you fight!"[5]

Financially the fight was a huge success. Depending on the source, between 10,000 and 12,000 fans were in attendance at Sydney Stadium, with the takings approximately £1,300. *The Sydney Sportsman* stated that "the depression was run out of town on a set of boxing gloves"[6] and praised the matchup between two top domestic fighters after the series of disappointing bouts featuring overmatched imports. The logical next match to make was a third fight between the two men, and there were talks of staging the contest in Melbourne at the end of November. Dick Lean, however, suspended the boxing season in Melbourne for the remainder of 1930, due to poor showings, shooting down any talk Melbourne hosting the third fight.

A nose injury then ruled Palmer out until at least December, and he returned to Melbourne to recover. Haines would keep busy by facing Italian import Emiliano Bernasconi on 29 November. Little was known of Bernasconi outside of Italy. A special clause in regards to the weigh-in was introduced into the contract when he arrived in Australia as Bernasconi looked much larger than a middleweight. The Italian would have to make the middleweight limit at 2 pm on the day of the fight or forfeit £100. The weigh-in drama proved to be just that as both men made the middleweight limit with Bernasconi having a slight weight advantage on the scales.

Many Italian-Australians living in Sydney were in attendance to support their countryman and while Bernasconi had impressed reporters with his workouts in the lead up to the contest, his performance on fight night was anything but impressive. Haines took control immediately, proving too quick for the crude style of the Italian, and while Bernasconi took his shots well and fired back initially, he began employing dirty tactics from the second round. The fouls only spurred Haines on, and he started dishing out a one-sided beating in rounds three and four while the import landed mostly low punches and kidney punches.

Bernasconi came back and fought well in round five and started round six well until he landed a hard low blow that almost had him disqualified. Haines scored with a pair of vicious body punches that made Bernasconi visibly wince at the end of the round. Another hard left rip to the liver landed early in the seventh before an uppercut to the chin deposited Bernasconi on the canvas. He beat the count, but he had nothing left. Bernasconi tried to hold and run, but after taking a right hook, he turned his back and quit forcing referee Joe Wallis to stop the bout and award it to Haines on a technical knockout.

Many called for Bernasconi to be put on the next ship out of Australia after his poor showing. Haines was to meet Belgian import Walter Libert the following weekend, but Libert suffered a severe cut to his eye in his last spar two days before the fight. Sydney Stadium offered American Herman Bundren, who had knocked out Bob Thornton in his Australian debut, as a short notice replacement but the Haines camp turned it down as he had a slight hand injury and didn't want to risk it before the third fight with Palmer. Bernasconi did fight once more in Australia, losing a first-round knockout to Bundren in January before he returned to Europe where he fought professionally until 1935.

Palmer's nose injury had healed by the time of the Haines-Libert cancellation and on 10 December Palmer travelled north to Sydney to prepare for the third contest with Haines, which would take place on 27 December at Sydney Stadium. The Melbourne fans were disappointed that the bout occurred in Sydney, but the Sydney fans were again expected to attend Rushcutters Bay in record numbers. Haines resumed training the following week, but at first, it appeared he would be working with a new corner after a disagreement with regular trainer Jack Dunleavy led to the pair dissolving their relationship. The two men sat down the following day and came to an agreement and Haines would go into the biggest fight of his career with his long-time Sydney trainer.

Palmer returned to Pat Kearon's gym to complete his preparations for his second tilt at the title where he drew a large crowd for his workouts in the weeks leading up to the bout. Before his afternoon gym workouts with sparring partners Bob Thornton, Jack Heeney and Norky Fowler, Palmer did his morning roadwork at Balmain. Haines was also drawing a large crowd at Dunleavy's, sparring Tommy Cribb, Lex Tyers and Denny O'Donnell while his morning roadwork was usually in Centennial Park. The attention both men received during training showed the public's anticipation to see who the best middleweight in the country was.

Further to this, many local hotels in the area were being booked out for the weekend of the fight. Many were expecting the takings on fight night to almost double that of the second bout between the two men. Both men skipped their Christmas dinner to make sure they were under the weight limit, completing their last spars on Christmas Day. Palmer reportedly had a small amount of weight still to lose when he checked his weight on Christmas, but there were no dramas on the day of the fight, both men tipped the scales under the middleweight limit of 11st-6lb placing the championship on the line.

The attendance for the third bout between the two best middleweights in the country was the largest seen at Sydney Stadium in close to ten years, with close to 13,000 in attendance. Haines entered the ring first to a massive ovation with Palmer, who also being received well by the crowd, arriving a few minutes later with a big grin on his face. Haines established his jab in the opening round and looked to land his left hook off it while Palmer boxed cautiously and picked his shots, focusing mainly on the body of the champion. Haines speed gave him the edge in rounds one and two, and his best punches were right hands to the heart. However, Palmer's defence was tight, and he blocked many of the shots, beginning to open up more towards the end of the round.

Palmer got going in the round three, landing a hard right hand to Haines' chin in the opening seconds. The challenger backed the champion up with his jab and landed another right hand. Haines fought back on the inside, but Palmer got the better of the exchanges and took the third round. The champion had the edge in the fourth with his superior hand speed. Palmer received a warning for a low blow in the fourth round, but the shot did not faze

Haines, who landed his left hand at will at the end of the round. The Victorian scored with a left to the body in round five that drew another complaint from Haines, but the referee told him to keep fighting, and Palmer opened up, landing his own left hook a number of times to take the fifth.

Haines showed his class and began to pull away in the middle rounds, drawing blood from Palmer's troublesome nose in round six while using his superior hand and foot speed to outbox the Victorian in the seventh. The champion landed heavy blows in the eighth, and a right hand sent Palmer to his knees, although he was up before a count began. The crowd sensed Haines was on the verge of a knockout and wildly cheered as he punished Palmer with both hands following the knockdown. Palmer stood up to the onslaught, returning to his corner with blood streaming from his nose and a cut over his left eye, but Haines had the clear advantage on points going into the second half of the fight.

Despite the blood, Palmer marched forward in round nine and Haines gave ground and boxed on the back foot in an evenly fought round. Palmer continued to dig shots into the body of Haines in the tenth and, sensing he was behind on points, fought at a much faster pace to try and close the gap on the referee's scorecard. Haines still had the advantage in speed, but Palmer's body punching was beginning to slow him down. In the tenth, Haines was forced to clinch after a left hook to the head rattled him and the challenger continued with his body assault in round eleven before he again wobbled Haines with a left hook to the head halfway through the round. Haines clinched to clear his head then rallied, landing body shots of his own in return before scoring with a pair of right hands to the head to even up the round.

Haines looked unsteady as he came out for round twelve and early in the round Palmer landed with a left hand to the body which hurt Haines, who tried to complain the punch was low but referee Joe

Wallis dismissed this and told him to continue. Sensing Haines was tiring, Palmer backed the champion up with his left and landed heavily with a right hand to the side of the head before dropping him with a left hook. Haines was clearly hurt as he beat the count and Palmer immediately dropped him a second time. The champion beat the count but had nothing left, and a barrage of punches put him down for the third time in the round, and Joe Wallis counted him out at 1min 20seconds of round twelve.

Palmer was ecstatic after the fight and embraced with his father Bill who had worked his corner as the crowd wildly reacted to the dramatic ending. The live gate totalled £1,700 leaving both men just under £420 each, an amount that was surpassing the entire takings at the Stadium before the emergence of Haines. Although he was conscious, Haines remained on the canvas following the knockout where he was assisted by his seconds to Palmer's corner. He was at first unable to rise from the stool, but after a few moments had passed, he left the ring unassisted and returned to his dressing room.

The stadium medical officer Dr Sydney Jones examined him and advised him to rest, and Haines returned to his home that evening. Not long after arriving home, Haines collapsed and was taken by Ambulance to St Vincent's Hospital. Haines was diagnosed as having suffered a cerebral haemorrhage but did not require surgery and was placed under observation while he remained in hospital. Haines' family were by his side when he regained consciousness on Sunday afternoon, and he was able to communicate with them. By Tuesday his condition was described as improving, and although he was still critical, there was greater hope for his recovery.

Palmer, who celebrated his victory immediately after, found out about the injuries of his opponent the next day, which ended his celebrations. The new champion attempted to see Haines in the hospital on the day after, but the hospital staff informed that he was not in a condition to receive visitors. Palmer returned to Melbourne a few days after the fight to a large attendance who were there to congratulate the 21-year-old champion. Palmer's return would be short-lived as he was booked in to fight in Sydney a few weeks into the new year, although Palmer delayed the bout as he stated he was not mentally fit to train while Haines remained in hospital.

Haines' condition declined and improved during the week before he was eventually released more than a month after losing his title. The sudden fall from grace of Jack Haines had many criticising his schedule and the number of big fights he had taken on so quickly. Described only thirteen months ago as the new Les Darcy, Haines had fought his last bout at the age of 23. He stayed involved with boxing, working as a referee at Leichhardt Stadium for the next 20 years. Although Haines was not around to profit from his popularity, the trilogy between him and Palmer was the economic boost that Australian boxing required and. With Palmer hailing from Victoria, many in Melbourne were now keen to see him in action. Victoria now had two Australian champions as Carroll was also still recognised as the welterweight champion, and the ensuing popularity of Palmer nationwide would propel boxing back to the mainstream in Australia.

THE TITLE CLAIMANTS

Carroll returned to training following his loss to Meyer Grace in 1929 with a rematch scheduled for 15 June at West Melbourne Stadium. Grace however injured his hand during an exhibition bout used to drum up interest for the rematch just days before and Carroll instead faced last-minute replacement Jim Mollette, a stablemate of Grace's. Mollette, from Chicago, had looked good during his workouts but not many gave him a chance with Carroll. The opening round proved this as Carroll systematically broke down the American. Carroll rarely missed with his left jab, bloodying Mollette's nose and mouth in round three and set a pace so high that Mollette was tired by round eight. He finally went down in round eleven but soldiered on until the end of the twelfth, where his corner pulled him out.

It was an impressive return for Carroll, who showed no ill effects from the knockout loss to Meyer Grace just one month before. There were attempts to make the rematch once again after the Mollette bout, but this time it was Carroll who had to withdraw due to a hand injury. Grace headed to Sydney to meet Ted Monson at which point Carroll accepted an offer to travel to Brisbane for a fight against former opponent Billy Richards on 26 July. Richards, based in Sydney, had a massive following in Brisbane having fought there regularly since 1926 and he hadn't lost to an Australian since the bout with Carroll. While Carroll made arrangements to travel to Queensland, Richards fought a warm-up with Mollette in Brisbane on 12 July.

The warm-up proved disastrous as Richards first injured his right hand early in the bout and then, while ahead on points, Mollette caught him with a right hand in the thirteenth round, dropping him heavily. He barely beat the count and was on unsteady legs before going down a second time without being hit, forcing referee Fred Craig to disqualify Richards. The result and the injury to Richards meant that Mollette would get his second chance with Carroll on 26 July. With more ring time under his belt and two weeks, rather than two days, to train for the return match, the Brisbane fans were looking forward to seeing the contest.

On the same night as the Mollette-Richards contest, Sydney welterweight Wally Hancock, who had taken Charlie Purdy's claim as the welterweight champion of Australia with a controversial 4th round knockout in June, again stopped Purdy, this time in 12, to strengthen his claim and interest in a fight with Carroll. Hancock, who was born in Britain but had fought his entire professional career in Australia, was wildly inconsistent. The ex-sailor had all but ended the career of former Australian champion Eddie Butcher and also knocked out Al Bourke as well as Purdy but had lost bouts to Newcastle fighters Jimmy Pearce and Bluey Jones as well as a one-sided loss to Jack Sparr. His first win over Purdy came from a punch that was landed "long after the bell,"[1] but his second win proved his claim. Despite Carroll's success against international opponents, Hancock's claim was strengthening in the media, and many were referring to Carroll as the ex-welterweight champion.

Carroll journeyed to Brisbane with his trainer Bill O'Brien on Sunday 21 July. It was the first time O'Brien had travelled interstate with his charge as Carroll had used Sammy Chapman before the pair severed ties. Carroll held a weight advantage of close to half a stone at the 3 pm weigh-in for the rematch. Despite Mollette having more time to prepare for the rematch, Carroll thrashed him in half the time. Mollette attacked more than he had in Melbourne but again had no answer to Carroll's jab and faster footwork. Carroll picked him off from a distance in the opening four rounds, leaving Mollette's counters missing by a whisker, before he outpunched him on the inside in the fifth round, dropping him with a body shot at the bell. Mollette was finished but came out for the sixth round where he was "punched into such a state that the referee stepped in."[2]

With Carroll back to his winning ways, many fans were after clarification as to who was the welterweight champion of Australia. Stadiums Ltd stated that they still regarded Carroll as their champion despite Hancock's claim. Because Carroll had not defended the title against an Australian in the twelve months after he won the title from Bourke and that he had not fought a rematch with Purdy for the title, many in the press disagreed with Stadiums Ltd and regarded Hancock as their champion. Carroll returned to Sydney, hopeful of a rematch with Meyer Grace, but when Grace returned to the United States while still under contract with Stadiums Ltd, any chance of the rematch had finished. Grace defeated Ted Monson before leaving, and there were talks of him facing Hancock, but he departed for home suddenly, leaving Stadiums Ltd contemplating an appeal to the New York Boxing Commission to have his licence suspended until he fulfilled his Australian contract.

Carroll stayed in Sydney where Sydney Stadium scheduled him to face Welsh welterweight champion Ben Marshall on 10 August. Marshall, who was a British amateur champion before turning professional, was considered a dangerous puncher and was undefeated in his professional career. Out of his 26 contests, he had only suffered two draws, and 17 of his wins were by way of knockout. Despite Marshall having not fought in six months, and Carroll's being a step up in opposition, many of the reporters in Sydney expected Marshall to be too much for Carroll.

Wet weather caused a "scant attendance" for the bout,[3] which turned out to be one-sided. Carroll started well, drawing blood from the Welshman's mouth in a fast-paced opening session. The Australian outworked Marshall, who repeatedly threw and missed with his right-hand counter, on the inside in rounds two, three and four before Carroll opened a gash under his right eye in round five. Marshall's right eye was swollen shut by the end of the sixth, and Carroll opened another cut over his left eye in the seventh. Despite being hampered by the injuries, Marshall continued to look for his right hand, but with his eyes swelling shut he was unable to fight back effectively against Carroll and after he staggered to his corner at the end of the tenth round, the referee stopped the contest.

The bout further solidified Carroll's claim as the country's best welterweight with Marshall now added to the list of international opponents on his record. Speaking to Melbourne newspaper *The Sporting Globe* upon his return to Melbourne, Carroll stated that "if Hancock considered himself a champion he could have his chance to try for the welter title any time he liked."[4] The main difficulty in making the match was that Wally Hancock was under contract with Pat McHugh, who ran a rival stadium in the Sydney suburb of Leichhardt. Hancock added fuel to the matchup with a sixth-round knockout over an American import Jimmy Carter on 6 September.

Hancock lost his next bout three weeks later in a controversial decision against Bluey Jones at Leichhardt Stadium but his trainer 'Slam' Sullivan, the man who replaced Sammy Chapman in Carroll's before the return with Sparr, looked to make the match with Carroll next. Leichhardt Stadium and Sydney Stadium were both keen to stage the bout but were unable to come to a deal, and Hancock instead fought Tommy Fairhall. Pat McHugh made a bid to get Carroll under contract so he could secure the big domestic clash with Hancock and announced that Carroll would battle another Welshman, Billy Thomas, a week after Hancock fought Fairhall.

Sydney Stadium countered quickly and upon Carroll's arrival (at McHugh's expense) stating that Carroll was under contract and would only be able to fight bouts fought under roofs managed by Stadiums Ltd. The match with Billy Thomas fell through, and after Hancock outpointed Fairhall in a slow fight, the matchmaking of Carroll and Hancock still had not progressed any further. Meanwhile, Harry Casey, the man who outpointed Carroll in New Zealand, defeated Billy Richards in his home town of Rockhampton in Queensland in a fight advertised as an eliminator for the Australian title. Casey was unbeaten in his previous eleven contests after he had started his return to Australia with a run of poor form. Carroll agreed to fight Casey at Brisbane Stadium, which was under the umbrella of Stadiums Ltd, in a match billed as being for the Australian welterweight title.

The failed negotiations and the lack of a suitable contender had left Carroll idle for three months heading into the bout with Casey. However, with his poor performances against Casey in New Zealand, Carroll was eager to show dominance over his former opponent. Casey had stayed active following the win over Richards, scoring a fifteen round decision over Newcastle's Dan Ritchie in Rockhampton on 1 November. The champion arrived in Brisbane one week before the fight to help advertise the contest before resuming training.

In what was Carroll's first official defence of his Australian title, he put a huge exclamation point on his claim as Australia's best welterweight. Carroll beat Casey both at long range and on the inside, scoring with hard jabs from a distance and pasting the Rockhampton man's body on the inside. Casey was game and attacked throughout, but Carroll handled him easily. The challenger was bleeding from the mouth at the end of the third round and, by the fifth, he was having trouble breathing. In rounds six and seven Carroll handed out a one-sided thrashing, and Casey only had the energy to tie him up when he reached punching distance, and his corner wisely pulled him out of the contest at the end of round seven.

The bout with Casey was Carroll's last in 1929. Wally Hancock was hospitalised with tonsillitis shortly before, which placed him out of action until mid-November. Tommy Fairhall was discussed as an opponent for Carroll in the interim, but Fairhall travelled to Wollongong, south of Sydney, for a fight with Bluey Jones, a man who he had just defeated, with this contest ending in a draw. Carroll was then matched with Billy Richards in Melbourne on 21 December for another defence of his title, but Richards withdrew due to his wife being seriously ill, leaving Carroll inactive until 1930.

When Carroll became ill in the first week of January, the rematch had to be rescheduled from 15 January to 1 February. The bout represented a chance for Richards' trainer Sammy Chapman, who trained Carroll during his stint in Sydney, to gain some revenge over his former charge. The winner was to meet Wally Hancock in the weeks after the bout for the championship. Richards had fought Hancock in Hancock's first bout, with Hancock, appearing in his first fight following his tonsillitis, avenging two previous defeats to Richards. Hancock had thoroughly outboxed Richards before the referee disqualified Richards in round eleven for repeated rabbit punches. Hancock, however, had since put his title on the line at Leichhardt and was held to a draw by Tommy Fairhall.

Both Richards and Carroll showed good form in the lead up to the contest, with the bout viewed as a battle of Carroll's speed against Richards' punch. It was Carroll's first fight at Sydney Stadium since the loss to Grace and was a chance for him to show the Sydney fans that he was still the best welterweight in the country. The match drew a small to moderate attendance, and both men comfortably made the welterweight limit for the contest. Carroll had no trouble finding Richards with his jab or his left hook in the first round, and the champion continued to score with short left hands to the body and right uppercuts to the head in the second as Richards tried to hold on. A left hook put Richards down for the count of eight in the third, but Richards lasted the rest of the round and avoided further punishment in the fourth.

Richards came back well in the fifth, landing with a hard right hand at the start and again at the end of the round but Carroll took the shots, and Richards' left eye was swelling shut at the end of the sixth. Carroll took his foot off the gas in the seventh and Richards fought himself back into the fight while Carroll fought on the back foot. Many in the crowd were anticipating an unlikely comeback as Richards took rounds nine and ten, but Richards needed a knockout after Carroll's early domination. Carroll stood his ground in round eleven, punching more with Richards who began to slow down. A barrage of lefts and rights put Richards down at the bell to end the eleventh, and he was carried back to his corner by his seconds. Carroll finished the job in the twelfth, scoring two knockdowns before the Police Inspector supervising the bout at ringside stopped the contest.

Remaining in Sydney after the bout, likely looking to be matched with Wally Hancock, Carroll stayed busy by taking on the crowd-pleasing "Tiger" Anderson two weeks after beating Richards. Anderson had proved no match for Jack Haines in either of their bouts, but had a massive following after his come-from-behind knockout against Frank Vann, and agreed to make the welterweight limit for the bout with the Australian champion. Despite Anderson's popularity, the contest did not draw a large crowd, and it was horribly one-sided. Carroll's hand speed gave him a clear edge, and he allowed Anderson to walk up to him while scoring with clean punches and moving out of the way of the American's ponderous attacks. Anderson took everything Carroll gave him, but the referee had seen enough by the eleventh round and stopped the bout to save him from further punishment.

With Carroll's dominating performances in Sydney, he had re-established himself as the top welterweight in the eyes of the Sydney fans. After the bout with Anderson, many called for Hancock to fight the Victorian. *The Sydney Sportsman*, who still regarded Hancock as the champion, responded to this, stating that Hancock would "go out and battle a room full of wild-cats if the instruction came from his trainer" although conceding that a bout with Carroll had to take place:

> "But the public demand that Hancock shall battle Carroll, and the cry of the crowd cannot go unheeded. The mob may not make a fighter, but it can go mighty close to breaking him."[5]

Stadiums Ltd offered a purse of £450 for the bout if Hancock would fight Carroll for the undisputed title at Rushcutters Bay, but Hancock and his trainer "Slam" Sullivan turned this down, stating they would make the same at Leichhardt and had no reason to fight for Stadiums Ltd unless they were offered more money. The offer was raised to £500, but again turned down, with Sullivan stating "it might be months before we get an offer that we consider suitable."[6] Leichhardt countered the next day and offered Carroll £550 to fight Hancock at Leichhardt, an offer that was accepted by Sullivan and Hancock. Carroll agreed but once again was not permitted to compete outside of Stadiums Ltd promotions. Hancock, who had just defeated little known Queenslander Stan Goode, instead decided to defend his claim of being champion in a rematch with Fairhall at Leichhardt on 7 March.

The Hancock-Carroll bout was dealt a considerable blow when Tommy Fairhall outpointed Hancock on 7 March. Fairhall, who usually competed as a lightweight, and won the British Empire title in that division in 1928, outboxed Hancock to take his claim as the champion. Carroll, who was still regarded by many as the welterweight champion, was frozen out of title picture as Hancock and Fairhall were in talks for a fifth meeting, expected to take place in the coming weeks at Leichhardt Stadium. When Hancock travelled to New Zealand for a series of fights, Fairhall, who now lead in the series with Hancock 2-1-1 with his recent win, scheduled his next bout with Australian lightweight champion Norm Gillespie. These matchups left Carroll without a chance to prove his claim that he was Australia's best welterweight.

Wally Hancock
(National Library of Australia, nla.obj-148607703)

Without an opponent for a match in Sydney, Carroll made plans to return to Brisbane to meet the Italian middleweight Orlando Leopardi, who had lost his Australian debut by one-sided tenth round stoppage against Jack Haines but bounced back with a 4th round stoppage over Dave Jackson. The bout was to take place on 10 May at Brisbane Stadium, but Carroll's misfortunes continued, and he was forced to withdraw from the bout after injuring his back. He returned to Melbourne and resumed training after recovering from the injury. Carroll's next contest would take place in Melbourne against the Western Australian welterweight and middleweight champion Danny Ryan. The fight, which took place on 18 June, ended four months of inactivity for Carroll. Ryan was game but, despite having a weight advantage of over half a stone, he was ultimately knocked out "with a perfect left hook" in round five.[7]

Wally Hancock meanwhile had returned from New Zealand after three bouts in which he won two and lost one and was keen to get back into the Australian welterweight title scene after he was reportedly paid well for his overseas bouts. Fairhall defended his championship claim with an "uninteresting" win on points against Norky Fowler at Leichhardt on 18 July. Carroll was to meet Welshmen Billy Thomas on 10 July, a midweek card in Melbourne, but Carroll refused to be relegated to Wednesday shows and held out for a better bout. The offer came from an unlikely source with Brisbane Stadium putting up the necessary money to stage the much-anticipated fight between Carroll and Hancock. The contest was set to take place on 13 August, which was Exhibition night during the week-long Brisbane agricultural show and was expected to draw a huge crowd:

> "Carroll and Hancock are expected to attract the biggest crowd seen in the Stadium for some years, for a match between them has been the principal topic in boxing circles all over the Commonwealth for months, and the event has been

eagerly sought by promoters all over Australia and New Zealand."⁸

Both fighters were in excellent condition, and neither man had any issues making weight with Hancock holding a 3lb weight advantage, despite weighing in well under the welterweight limit. A competing wrestling match that was double booked did affect the crowd, but the bout still proved to be a near sell-out, and the fans got their money's worth. The Victorian was a 2-1 favourite at the start of the fight, and both men entered the ring at 9 pm to face each other in the most anticipated clash in Australian boxing of the year.

Both men were cautious early on and sparred for openings in the first round. Carroll landed well with his jab in the opening round, but Hancock scored with the better punches, and Carroll was having trouble seeing his left hook, two of which landed flush on his jaw. Carroll was the quicker man and was busier, but Hancock's punches were more damaging, especially his left hook. The second round saw Hancock land again with the left hook, which momentarily wobbled the champion but Carroll used his jab and his superior speed to stay out of trouble for the rest of the round. Carroll's educated jab gave him round three, and he used it to set up combinations to the body on the inside. Hancock continued to look for his left hook, but although he did land it again in the third, Carroll was beginning to see the blow coming and was landing his own left hook as a counter.

Hancock was busier in the fourth, sensing he wasn't going to be able to catch Carroll with his single shots and he scored well to the body in this round but was unable to get away from the champion's jab. Carroll's defence allowed him to fend off many of Hancock's blows, but neither man was able to gain a clear advantage thus far. Hancock looked for the left hook to the head more in round five, but Carroll was now countering the shot more and tripled his left hook as the crowd cheered the action. Hancock kept the pressure on in the sixth, and again found a home for the left hook, landing now to both the body and head to keep the bout fought on even terms.

The champion focused more on his defence in rounds seven and eight and even when trapped on the ropes, he used clever footwork and skilful blocking to make Hancock miss and continued to score with his jab. Hancock was beginning to grow frustrated by Carroll's evasiveness and threw wildly, at one point falling to the canvas after missing in the eighth. The crowd sensed the momentum was shifting towards Carroll in round nine as he continued to pile up points with his jab and frustrate Hancock with his elusiveness while punching evenly with him when Hancock was able to force him into an exchange. Round eleven was the champions best round of the fight thus far, as he "boxed the other man's ears about a dozen times with the left" and "foiled him cleverly in close."[9]

Hancock became more urgent in round twelve and pressed the action more, fighting on even terms with the champion, who continued to score and opened a cut under Hancock's right eye in this round. Sensing he needed a knockout in round thirteen, Hancock had more success than in previous rounds but never looked like ending the fight, as Carroll's superior skill-set kept him out of trouble even when Hancock trapped him on the ropes. A hard right hand landed for Hancock early in round fourteen which gave him hope, but Carroll rallied back to take the round with both men still exchanging blows as the bell sounded. The champion was in complete command in the fifteenth round despite Hancock's aggression and referee Fred Craig crowned him the winner on points at the final bell.

The Brisbane audience thoroughly enjoyed the contest and, despite the lack of drama, the fans enjoyed Carroll showcasing his skills and gave his performance a great reception. Sydney Stadium had even sent matchmakers to the bout, and they were so impressed with both men that they began negotiations for a return bout to take place at Rushcutters Bay in ten days. Carroll was also offered a match with the Welshman Billy Thomas in Brisbane on the same date. Thomas had outpointed Al Bourke days before the Carroll-Hancock bout and had also scored wins over Les Robson and one of the country's best middleweights in Norm Johnson. The fight with Thomas would also be for the Australian title as Thomas been in Australia for more than twelve months. Carroll took both matches, agreeing to fight Thomas then returning to Sydney to meet Hancock the week after.

Hancock returned to Sydney and began preparing for the rematch while Carroll remained in Brisbane to prepare for Thomas. Thomas was another technical boxer who possessed a jab that could match that of Carroll, although he lacked consistency during his time in Australia. Apart from his three recent wins over Bourke, Johnson and Robson, Thomas had also defeated Tommy McInnes and Artie Hay, but two draws and a loss in his three fights with Billy Richards, and a loss to Fairhall offset these wins. While there are only records of eleven fights in Thomas' career before his trip to Australia, *The Telegraph* reported that he had fought 95 career contests for 75 wins.

In his recent fights, Thomas had fought above the welterweight class and had to boil down to the welterweight limit for the title bout with Carroll. Weighing in at 10st-6lb, he was heavier than Carroll, who was well under at 10st-4.5lb, but his efforts to make the weight division took a lot of the fight out him. Thomas started well in the first round, and his jab was proving difficult for Carroll to deal with, and both men fenced with their left leads with the honours even. Carroll adjusted his defence in the second round and had success stopping the Welshman's jab with his right glove while finding a home for his left hook.

A hard left hook caught Thomas early in the third round which stunned him, and when Carroll dug a follow-up shot to the solar plexus, it crippled the challenger. Thomas rose at the count of nine but was in obvious pain, and Carroll swarmed, throwing a barrage of punches, punctuated with another shot to the body, that left Thomas on the floor again. Thomas was up at the count of seven, but another barrage of punches to the head and body sent him down two more times in the round and opened a huge gash over his right eye. Thomas staggered back to his corner where the referee called in the ringside doctor, who put a stop to the bout.

Thomas praised Carroll after the bout, telling Brisbane newspaper *Truth* that he had met a better man and that "I thought I had a good left hand, but I am satisfied that Carroll is my master."[10] Carroll was on the train to Sydney shortly after the bout and arrived in Sydney on the Tuesday before the return with Hancock. 'Slam' Sullivan had Hancock training hard for the return bout, sparring with Welsh boxer Fred Welsh in the afternoons and covering 8 miles on the road each morning. Despite his loss to Fairhall in March, the Sydney fight between the two top welterweights was still a big hit, and the excellent reports of the first Carroll-Hancock match had many people anticipating the rematch. Carroll and Hancock gave public training displays on the undercard of the Wednesday show at Rushcutters Bay, with both men looking in excellent condition.

There was confidence in the Hancock camp before the bout. His trainer Sullivan told reporters that "Wally will have Carroll out on his feet before the sixth round."[11] Carroll was again the favourite with most thinking his speed and cleverness would be too much for the hard-punching of Hancock. The champion was in tremendous shape off the back of his recent ring activity and weighed in the lightest that he had weighed since his days as a preliminary fighter in Melbourne, coming in at 10st-3lb, giving Hancock, who weighed 10st-6lb, a significant weight advantage. When the interest for the bout was at its highest, the combatants were to share in a £550 purse. Despite the interest in the rematch, the depression affected the crowd, and both men were paid only £83 for their fifteen round contest.

Hancock came forward in the opening moments of the bout, but it was Carroll who did the leading, using his left hand to score and his feet to keep Hancock at bay. The ex-sailor surprised Carroll one minute into the round when he quickly shifted into range and delivered a left hook to the body followed by a hard left hook to the head that deposited Carroll onto the seat of his pants. Carroll rose quickly, and the speed of his footwork increased while he glued his right hand to his chin to avoid Hancock's primary weapon. Hancock attacked but was unable to get close enough to do any further damage, and although he took the round, Carroll had recovered at the bell.

Carroll was never in range to be hit in the next two rounds, using his superior speed to its full advantage as Hancock couldn't close the distance. Hancock came back in the fourth, driving the Victorian back with a flurry of rights and lefts but Carroll responded by outpunching him on the inside for the remainder of the round. Carroll's lead continued to build in the next few rounds, and Hancock's face was showing the effects of the champion's punches, with both eyes beginning to swell by the sixth. The boxing lesson continued in rounds seven, eight and nine and Hancock was growing frustrated with Carroll's speed and non-stop motion. Carroll switched his attack to the body in the tenth and sunk a left rip into his solar plexus which dropped Hancock for a nine count. Hancock recovered well and even forced the pace in the next round but was unable to close the distance.

Hancock fought back well over the next five rounds but never looked like winning a round, much less the fight. In round eleven he landed his best punch since the opener in the form of a left hook, although this just spurred a Carroll rally and in round fourteen

Hancock forced matters for the duration. At the end of the contest, there was only one winner. Carroll had put on a magnificent display and was cheered when referee Joe Wallis declared him the winner. While most reporters were vastly impressed with Carroll's dominance, Sydney newspapers *The Referee* and *The Labor Daily* both criticised Carroll's defensive tactics and were not impressed with his performance. *The Referee* stated that Carroll would be no match for Fairhall, who was still claiming the Australian title despite fighting in the division below, and *The Labor Daily* stated that Carroll's "scheme of scrambling his punches and flying around the ring like a scared kangaroo" was possibly down to the poor turnout for the bout.[12]

The champion returned to Melbourne after the fight for the first time since July after being interstate since the start of August. Fairhall was due to meet Len White on 12 September, with many fans hoping he would face Carroll after this bout. Fairhall scored a fourteenth round stoppage over White and announced he was willing to meet Carroll "but at Leichhardt Stadium unless Stadiums Ltd offer me a better guarantee."[13] Carroll agreed to meet Billy Thomas in a rematch at middleweight in Melbourne on 11 October to keep ring fit. The rematch proved that Carroll was the better man, Thomas was only able to last four rounds this time. After a cautious opening two rounds, Carroll opened up in the third and had Thomas in trouble at the bell before three knockdowns in round four forced the stoppage.

Two weeks later the 29-year-old Fairhall faced off with Hancock in what was the fifth meeting between the pair and outfoxed the younger and larger Hancock to win a clear fifteen round decision. Dick Lean looked to bring the Fairhall-Carroll bout to Melbourne to avoid having to negotiate with the managers of Leichhardt Stadium but then suspended the season in Melbourne due to poor showings. Fairhall subsequently lost his claim to the title when he dropped a fifteen round decision to Russ Critcher on 7 November at Leichhardt. Critcher was a young welterweight who earlier in the year had been knocked out sensationally in two rounds at Sydney Stadium by Newcastle lightweight Jack Roberts. Although he had won his last eight contests, Critcher did not claim the welterweight title at this time and few disputed Carroll's claim to welterweight supremacy.

With boxing suspended in Melbourne, Carroll returned to Sydney to meet imported middleweight Tony Tuzzolino on 22 November. If Carroll was victorious over Tuzzonlino, who had just defeated Frank Vann and Jimmy Pearce, many were speculating that Carroll would challenge middleweight champion, Jack Haines. Carroll had decided that it was necessary for him to fight more regularly at middleweight to earn a better living. His debut at the new class was delayed, however, when Carroll was forced to withdraw from the Tuzzolino bout due to illness Upon his recovery, Carroll would only fight once more in 1930, against the American Herman Bundren, who fought under the name Jack Kilbourne. Carroll was ahead on points heading into the eighth round when Bundren struck him with a crippling low blow and earned himself a disqualification.

After defeating all of the top welterweights in his division and earning just £23 for his bout with Bundren, Carroll considered travelling to Britain or Europe to try and make more money fighting men his size. With the emergence of fellow Victorian Ambrose Palmer as the middleweight champion of Australia, Carroll was hopeful of a boxing revival in Melbourne so he could fight closer to home. When another Victorian boxer Michael White, who fought under the alias "Young Llew Edwards," won the Australian featherweight title in January, talk of a revival of the fight game in Melbourne heated up.

Ambrose Palmer returned to the ring for the first time since stopping Haines for the middleweight crown, finally meeting Tony

Tuzzolino in February at Rushcutters Bay. In front of what was a solid attendance, Palmer won every round against the game American before referee Joe Wallis was forced to stop the contest due to the cut above the import's right eye. With the £736 gate, Stadiums Ltd saw to make money again in Melbourne and re-opened the season in March. The first matchup on 7 March would be a rematch between Palmer and Tuzzolino before Carroll returned to the ring a week later in a rematch with Bundren.

Bundren had proved very successful since the loss to Carroll, scoring a string of knockouts since over Frank Vann, Jimmy Pearce and Al Bourke as well as international opponents Walter Libert and Emilio Bernasconi. He had fought six times in just nine weeks, winning every bout with five by knockout. Without any suitable opponents, Carroll had taken a holiday in January and returned to training with O'Brien a week before the announcement that he was to meet Bundren. Due to his inactivity and Bundren's recent ring time, combined with the height and weight advantage that Bundren held, Carroll turned down the opponent and requested "Tuzzolino, Critcher, Hancock or any other logical opponent put forward by Stadiums Ltd."[14] Carroll agreed to a fight with Belgian middleweight Walter Libert on the same date.

Libert had little success since coming to Australia. Both Bundren and Jimmy Pearce had stopped him, and he wasn't expected to give Carroll any trouble. Palmer and Carroll sparred in the days leading up to the Tuzzolino bout, with many eager to see the new middleweight champion who had taken control of the division in such a short amount of time. A large crowd witnessed Palmer again stop Tuzzolino, and outside of a cut to his eye, Palmer had no issues. The import fought in a negative manner, which allowed him to last until the ninth round, where Palmer ended matters with a right hand to the body and a left hook to the head. Carroll drew a much smaller crowd but had little trouble with Libert, stopping the Belgian on a cut in the fourth round.

Palmer's injured eye forced him to sit on the sidelines for several weeks and delayed a much-anticipated matchup between him and Herman Bundren, who chose to wait for Palmer and not risk the payday. Russ Critcher, meanwhile, placed himself as an obvious contender to Carroll with a draw and then a win over Wally Hancock at Sydney Stadium. The win came in their rematch on 14 March with Critcher holding on to an early lead and surviving a torrid final two rounds in which the more powerful Hancock badly hurt him. Carroll returned to Sydney in April, where he was to meet Tuzzolino on Easter Saturday at Rushcutters Bay, but told *The Labor Daily* that he hoped to meet Critcher before returning to Melbourne. Tuzzolino was no match for Carroll, and his right eye was opened up in the second round before his corner asked referee Joe Wallis to stop the bout at the end of the fifth.

The welterweight champion returned to Melbourne for a few days before coming back to Sydney and, while waiting for a fight with Critcher, Carroll agreed to face Billy Richards for the third time. Richards had won four contests so far in 1931, beating Frank Vann twice as well as Alby Roberts and Billy Thomas. A "disappointing" crowd of between 2,000 and 3,000 spectators witnessed a one-sided, but a thrilling contest between the two.[15] Despite stunning Carroll in the first round with a left hook, Richards was thrashed throughout, and Carroll put Richards through the ropes in the sixth and dropped him again at the end of the seventh, with Richards saved by the bell. The contest was stopped before the start of the eighth round with Richards not in any shape to continue.

Ambrose Palmer's eye had finally recovered, and he made his way to Sydney to battle Bundren, the bout taking place on 16 May. Palmer concluded his training at Pat Kearon's gym as he had in preparation for his fights with Haines while the American trained at the gym owned by Haines' old trainer, Jack Dunleavy. The bout was expected to produce the largest gate since Palmer's fights with Haines, with bookings coming from all around Australia for tickets to the contest.[16] Hundreds of spectators showed up at the boxers' respective gyms to get a glimpse of the two men training. At 2 pm on the day of the contest, Palmer weighed in 11st-10lb, 4lb more than the experienced American, with the bout taking place above the middleweight division.

The bout drew as expected, with 12,000 filling the Rushcutters Bay Stadium for the fifteen round contest however they did not get the battle they were hoping for. Palmer proved his class, winning a decision over fifteen rounds in a dull fight. Bundren attempted to use his height and reach to his advantage but had trouble punching through Palmer's guard. Palmer walked forward and picked his shots as he got into range while Bundren struggled to get any attack going. By the eighth round the tall American was tiring, and Palmer swept the second half of the fight as Bundren offered little in the way of offence. The crowd "counted out" Bundren at least once in each of the last rounds but despite their hostility towards the foreigner, they cheered their champion when referee Wallis declared Palmer had won on points.

The live gate for the bout was £1,700, earning Palmer another tidy payday. Jack Carroll, meanwhile, was announced to meet the winner of this bout in a few weeks, although this was unlikely he was already matched against Canadian boxer Tommy Fielding in a contest that was to take place the following week at Leichhardt. Management at Leichhardt sensed Carroll was getting a raw deal with Stadiums Ltd and offered him £125 for a one-time appearance. While Fielding had been mostly unsuccessful during his time in Australia, he was coming off a ninth-round knockout over Wally Hancock in April.

Fielding took the fight to Carroll but was never in the contest after the third round, in which Carroll drew blood from his mouth. Carroll opened up cuts over both of the Canadian's eyes in the fifth round, and Fielding could do little in return after this other than take what was coming to him. Although he was never off his feet, referee Yank Pearl saved Fielding from further punishment in the eleventh round, giving Carroll a technical knockout win. The £555 live gate was thought to be the highest ever produced at the time at Leichhardt Stadium, and the win was Carroll's 16th in a row.

Palmer returned to Melbourne to meet Bundren in a rematch and Carroll agreed to another fight at Leichhardt, again with Wally Hancock, which shot down any talk of the two men fighting each other. Carroll's stay at Leichhardt looked lengthy as foreign welterweights were sort after to take on the company's new welterweight star. The Palmer-Bundren rematch took place on 6 June with both men once again weighing over the middleweight limit. The Melbourne contest was no more entertaining than the Sydney one, although Palmer's troublesome left eye was opened up yet again in this bout, he had little trouble with Bundren, who seemed unwilling, or unable, to get any of his punches off at Palmer. The champion was able to frequently score with his jab and use his superior defence while taking no risks to outscore the American.

Carroll returned to Leichhardt on 5 June to face Hancock, a man who he had beaten twice, but who had given him trouble both times. Carroll immediately showed that he had Hancock's number this time and he took control from the outside and never let the ex-sailor get off his vaunted left hook. After four rounds he was in complete control, and he opened up in rounds five and six, driving Hancock back with both hands. Towards the end of the sixth round, Carroll sunk in several blows to the body that dropped Hancock to his knees and the bell saved Hancock. At the beginning of round seven, the bout was terminated but not in Carroll's favour. The referee, Yank Pearl, ruled that the body shots that did the damage were below the belt and gave the fight to Hancock on a foul.

It was the second time Carroll had been beaten in a non-title fight controversially by a foul. After having just cleaned up the welterweight division over a two-year period following the disqualification against Purdy, Carroll was back where he started with Leichhardt planning on making another bout between Critcher and Hancock to decide the championship. Critcher had returned to the welterweight division after splitting a pair of fights with a young fighter based in Sydney named Fred Henneberry. Henneberry, from Albury, near the border between New South Wales and Victoria, had quickly outgrown the welterweight division before the Critcher bouts and was a fully fledged middleweight by the time he beat Critcher. The addition of Henneberry to the middleweight rankings and his fights with Carroll and Palmer in the coming months would bring Australian boxing back to the spotlight.

FRED HENNEBERRY

Fred Henneberry was born in 1911 in Port Pirie, South Australia. Like Ambrose Palmer, Henneberry was from a boxing family. One of ten children, Fred's father, Michael, was reportedly a bare-knuckle fighter. His older brother Alf, who fought under the alias 'Yank,' was a successful heavyweight who headlined at Sydney and Melbourne Stadium and another older brother Bill was Fred's trainer and manager. Also like Palmer, Fred's rise to the top of the Australian scene was meteoric. He made his pro debut at the age of 18 under the alias 'Dick' Henneberry, earning a four-round draw with Stan Harris on 14 March 1930 in Leichhardt.

Fighting in four round preliminary bouts, Henneberry won his next eight contests in a row, seven by knockout with the other coming via disqualification. A fourth-round knockout over Billy Welsh in his first ten round earned him his first main-event slot, where he met Newcastle based journeyman Billy Woods in Broken Hill, on the western border of New South Wales. Woods, who was originally from Broken Hill, was no match for Henneberry, even in front of his home crowd. Henneberry's pace and powerful infighting overwhelmed the experienced Woods and, after taking a knee in the ninth round of a scheduled fifteen, the referee mercifully halted the bout. Henneberry spent the next two weeks in Broken Hill fighting two more times, scoring a 15 round decision over the experienced Jack Heeney and a third-round knockout over Sid Sampson.

Returning to Sydney in 1931, Henneberry added four more victories to start the year, including a seventh-round knockout over Norky Fowler in an action-packed, foul-filled fight at Leichhardt Stadium. This bout started the reputation for Henneberry as a rough and aggressive fighter who often bent the rules:

> "The rules were broken frequently, and really one was as much to blame as the other, although when Henneberry got properly nasty he was a little more nasty than Norkey."[1]

The win over Fowler earned Henneberry his first headline bout in Sydney, against the Canadian Tommy Fielding at Leichhardt Stadium, where Henneberry was immensely popular. The 15x2 minute round bout took place on 13 March. After a close opening five rounds, Henneberry's aggression allowed him to take over. Fielding did his best, but couldn't match his youthful opponent and, despite good rounds in the eighth and eleventh, Henneberry was in command of the contest after the sixth round, and he won the referee's verdict on points. A ninth-round stoppage over Walter 'Kid' Lee in April earned Henneberry a shot at the ex-sailor Wally Hancock.

Henneberry, only 19 years old, had not yet fully developed as his future bouts with Carroll, Palmer and Richards would be at or above the middleweight limit. Hancock was the more experienced boxer, with 64 bouts and 42 wins (29 by knockout) compared to Henneberry's 20 career bouts, but Henneberry emerged as a new star in Australian boxing with a fifteen round decision win. Both men weighed in at 10st-7.5lb, slightly over the welterweight limit, and Henneberry dominated the fifteen round main event at Leichhardt Stadium, showing he was one of the top welterweights in the country:

> "Boxing with the skill of a veteran scientist, displaying the cunning of an old-man fox, and exhibiting ruggedness not in keeping with his outward frailty, young Fred Henneberry administered to welterweight champion Wally Hancock a sounder and more convincing thrashing than he has received from the gloves of anybody with the exception of Jack Carroll." [2]

The win put Henneberry among the top welterweights in the country alongside Carroll, Fairhall and Russ Critcher. Critcher, from Woonona, south of Sydney, had claimed the welterweight championship of Australia after outpointing Wally Hancock in October. A dispute about the weigh-in time was the only obstacle in a bout between Henneberry and Critcher, and the match was set to take place after Henneberry agreed to make the welterweight limit by 2 pm. The bout took place on 29 May, and Henneberry surprised everyone by coming in well below the welterweight limit, weighing in at 10st-4lb.

Critcher won the bout with surprising ease, winning a fifteen round decision to hand Henneberry the first defeat of his career, although his tactics of "sneak punching" and tying up the young man turned the crowd against him. Henneberry rallied in the final round, hurting Critcher with a right hand, but he left it too late, and while the crowd booed the decision, Critcher was the rightful winner. Jack Carroll, ringside to have a look at the man who claimed his title, was "unperturbed at his challengers efforts." [3] Henneberry's reputation as a dirty fighter continued to build in this fight. *The*

Maitland Mercury reported that in this fight Henneberry was warned for "deliberately using his shoulder in the 13th round and made frequent use of the 'rabbit killer' punch." [4]

Critcher defended his claim to the welterweight title in his next bout, scoring a points win over Wally Hancock. This bout came three weeks after Hancock had beaten Jack Carroll by disqualification in a non-title bout and, despite Critcher claiming the title, many still classed Carroll as the real champion. A rematch between Critcher and Henneberry was set for 10 July 1931. Henneberry, who had fought nine times already in 1931, had an uncharacteristic layoff and didn't fight between the two Critcher bouts. The rematch would be fought above the welterweight limit after negotiations to make the bout for the title failed.

The rest and the extra weight (Henneberry weighed in at 10st-12lb) seemed to do wonders for Henneberry, as he avenged his only professional loss with a unanimous decision over the Australian welterweight champion. Critcher took more chances in the rematch than he did in their first fight, taking the fight to the younger man at the opening bell. Henneberry worked Critcher's body in the early rounds with his left rip in an effort to slow him down in the later rounds, and the plan worked. With the fight in the balance entering the final five rounds, Henneberry battered a tiring Critcher with short right hands to the head and left hooks to the body to take the unanimous decision. Henneberry could have put Critcher away in the 15th round had he been less wild and picked his punches better. Critcher reportedly fought "the best fight of his career," and he was "more popular in defeat than he has ever been in victory." [5]

Henneberry decided to make the jump to middleweight after this fight.[6] Three weeks after avenging the loss to Critcher, he weighed in at 11st-1.5lb for a bout with Newcastle's Jimmy Pearce at Leichhardt Stadium. Pearce was in his 11th year as a professional. He had previously challenged for the Australian welterweight title in

1926, losing to Eddie Butcher in the 16th round of a 20-round fight. After struggling with Pearce's jab in the opening two frames, Henneberry found his range in the third and battered the veteran for the remainder of the fight. Henneberry set a pace that was too high for Pearce to deal with and by the end of the sixth round, Pearce was out on his feet. Pearce finally went down in the eighth, and his corner stopped the bout before the referee could administer a count. This victory not only established Henneberry as one of Sydney's best draw cards, but it put him in line for a shot at the Australian middleweight title.

AMBROSE PALMER VS FRED HENNEBERRY

Following the rematch with Bundren, Palmer was advised not to box for three months while his eye healed. An offer that was too good to pass up, however, had Palmer disobeying his doctor's orders. The opponent was Norm Johnson, the man who had beaten Palmer by disqualification 18 months prior and still the only man to beat the young Victorian. Palmer was to travel back to Brisbane to take on the Queenslander on 10 July. Johnson had shown with his recent form that he was not on Palmer's level. Since being sensationally knocked out in the first round by Merv Williams, Johnson was outpointed by the Welshman Billy Thomas as well as losing by knockout to Tony Tuzzolini and Jimmy Pearce. He was also held to a draw by the Belgian Walter Libert, but he had defeated Les Robson and Andy Anderson.

The middleweight champion stopped in Sydney for a few days, training at Sammy Chapman's gym, before heading to Brisbane for the bout with Johnson. This fight was purely for revenge as Palmer did not put his title on the line in the contest and weighed in over the middleweight limit. The bout drew a large crowd, many of who were expecting Johnson to spring another upset on Palmer. Johnson was confident as he entered the ring to the cheers of the crowd, but his confidence was quickly shattered by Palmer's left hook, which found the target early in the first. From there it was carnage, Johnson offered little in return, holding on as Palmer went to work. An uppercut rocked Johnson at the bell, and he looked tired before the start of the second round.

Palmer stepped up the pressure in the second round but remained patient and did not rush his blows and while Johnson fought better in the second, he couldn't land anything to keep the champion off him, who was. There was blood from Johnson's mouth as he went back to his stool at the end of the second and although he came out fast in the third, Palmer soon had him on the back foot. A barrage from both hands forced Johnson to the ropes where Palmer hammered him the referee stopped the fight. It was an emphatic performance by Palmer, who "made a chopping-block of Johnson's head from the time they shook hands."[1]

Returning to Melbourne, Palmer agreed to box a three-round exhibition bout with Jack Carroll as part of a charity show on behalf of the widow and children of Bert McCarthy, a featherweight from Melbourne who died of injuries sustained in a bout with Alby Roberts on a smaller show in the Melbourne suburb of Brunswick. The charity bout took place on 18 July and proved to be a good tune-up for Palmer, as he was to defend his title the following week against Bob Thornton, a puncher from Sydney who was undefeated in close to a year. Thornton had won his last three bouts inside four rounds by knockout and looked to be a suitable contender for Palmer's first official defence of his Australian title. The two men had previously sparred at Pat Kearon's gym in Sydney and Thornton's trainer Kearon claimed to have learned how to defeat the 19-year-old champion from his time watching him in the gym.

The champion showed he could still make the middleweight limit comfortably and hit the scales at 11st-5lb with Thornton weighing 11st-2.5lb. The crowd was disappointing, a gate of just £190 meant that the boxers earned just £46 each for their title bout. Those in attendance got to witness a savage fight with an unsatisfactory ending. It didn't take long for Thornton to land his hard right hand and it landed hard on Palmer's jaw in the opening seconds of the first round, staggering him. The crowd cheered as Thornton followed-up but Palmer boxed cleverly and, despite taking the right hand a number of other times, Palmer had cleared his head and began landing his left hook to Thornton's body.

The champion started the second well, and it was his turn to hurt Thornton, landing a left hook on the point of the challenger's chin that made his legs wobble. Palmer put more pressure on but was rocked by a left hand in return which spurred him on further. The two men traded for the remainder of the round, which was won by Palmer. Thornton looked for his right hand again in the third and had some success, but Palmer was seeing the blow coming more easily now and defended it well. He also put work into Thornton's body, landing vicious body assaults with both hands. Palmer continued working the body in the fourth round and, after backing Thornton into the ropes, another barrage hammered into his midsection. Unfortunately one of the right hands strayed low, and Thornton went down and was severely hurt. The referee had no hesitation in disqualifying Palmer, handing the Victorian his second loss by a low blow and the Australian title to Thornton.

Even the new champion was disappointed with the result. Talking to *The Daily Telegraph*, Thornton stated that he "would rather have won the fight with fighting and not on a foul." Thornton also said that Palmer did not hurt him before the low punch and that he felt he could have beaten him regardless.[2] News broke after the fight that Palmer had been suffering badly with influenza in the lead-up and, after he was bedridden for a week after the bout with Thornton, he took an extended break from the training. With Palmer out of action, Thornton looked for a payday on 12 August against Herman Bundren, who was still selling tickets in Brisbane, despite his poor performances in his bouts with Carroll and Palmer down south. The result of this bout further shook up the middleweight division in Australia.

In front of a "very large attendance" at Brisbane Stadium, Thornton had no answer for Bundren's height and reach advantage, and was anxious about exchanging after tasting the American's power early in the fight. From there, the new Australian champion tried to fight off the back foot, which played right into Bundren's hands. The American kept his left jab in Thornton's face and took his time until he found his opening, which came in round eight, and he landed a flush right hand on Thornton's temple that "pancaked" the champion on the canvas where he was unable to beat the count.[3]

With the win over Thornton, Bundren earned a third shot at Palmer, this time in Queensland, where he stated he had been anxious to meet Palmer, as his trainers blamed the climate for his other losses while in Australia. Bundren had won all five of his Brisbane bouts, with four by knockout, and looked to avenge his two losses to Palmer on their 21 August bout. In his time in Australia, Bundren had lost only four times, the other two losses coming to Jack Carroll. Carroll had outpointed Bundren on 11 July, in his first fight back from the shock loss to Hancock, despite being outweighed by almost a stone. Unfortunately, Carroll had injured his hand not long after this bout, which, along with Palmer's flu, had cancelled a mega fight between the two men from taking place on 15 August.

Palmer arrived in Brisbane just a few days before the bout after training in Sydney for a day during the journey up from Melbourne. While at Sammy Chapman's gym in Sydney, Palmer told reporters he would return there after the bout with Bundren to begin preparing to face Thornton in a rematch for the title.[4] Despite the one-sided, slow nature of their first two bouts, "one of the largest crowds that has ever assembled inside"[5] Brisbane Stadium witnessed the third contest between Ambrose Palmer and Herman Bundren.

While Bundren put up a much better performance than he did in their previous two fights, Palmer was his master. Palmer outscored the American with his jab from the outside and landed his left hook on the inside while cleverly avoiding Bundren's dangerous right. Even when Bundren scored with his right hand in rounds four and ten, he was outpunched and was on the defensive as Palmer immediately fired back after the blow. The decision was never in question, and Palmer was crowned the winner by referee Fred Craig. Although Bundren disputed the decision, even challenging Palmer to a fourth fight with a £100 side bet, it would be his last bout in Australia.

Talk immediately went to the Palmer-Thornton rematch, which had been all but agreed to. The bout was to take place on 12 September in Sydney however Thornton did not want to risk his title. This angered Sydney Stadium management, who stated that "if he was a real champion he would defend his title and shut up."[6] Palmer and his team called Thornton's bluff and telegrammed an offer to Tasmania's middleweight and heavyweight champion Pat Appleton for a fight in Melbourne on the same date. It turned out to be Thornton's manager, Pat Kearon, who had insisted on the title not being on the line and after Thornton told Stadiums Ltd that Pat Kearon was no longer his manager and that he was now under Sammy Chapman's control, the fight with Palmer for the title went ahead on 19 September.

Thornton training with Sammy Chapman meant Palmer would need a new place to train for his bouts in Sydney. Palmer completed most of his training in Melbourne and found the time to get married during his hectic schedule. He married May Gibson at Footscray Baptist Church on Sunday 13 September before leaving with his wife and father on the train to Sydney to try and regain his middleweight title. After arriving in Sydney, he eventually set up his training headquarters in Balmain in Sydney's inner west. Days before the bout, Sydney Stadium announced that the winner of the championship fight was to meet Fred Henneberry on Derby night in what was sure to be a big payday.

Unlike the first bout, the opening round was quiet. Both men prodded for openings with their jabs and were cautious about taking risks. Palmer made one big adjustment in this fight from the first. When Thornton threw his right hand, Palmer stepped back, which made it fall short, and, after getting the timing of the dangerous blow, Palmer began to take the fight to the champion in the second round. He landed with his left hook to the head and body, one particular shot to the body strayed low, and Palmer earned a warning. Thornton scored with a grazing right hand towards the end of the round, which opened a cut over Palmer's left eye. Palmer responded in the third, bloodying the champion's nose with his jab but again he received a warning for a low blow. The pace in the fourth round was fast, with the two men exchanging at close quarters. Palmer's punches, however, were stronger and his defence was better before a glancing blow put the Victorian on the seat of his pants at the bell to end round four, but it was not an official knockdown.

Palmer took more chances in round five, and it paid dividends as he landed two hard right hands that looked like they hurt the champion. Round six was the former champion's best round as he landed hard lefts to the body and numerous right hands to the head as Thornton went on the defensive. An uppercut landed flush on Thornton's chin towards the end of the round, and many were questioning how much longer the fight would last. The champion came back in the next few rounds but was mostly ineffective against Palmer's defensive skills and, although Thornton fought gamely in these rounds, the punishment he had taken in rounds five and six was taking its toll. Thornton fought for the first minute in tenth and eleventh before he was beaten up for the remainder of the round.

The 20-year-old Victorian showed his inexperience in the final few rounds and, although he had his man hurt, he fought wildly and couldn't finish Thornton off. Thornton used the challenger's aggression against him, landing a solid right hand in round twelve, which Palmer took well but the blow was enough to make Palmer cautious. Palmer boxed carefully over the final three rounds, using his jab and keeping the champion off balance where his right hand was ineffective. The 4,000 in attendance cheered as Palmer was declared the winner on points at the final bell.

In the days after the bout, the fight between Ambrose Palmer and Fred Henneberry was set for 3 October 1931 at Sydney Stadium with the middleweight championship of Australia at stake. Boxing fans were anticipating the clash, with *The Referee* labelling the matchup "perfect."

> "All boxing enthusiasts for miles around Sydney Stadium (N.S.W) will centre their attention on the defence of the middleweight championship by Ambrose Palmer, of Victoria, against Fred Hannaberry, of N.S.W., on Saturday night. The bout is perfect. The champion is risking against a logical contender, and the champion may be beaten."[7]

Henneberry had fought just once since defeating Pearce, scoring a fifteen round decision over the American Eddie Daniels before signing for the fight with Sydney Stadium. He was reportedly the first man to fight for a championship in his debut at Sydney Stadium. There were 8,000 spectators in attendance to see Palmer's first defence of his 2nd reign as Australian champion, with the live gate totalling £1200, earning both Palmer and Henneberry £287 each. The Australian title fight, scheduled for 15x3 minute rounds, was the first time Henneberry would fight over the championship distance. The Victorian was a slight favourite in the betting at the time of the opening bell.

Both men started the fight cautiously, trying unsuccessfully to feint one another into a bad position. The second was more of the same, and while Henneberry rallied towards the end of the session, Palmer was starting to score with right hands that gave him the round. Palmer sensed that Henneberry wasn't comfortable and picked up his pace in round three. Henneberry was defending well and keeping himself out of danger, but Palmer was beginning to show his superiority. In round four Palmer hurt Henneberry with two left hooks to the body that made Henneberry grimace with pain. Henneberry was looking nervous and unsure about when to punch and, while he continued to show good defence and made Palmer miss wildly on occasions, his lack of punching left him well behind at the end of the sixth round.

Palmer hurt Henneberry with a left-right combination to the head early in the seventh, but this seemed to bring Henneberry to life momentarily. Henneberry landed his best punch of the fight in the form of a left hook to the head and followed it up with a body attack but he was still too defensive minded, and Palmer continued to push him around in clinches and outwork him with combinations to the head and body. Rounds eight and nine were one-sided as Palmer outpunched Henneberry "four punches to one."[8]

Henneberry began to take more chances in the tenth and started to take the fight to the champion. A big right hand forced Palmer back onto his heels, and the two men traded punches. After such a one-sided first nine rounds, Henneberry was fighting evenly with Palmer, and the two exchanged heavy blows through round eleven. Palmer retook control in the twelfth round and scored heavily with both hands, and Henneberry's defence was the only thing that kept him in the fight. This onslaught from Palmer seemed to be the last in his gas tank as the tide turned dramatically in round thirteen.

Henneberry stormed out for the thirteenth and hurt Palmer with a hard right hand. Forcing him to the ropes with a two-handed barrage, Palmer was now the one covering up as Henneberry unloaded an attack that seemed to surprise Palmer with its suddenness. Henneberry shoved Palmer through the ropes and out of the ring towards the end of the round and Palmer somehow lost his fighting trunks during the fall. A new pair was searched for while the action continued. Henneberry continued to outwork Palmer until the bell to end round thirteen.

Palmer's trunks were replaced, but he was showing severe signs of fatigue as round fourteen began and Henneberry, likely needing a knockout to win, continued to batter him across the ring. Palmer tried to fight back but Henneberry's defence, in particular, his ability to duck under Palmer's hooks to the head, were making Palmer miss badly and setting Henneberry up to drive the champion into the ropes with his ferocious punching. The round ended with Palmer's mouth dripping blood, and the Sydney fans were cheering for the New South Welshman to pull off an unlikely comeback victory.

The final round saw a rejuvenated Palmer stand his ground and attempt to fight off Henneberry's charge. Henneberry took the fight to Palmer again and was clearly on top, but Palmer exchanged blows with him, and the two fighters traded punches throughout the fifteenth. Henneberry never looked like scoring the knockout he needed in this round, and at the bout's conclusion, Joe Wallis crowned Palmer, the winner on points. The crowd was mixed in their reception of the referee's decision, but all newspapers seemed to agree with the verdict of Joe Wallis.

The Sydney Sportsman stated that Henneberry "made a wonderful bid for victory, but only Phar Lap can give 'em a start - and Phar Lap has twice as many legs as the greatest fighter that was ever bred."[9] Many felt that had Henneberry started his late rally earlier, that he could have taken Palmer out before the end of the contest. A rematch was already being talked of moments after the fight ended, with former Australian heavyweight champion Dave Smith, who trained Les Darcy, stating he fancied Henneberry in a return bout.

JACK CARROLL VS FRED HENNEBERRY

After being disqualified against Hancock, Carroll had taken a holiday in country Victoria, but he was soon tracked down by Stadiums Ltd. After Bundren's second loss to Palmer, Bundren said that he would only remain in Australia if a fight with Carroll could be made. Carroll had been in the country with his new wife; having married a girl from Kensington, Doreen Thomas, on 9 June after arriving back in Melbourne following the bout with Hancock. Carroll had no trouble with Bundren in the rematch and, after a slow opening three rounds, he outpunched the American easily over the final twelve rounds to win a wide points decision.

The first talks of a Henneberry-Carroll clash had come after Carroll's victory over Bundren, which was also the night after Henneberry avenged his loss to Critcher. Both Stadiums Ltd and Leichhardt were keen to stage the contest, but Carroll returned to Melbourne, where he signed to meet Ambrose Palmer on 15 August in a fight between the two stars of the Victorian boxing ring. Unfortunately, the fight was not meant to be; it was at first delayed for two weeks after Palmer came down with the flu and Carroll jarred his left hand. The fight was then moved to Sydney, but then ultimately cancelled when Carroll again broke his hand sparring Bobby Blay. Carroll had considered travelling to America at this time, after an offer from American manager Tom O'Rourke, but the hand injury also cancelled those plans.

After Henneberry's loss to Palmer, there were talks of a rematch, scheduled for 31 October, but the bout was at first delayed until 7 November and then put back until December. Palmer was under the impression that the rematch would be a non-title bout and stated that he was unable to make the weight limit by the time of the contest. Henneberry's team insisted that the middleweight title would be on the line for any rematch. Carroll's hand looked to have healed in October, and his manager expressed interest in a fight with Henneberry for mid-November. Scheduled for 21 November, Carroll was forced to withdraw after he injured his arm in training, cancelling the bout.

Carroll's injuries, combined with Palmer's choice to tour New Zealand for a series of bouts left Henneberry without the elite opponent he desired until 1932. He stayed active with knockout victories over former Australian welterweight champion Al Bourke in nine rounds at Sydney Stadium on 18 November and Queensland middleweight champion Merv Williams in eleven rounds at Leichhardt on 4 December. He closed out 1931 with a fight against Tasmanian Pat Appleton on 18 December. Appleton was coming off an impressive 2nd round knockout over Melbourne light heavyweight Leo Bandias, who outweighed Appleton by a stone.

Appleton was a 6-1 underdog in the bout but, after a slow start, showed surprising success with his crouching, wild punching style, which drew Henneberry into wild exchanges. Henneberry hurt Appleton in the second round, but the Tasmanian survived, a theme that would continue throughout the fight. Appleton roared back in the fourth but was again staggered, and Henneberry continued to be in command of the battle. The bout turned messy in rounds five and six with Appleton throwing wild punches from the outside and referee Yank pearl having to separate the inevitable clinches that resulted from the windmilling style. Henneberry continued to dominate in rounds seven through nine but couldn't find the punches to put his game opponent away.

Appleton had success with a wild left hook lead to the ribs in these rounds, but a Henneberry right hand had Appleton badly hurt in the tenth and Henneberry continued to punish Appleton in rounds eleven and twelve. The Tasmanian rallied in rounds fourteen and fifteen, winning the rounds clearly, but it seemed to be a clear cut decision for Henneberry based on his early work however referee Yank Pearl inexplicably ruled the contest a draw. Henneberry's brother and trainer Bill was livid with the decision. He vowed that Fred would never again fight at Leichhardt Stadium or with Pearl as the referee. Appleton went back to Tasmania after the bout to spend Christmas with his family, but stated that he would be back in Sydney in the new year to "fight Henneberry or anybody else, anywhere and at any time."[1]

Jack Carroll was inactive for the remainder of 1931, but by the start of 1932, he had recovered from his injuries. During his time away from the ring he had become a father, with Doreen giving birth to a daughter, who they named Betty. Henneberry had a list of possible opponents including Carroll and New Zealand middleweight champion Fred Parker, who had travelled to Australia for a series of bouts. After Palmer scored wins over Bob Thornton and Australian heavyweight champion Jack O'Malley in New Zealand at the end of 1931, he returned to Australia, and a rematch between Palmer and Henneberry was set to open the boxing season for 1932 at Sydney Stadium. Palmer, however, wasn't interested in making middleweight, and instead challenged Australian heavyweight champion Jack O'Malley, whom he had already beaten in New Zealand.

The decision by Palmer to fight for the heavyweight title had many expecting him to vacate the middleweight crown and Sydney Stadium instead opened its season with a matchup between Jack Carroll and Henneberry on 29 February. The winner of this bout was to either fight Palmer for his title, should he make the weight, or face former champion Bob Thornton for the vacant title. Thornton had snapped his three-fight losing streak with a knockout win over Appleton at Leichhardt on 22 January to re-establish himself as one of the top middleweights in the country.

The return of Carroll to Sydney Stadium was a significant boost for Stadiums Ltd as he was still one of the Stadium's main draw cards and both men drew large attendances at their training camps. Carroll's hand was strong, and he was in excellent shape, although he expected "the hardest fight of his career."[2] 10,000 spectators came in to see the Carroll-Henneberry clash, and it was a good sign for Australian boxing after some poor showings in attendance to end 1931. Henneberry weighed in at 11st-2lb for the bout, half a stone more than the welterweight champion Carroll, who came in at 10st-9.5lb. Palmer, meanwhile, had defeated Jack O'Malley to become the first man since Les Darcy to hold both the Australian middleweight and heavyweight titles simultaneously. The winner of Carroll vs Henneberry would meet Palmer, and Palmer's middleweight title would be at stake.

Both men started very fast, with Carroll using his hand and foot speed while boxing from the outside at a high work rate. Henneberry used his smart defence to manoeuvre Carroll to the ropes or corner, where his size and strength advantage could be of use. Carroll had a slight edge in round one due to his speed but lost the second round when Henneberry trapped him on the ropes and scored well with his right hand. In round three it appeared as though the more experienced Carroll had figured Henneberry out in the first two rounds and he began to take over the contest. Scoring with his left jab from a distance and ripping Henneberry with short uppercuts on the inside, Carroll's work rate and his slick defence was befuddling the larger man. Henneberry continued to march forward, but his inability to mix up his attack was allowing Carroll to get away from his punches without taking too much damage. In rounds six and seven Carroll was so in command that Henneberry barely landed a punch.

Carroll was showing none of the effects that the seven months out of the ring could have caused him in terms of his sharpness, but his lack of match fitness began to even the fight out as the tenth round began. The Victorian's hand speed started to drop off, and Henneberry began to make him miss with his jab. After nullifying the smaller man's jab, Henneberry countered it with a huge right hand that landed on Carroll's jaw. Carroll was hurt, and he spent the rest of the round trying desperately to fight Henneberry off as Henneberry moved in for the kill.

Henneberry continued to pour on the pressure in the eleventh and twelfth, while Carroll was looking "tired of mind, eye and limb and his counter attacks against the fierce onslaughts became very feeble."[3] Unlike his bout with Ambrose Palmer, Henneberry had started his onslaught early enough to wipe out the early deficit, and in round thirteen, a right hand to Carroll's jaw dropped him face first to the canvas. Carroll looked as though he might beat referee Joe Wallis' count, but "the flesh could not respond to the willing spirit"[4] and Henneberry scored a dramatic knockout victory.

Commercially, the bout was a success with the live gate totalling £684. Fred Henneberry's stock rose dramatically with the win, and he cemented his place as one of Sydney's best drawcards as well as the rematch with Palmer. The fight was a big blow to the middleweight championship hopes of Carroll and a massive setback for one of Australia's best fighters after his seven-month layoff. It was the first time Carroll had been knocked out since his 1929 loss to American Meyer Grace. With a wife and a daughter to now provide for, it was also the loss of a potentially large payday against Ambrose Palmer. While Henneberry and Palmer would increase the public's interest with their rematch and subsequent bouts, Carroll was about to begin a run that would cement his place among Australia's greatest ever boxers.

AMBROSE PALMER VS FRED HENNEBERRY II

Immediately after the first bout between Palmer and Henneberry the talks turned to a rematch. The two men were set to box for the title on 31 October but Palmer's efforts to make the middleweight division were beginning to drain him and his father objected to the idea of his son having to make the weight limit for the third time in as many months as he feared it would burn the 20-year-old out. Against the wishes of Stadiums Ltd, Palmer travelled to New Zealand with his wife and his father to take some fights above the middleweight limit. With Jack Carroll still on the sidelines with his hand injury, this was a massive blow for Stadiums Ltd.

Palmer stated to the press in New Zealand that he was actually there for a break from boxing but would fight if a suitable opponent could be found. Palmer ended up fighting twice while in New Zealand, both against Australians. His first bout was against the Australian heavyweight champion Jack O'Malley, who had been in New Zealand since June, losing twice to their heavyweight champion Alan Campbell. O'Malley was no match for Palmer, who "severely punished and easily defeated"[1] the Australian heavyweight champion. There were talks of Palmer facing Campbell after this bout, however, Campbell wouldn't agree to Palmer's conditions of a ten round bout and a catch weight of 12st and the bout wasn't made. Palmer fought Bob Thornton for a third time three weeks after defeating O'Malley, winning on points over a slow fifteen rounds.

Both Palmer and Thornton returned to Sydney early in 1932, at the request of Stadiums Ltd, and with Carroll back in the gym, many were calling for a middleweight series between those three, Henneberry and Appleton, who had fought their controversial draw just days before the end of the year. Palmer requested more time to make the middleweight limit but agreed to meet the winner of the Carroll-Henneberry clash during the Sydney Harbour Bridge Opening Sports Carnival. In the meantime, Palmer travelled to Queensland to fight O'Malley in a rematch, with the Australian heavyweight title at stake.

O'Malley, who was born in Christchurch, New Zealand, before moving to Sydney, had won the Australian heavyweight title in March 1931 against George Cook. O'Malley was only slightly larger than Palmer, weighing close to a stone more than the middleweight champion for their bout at Brisbane Stadium. Both men were expected to depart overseas after the contest, O'Malley to Great Britain and Palmer to America. As in their New Zealand matchup, O'Malley was no match for Palmer, who "out-boxed, out-sped and out-punched the tough O'Malley."[2] Many were amazed that O'Malley was able to stand up to the punishment that he did.

With the talk after the bout of Palmer's intentions to leave Australia, Stadiums Ltd had grown frustrated with the lack of money in Australian boxing and the cost to import foreign fighters, and opted to lease Sydney Stadium to its former owner, Hugh D. McIntosh. McIntosh told of his plans to bring foreign fighters to

Australia to rebuild interest in the sport. Palmer had injured his shoulder during the bout with O'Malley but had stopped in Sydney on his way back to Melbourne and again stated that he would meet the winner of the Carroll-Henneberry matchup. When Henneberry knocked out Carroll in the thirteenth round, the Palmer-Henneberry rematch was set for the Monday of the Sydney Harbour Bridge Opening celebrations.

> "Henneberry's sensational win should make his match with Ambrose Palmer for the Australian middleweight championship draw more than £1000 worth of paying customers to Rushcutters Bay next Monday night week. Apart from the regulars, visitors here for the Harbour Bridge opening may make the "gate" even greater, and if the big arena is crammed to capacity enthusiasts will believe boxing has come back with a bang."[3]

Tennis, horse-racing, swimming, cricket, bowls and golf all staged tournaments to give the thousands of tourists entertainment in the days leading up to the opening ceremony and this bout would be boxing's big showcase during the carnival.

Despite Palmer holding both the middleweight and heavyweight championships of Australia, the middleweight title would be the only one at stake. Palmer had set up camp for the bout at Sydney Stadium while Henneberry trained with his brother Bill at Becky Brown's gymnasium in Leichhardt. Tensions were high between Palmer and Henneberry, with Sydney newspaper *The Truth* reporting that the two almost came to blows four days before the bout:

"Bristling with pugnacity, Young Palmer and Fred Henneberry, who will provide a fight for a share of something in the vicinity of £2000 at the Stadium, almost staged during the week - for nothing!

Following Thursday afternoon's matinee at Rushcutters Bay a heated argument developed between the two, and only the intervention of outsiders prevented a dressing-room sensation.

It was no showman episode but a real indication of the difference of opinions between the pair. There was hardly anyone to witness the sudden flare-up of tempers, but the few who did are certain if wiser counsel had not prevailed Palmer and Henneberry would have had no hesitation about mixing it with bare fists."[4]

Palmer surprised many when he successfully boiled himself down to the middleweight limit of 11st-6lb, and while Palmer's father told *The Sporting Globe* that the weight drop hadn't weakened the champion, he looked drawn at the weigh-in. Henneberry comfortably made weight, weighing in at 11st-1lb. A crowd of 12,000 filled Sydney Stadium at Rushcutters Bay to witness the highly controversial bout.

After his slow start cost Henneberry the decision in the first bout with Palmer, Henneberry was determined not to get too far behind early on this time, and he started fast. Palmer matched his early aggression, and while the two were trading punches, a clash of heads opened up a deep gash over Henneberry's right eye. Palmer immediately began targeting the injury, hoping that he could end the night early with a referee's stoppage. Despite the handicap and Palmer's aggressive style, Henneberry defended himself well, blocking most of Palmer's punches and the challenger was looking to land his right hand over the top of Palmer's left jab, which Palmer aimed at Henneberry's cut right eye.

With Henneberry's eye swollen shut by the third round, Palmer was building a comfortable lead, but unlike the first fight, Henneberry was more aggressive, and not pacing himself as much, and even though he likely trailed on points, the pace of the action combined with Palmer's tough weight cut was beginning to wear on the champion. By the seventh round, Palmer was tired, and Henneberry landed a hard right hand to the champion's jaw which hurt him badly. Henneberry rushed at the champion and wailed away with both hands until the bell sounded to end the round. The Sydney crowd were on their feet cheering for Henneberry, and while many were expecting a knockout early in the 8th round, Henneberry's inexperience in trying to finish the fight had seen him temporarily punch himself out, and Palmer was able to regain the strength in his legs during the 8th round.

The pace slowed through round eight, but Henneberry was still forcing the action and beginning to even up the bout on points as the ninth round began. Both men were tired, so the infighting was less intense as it had been earlier and both fighters were working less in the clinches. Early in the ninth round while working in the clinches, Palmer landed a left, either to the solar plexus or below the belt, depending on the source. Henneberry dropped to the canvas as a result of the punch, and referee Joe Wallis immediately awarded him the fight, and the Australian middleweight title, via disqualification.

It was the third time Ambrose Palmer had lost in his professional career and the third time he had lost by disqualification for low blows. Palmer denied the punch was low, stating that it landed on the solar plexus, but Sydney newspaper *The Referee*, *The Sporting Globe* out of Melbourne and *The Australian Worker* all agreed that the punch was low and stated that referee Joe Wallis had warned Palmer on a number of occasions throughout the bout.

Another fight between Palmer and Henneberry was briefly

rumoured to take place in Melbourne but with a higher weight limit as well as a rematch with Jack Carroll for the middleweight title but both matchups fell through. Henneberry's cut eye he suffered in the bout with Palmer would keep him out of the ring until May, and after failing to get Palmer or Carroll to agree to a fight, Henneberry instead fought former Australian champion Bob Thornton at Sydney Stadium on 9 May 1932. The Henneberry bout would be the last time in his career that Ambrose Palmer would make the middleweight limit. Palmer and Henneberry would settle their score years later, with the Australian light heavyweight title on the line, but with Hugh McIntosh's talk of importing world class heavyweights, Palmer was about to take on the biggest challenge of his career.

AMBROSE PALMER VS YOUNG STRIBLING

Following the loss to Henneberry, Palmer stayed in Sydney and fought a pair of heavyweight bouts against imports. His first contest was with the New Zealand heavyweight champion Alan Campbell at Sydney Stadium on 2 May. Campbell was billed as the Australasian heavyweight champion following a win over then Australian heavyweight champion Jack O'Malley in December 1932 and was said to be New Zealand's best heavyweight since Tom Heeney, who had unsuccessfully challenged Gene Tunney for the World heavyweight championship in 1928. As well as being the New Zealand champion, Campbell worked as an executive in the New Zealand motor industry.

The winner was to meet Tony Gora, a Hawaiian heavyweight who was on his way to Australia for a series of bouts. Campbell appeared confident and was significantly bigger than the Australian when the two men entered the ring. Palmer, who weighed 11st-12lb, opened cautiously but once he realised Campbell couldn't match him on the inside that's exclusively where he worked. Campbell's nose and right eye were bleeding by the end of the third round as Palmer couldn't miss with his left hook. The New Zealand champion was tough and continued to try for a blow that would turn the tide, but Palmer's defence was too tight, and his work was methodical. Following a ninth-round knockdown, a further barrage brought about the end of the fight.

Tony Gora arrived from Hawaii in Australia on 1 June and immediately signed to fight Palmer with the bout taking place on 20 June. In November 1931, Gora had lost a disputed decision with future middleweight champion Ceferino Garcia in The Philippines with the decision being so unpopular that the referee Elino Flores was fired for awarding the decision to Garcia. Gora was brought to Australia by Hugh McIntosh, and McIntosh's original plan was to bring heavyweight contenders Primo Carnera and Paulino Uzcudun to Australia for fights, as well as British middleweight Len Harvey. While waiting for these fighters to arrive, McIntosh planned to stage some domestic matchups including a third fight between Henneberry and Palmer and a lightweight clash between Australian champion Bobby Delaney and contender Bobby Blay.

Following the success of the promotions involving heavyweight champion Tommy Burns in 1908, McIntosh continued to promote bouts with American imports, and many great fighters competed in Australia during the 1910s. African American heavyweight contenders Sam Langford and Sam McVea, two of the leading contenders for Jack Johnson's heavyweight title who never received a title shot because of the colour of their skin, fought each other six times in Australia between 1911 and 1913 after being imported by McIntosh. McIntosh was also the promoter behind the series of bouts won by Les Darcy against top American middleweight contenders and with ongoing bankruptcy hearings involving his purchase of the newspaper *The Sunday Times*, McIntosh was attempting to re-enter the industry that was so successful for him over 20 years ago.

While the offers to bring Carnera and Uzcudun to Australia fell through, in April it was reported that McIntosh had cabled an offer to 'The Georgia Peach' William 'Young' Stribling to come to Australia for three contests. While Gora was unknown to the boxing world, Stribling was a veteran of over 300 fights and the year before had lost in the fifteenth round in a challenge for the world heavyweight championship against Max Schmeling. Born in Bainbridge, Georgia on Boxing Day in 1904, Stribling turned professional in 1921 and fought a torrid schedule in his first few years as a professional, often fighting two or three times a month. In 1923, at the age of 18, Stribling challenged Mike McTigue for the light heavyweight championship of the world, initially winning the contest before referee Harry Ertle reversed his decision an hour later. Stribling avenged the loss in a non-title bout the following year and then defeated future light heavyweight champion Tommy Loughran in 1925.

Stribling lost in his second world title bid to new champion Paul Berlenbach in 1926, suffering a knockdown in round seven and losing a decision. He lost a return with Loughran the following year, but all the while continued to fight multiple times every month after which he began to campaign exclusively as a heavyweight. He lost in the first round of the elimination tournament to crown the new champion after Gene Tunney's retirement, losing a ten round decision to Jack Sharkey, who would win the title two years later from Max Schmeling. A pair of controversial bouts took place in Europe with another future champion Primo Carnera saw each man disqualified in fights that are widely believed to be fixed.

Even as he entered his tenth year as a professional, Stribling continued to fight multiple times every month. By the time he met Schmeling for the world heavyweight title in 1931, he had fought a recorded 268 times as a professional, winning 238 with 120 wins by knockout. Despite the high number of knockouts in his career, Stribling was a scientific boxer who preferred to use his clever defence and took no joy in hurting his opponent. Stribling gave Max Schmeling a hard fight for the first ten rounds until a right hand in the eleventh hurt him. He battled on until he succumbed in the fifteenth and final round, the only time he had been knocked out in 269 professional contests.

Young Stribling
(Photo Agence Maurice (1929) Bibliothèque de France)

Initially scheduled for 6 June, the Gora-Palmer bout was delayed to give Gora an extra week to prepare, but then an ankle injury to Palmer put the fight back to 20 June. Gora impressed reporters in his training exhibitions, described as a "fast ambitious youth" with "a sound knowledge of short punches, twinkling feet that dance to the attack throughout the rounds, and undoubtedly, a potent enough punch,"[1] however Palmer was favoured going into the contest, and his sprained ankle had fully healed.

Gora lived up to expectations early in the contest and landed several hard punches, including a right in round two that momentarily stunned Palmer. However, Palmer's work rate and tight defence gave him a clear lead after the first five rounds. A head-clash in round six opened a large cut over Palmer's left eye which would require four stitches to close, but despite the would bleeding profusely for the remainder of the contest, Palmer was in clear control as his superior stamina allowed him to take over. While Gora never looked like being stopped, he also never looked like winning after the sixth round, and although he was cheered by the crowd of 8,000 for his efforts, Palmer won the referee's decision.

Palmer praised Gora post fight for his toughness and his power. "I hammered him with everything I could yet he stood there and came back for more. Yes, he is game; and that little right-hander he hit me with in the second round was hard."[2] Palmer's inability to finish Gora had reporters already limiting his chances in the bout with Stribling.

> "Ambrose Palmer, the Australian heavyweight champion, does not appear to have the remotest chance against Young Stribling, after his failure to knock out the Japanese boxer Tony Gora, whom he hit with everything except the stool. Palmer apparently, does to pack a sufficiently powerful wallop to bowl his opponents over."[3]

Stribling arrived in Sydney on the ship 'The Monterrey' on 23 June with another heavyweight Clyde Chastain, who was to meet Tony Gora on 18 July, two weeks after the Stribling-Palmer contest, scheduled for 4 July. While many agreed that could Palmer upset Stribling that it would be a massive achievement for an Australian boxer, Stribling was considered too big and too experienced for the 20 -year-old. While he had outgrown the middleweight division, Palmer was not even a light heavyweight by American standards. Palmer often weighed in around 12st while Stribling was a fully fledged heavyweight who had not weighed in less than 13st since October.

The Australian promoters billed the Stribling-Palmer contest as a "world's heavyweight elimination contest"[4] suggesting that the winner would be fighting newly crowned heavyweight champion Jack Sharkey, who won a controversial decision over Max Schmeling in New York on 21 June. A twelve round co-feature between Australian featherweight champion Llew Edwards and lightweight contender Jimmy Kelso was also scheduled for the night in a rematch of an entertaining bout from Leichhardt Stadium six weeks prior. Hugh McIntosh also sought an injunction that prevented Stribling, an avid pilot with 1,200 hours flight experience, from being allowed to fly a plane until after he had completed his contest with Palmer.

Stribling impressed the Australian public in his workouts with many commenting on how little wear and tear his face showed despite so many career bouts. There were some concerns about the cut Palmer suffered over his left eye in the Tony Gora fight would delay the contest but the doctor cleared the eye, and the fight took place on the advertised date. The fight was expected to draw the largest crowd for an Australian bout since before World War I. Sydney's public transport agencies saw an opportunity to make some money off the bout also, doubling ticket prices on the Eastern Suburbs line that ran from the city to the stadium.

Weighing in at just over 13st, Stribling entered the ring with just over a one stone weight advantage over Palmer, who came in at 11st-12lb, lighter than he had against Gora. Sydney newspaper *The Referee* joked that Palmer had "fretted himself down" to that weight as his wife was due to have a baby around the date of the fight. The size difference appeared to be much more significant as the men started the contest as Palmer carried a lot of his weight in his legs while Stribling carried the bulk of his weight in his upper torso. Palmer fought out of a crouch to begin the opening round while Stribling established his jab and landed some shots to the body. Many of the American's jabs sailed over Palmer's head, but Palmer's retaliations were falling short in a tame opening round.

The crowd cheered wildly in the second round as Palmer backed Stribling to the ropes and landed a clean left hook. Stribling stayed patient and waited for openings while Palmer tried to capitalise on his success. The cheers of the crowd turned to concern at the end of the round as Palmer's previously injured left eyebrow was bleeding by the end of the round. Stribling stayed patient and used his enormous reach advantage, holding Palmer off in the third round with his jab and looking for openings for the right hand. Twice in the third round, he was warned for infractions, once a kidney shot and once for holding and hitting. This was the beginning of a rivalry with Australian referees that would last for the duration of his visit. Stribling landed several hard right hands to Palmer's body before the end of the round and shoved Palmer partway through the ropes.

Referee Joe Wallis' run-ins with Stribling continued into the fourth round as he ordered Stribling's corner to wipe excess water off him at the start of the round. The crowd was also turning on the American as he argued back after being warned for hitting Palmer's kidneys. All the while Ambrose Palmer, blood now dripping from his left eye, was being repeatedly backed into the ropes and punished by the larger American. Stribling repeatedly stayed an arm's length away from the undersized Australian, stepping back as his punches fell short, and hammered Palmer with counter shots while tying him up when he got within punching range. The crowd booed at the end of the fifth round as Stribling pushed Palmer back into the ropes.

Palmer was down in the sixth round for a count of two courtesy of a short right hand as the massacre continued. The 20-year-old continued to fight bravely by attacking Stribling again after rising, but Stribling tied him up and continued to stifle his attacks. Two clubbing right hands landed on Palmer's injured eye as the round came to a close. In the seventh, the crowd was calling for Stribling to fight with more venom and stop prolonging the beating but Stribling, ever methodical, continued to take no chances and continued to argue with the referee about various infractions. A pair of uppercuts hurt Palmer again in the eighth round, but Stribling continued to fight cautiously, showing impressive defence as Palmer tried in vain to land something to get him back in the fight.

The Australian's face was a mess as he entered round nine. His left eye was swollen and bleeding, and his mouth and right ear were also dripping blood. 'The Georgia Peach' dished out more punishment, finding an opening for his right uppercut three consecutive times that snapped Palmer's head back. The end finally came in round ten as Palmer went down a second time. Stribling feinted his left jab and threw another right uppercut which landed on Palmer's chin, dropping him heavily. Somehow Palmer was up at the count of four and Stribling threw and missed the same punch before the two men ended in a clinch. Palmer's chief second, Jack Warner, had seen enough and threw in the towel. Joe Wallis crowned Stribling, the winner by technical knockout.

The fight was a huge economic success. *The Sydney Morning Herald* reported that 12,000 were in attendance while Melbourne's *The Sporting Globe* reported the number at 14,000 and *The Referee* reported that while 12,400 were inside, a further 5,000 waited outside to hear the result. The live gate exceeded £4,000 with Palmer earning a purse of £940, the equivalent of one year's salary. Speaking to *The Sydney Sportsman* a few days after the contest, Ambrose Palmer was in good spirits despite the bad loss. "He picked me up and spun me round like a top when he wanted to. I hit him twice as hard as I was able in one round and he looked at me as if the flies were troubling him." Asked whether he would be interested in a return contest, Palmer stated "what would be the good? I couldn't hurt him. I'd just be wasting his time." [5]

Palmer would be the only Australian who Stribling would meet in the ring during his time in Australia. Three weeks after the win

Stribling was back in the ring at Sydney Stadium against the American journeyman Frankie Wine. Wine was never in Stribling's class, having lost to him three times previously in America, and he fought purely to stay the distance. Stribling fought cautiously, as he knew Wine was not in his league and that it was an easy nights work, but after the Palmer fight, the crowd wanted to see Stribling force the action more. They booed him early, and by the 14th round they were walking out. Stribling won a wide decision, but his safety first tactics had killed off his ability to draw a crowd in Sydney.

McIntosh took Stribling to Brisbane. Canadian heavyweight Jack Renault, who had been the distance with Jack Sharkey, Paulino Uzcudun and the great African-American heavyweight George Godfrey, was stopped in five rounds by Stribling. Fighting to please his new audience, Stribling tore into Renault to give the Australian crowd what they wanted. Displeased by the difference in skill level, the Brisbane crowd booed the mismatch and counted both men out numerous times from the second round. After five rounds Renault's corner halted the carnage due to a severely cut ear and, despite a £1,200 gate, Stribling's reputation in Queensland became that of a bully.

After Stadiums Ltd decided to challenge the N.S.C.A by staging a second Jack Carroll-Fred Henneberry clash in Melbourne, McIntosh brought Stribling south to try and build the American's following there. Stribling met Johnny Freeman, another man he had beaten before coming to Australia. Initially scheduled for 24 August, Stribling postponed the bout due to a hand injury he suffered against Renault, and the two met on 22 September. The bout was another commercial success, the gate was approximately £1,100, but like Stribling's previous three encounters in Australia, the crowd was unsatisfied. Freeman put up a stronger fight than even Palmer did, taking a handful of rounds and lasting the distance, but he was never a chance to win the fight. The majority of the crowd were booing early and left the arena as the two men were still fighting. McIntosh returned to Sydney with Stribling, matching him with Freeman to keep him busy while he wired Perth and Adelaide, the only two major cities Stribling had not fought in, to see if he could match the 'Georgian Peach' there.

The third bout between Stribling and Freeman, which took place on 21 October, was declared a no contest after the eighth round. In a fight that Stribling was reportedly winning easily, both boxers had been warned repeatedly by the referee during the contest for holding and hitting as well as kidney punching and fighting after the bell. An argument between the referee and Stribling's father and chief second broke out at the end of the sixth round after Stribling pushed Freeman through the ropes. After Stribling repeated the infraction at the end of the eighth round, the fighters began to trade punches after the bell. After the referee and both fighters respective corners failed to break the boxers up, the referee disqualified both fighters and ruled the bout a no contest. Hugh McIntosh announced both boxers purses would be withheld until an investigation had taken place. Both boxers claimed after the contest that they had not heard the bell.

Stribling did fight in Adelaide and Perth, defeating Tony Gora and George Thompson respectfully, both by decision. He returned to the United States in 1933 after fighting in South Africa and France after leaving Australia. In September he defeated world light heavyweight champion Maxie Rosenbloom in a non-title fight, which was the 251st recorded career contest of his career and tragically the last. While riding his motorbike to visit his wife and newly born child in the hospital, Stribling was hit by a car which crushed his left leg and fractured his pelvis. Stribling was taken to the same hospital his wife and child were at and lasted two days before succumbing to the injuries. He was only 28 years old.

FRED HENNEBERRY VS JACK CARROLL II

Following the knockout loss to Fred Henneberry, Jack Carroll stayed in Sydney and agreed to fight at Leichhardt Stadium against Russ Critcher on 1 April. Critcher had been a solid draw at Leichhardt and had recently travelled north to Newcastle for three fights in as many weeks before returning to Leichhardt to again defeat Wally Hancock. There were talks of the bout being for the welterweight title; however, Critcher's manager, Harry Stone, refused to put the title on the line and the bout was fought over 15x2 minute rounds. Carroll stated that he didn't care about the title and was only concerned with giving Critcher a lacing.

While Critcher was still officially the champion, Carroll was considered the uncrowned champion, with his only losses to Australian's at the welterweight limit being on a foul. His contest with Critcher proved this. Weighing in slightly over the welterweight limit, Carroll dominated the final six rounds to win a clear cut decision. Critcher was said to have given a good account of himself but could not deal with Carroll's fast left hand. After the fight, it was reported that Carroll had again fractured his left hand, and would be out of the ring for an extended period. There were talks of a rematch with Critcher with the title on the line, however, Carroll's injured hand kept him out of action until June. Bouts with Bobby Delaney and Ambrose Palmer were proposed, but when Hugh McIntosh leased the stadium at Rushcutters Bay, he did not have Carroll under contract. Palmer was matched with Gora and Delaney with Bobby Blay, leaving Carroll without a bout in Sydney.

During the layoff, Carroll was employed at an abattoir that was owned by his brother, marking the first time he had to work as well as box since he first won the Australian title. Carroll claimed years later that the work skinning sheep with his bare hands would have benefits to his career as a boxer. The physicality of ripping the skin from the carcass resulted in the toughening of Carroll's hands and wrists as well as building the muscles in his forearms and Carroll would stick with the job for the remainder of his boxing career. After his hands had healed, Carroll kept busy in the gym as a sparring partner for Tony Gora in the latter's preparation for his bout with Clyde Chastain before he was finally offered a third bout with Billy Richards in Newcastle.

Richards had regularly been fighting in Newcastle throughout the year. He had returned from Queensland earlier that month after a pair of bouts with Ron Richards, a young Aboriginal puncher to whom he had split a pair of 15 round bouts. Meanwhile "Bluey" Jones, from Newcastle, had just taken the welterweight title claim from Critcher and promoters were likely looking to expose Carroll to the Newcastle audience to stage the bout up there. Richards was again no match for Carroll, retiring after the ninth round, and a fight between Jones and Carroll was pencilled in for Newcastle on 13 August.

The cut eye that Fred Henneberry suffered in his title-winning effort with Palmer would keep him out of the ring until May, and after failing to get Palmer or Carroll to agree to a fight, Henneberry instead fought former Australian champion Bob Thornton at Sydney Stadium on 9 May 1932. Thornton was a logical contender based off of his short tenure as champion in 1931 and his January knockout win over Pat Appleton, who had drawn with Henneberry in December. There was a lot of confidence within Thornton's camp, with Thornton's manager Sammy Chapman even proposing a winner take all purse during negotiations. Henneberry accepted a guarantee of £300 for his first title defence.

Thornton appeared timid in the opening round, but Henneberry sat off him and used his jab almost exclusively, one of these jabs drew blood from Thornton's mouth. The challenger loosened up in the second round, and Henneberry had trouble with his timing as Thornton was always on the move and a series of right hands gave the second session to Thornton. Henneberry had greater success in round three by cutting off the ring and only working when he trapped his man on the ropes. Referee Joe Wallis cautioned both men for butting in a fourth round that was won by the champion. Henneberry was repeatedly landing with the left hook to the point that Thornton was becoming hesitant to throw his powerful right hand.

Thornton fought back in round five and found success by pawing with his left hand and throwing his dangerous right hand behind it while the champion's output slowed in rounds five and six. A hard right hand landed by Thornton in the seventh woke Henneberry up, and a slugfest ensued. Thornton was getting the better of the exchanges now, but Henneberry was still landing clean, accurate shots. Thornton was landing his right hand repeatedly in the eighth round and what at first looked like an easy night for the champion was now looking like much more of a battle.

The match ended in the ninth round but how the contest ended depends on the account. What definitely happened was Bob

Thornton was disqualified. *The Sydney Morning Herald* reported that he placed a number of low punches which hurt Henneberry. Joe Wallis cautioned Thornton after the fourth low punch in the round before a fifth low punch forced the disqualification, which seems to be discounted by other sources. Sydney newspaper *The Referee* reports that Henneberry ducked a counter from Thornton and his groin and the challenger's knee made contact, leaving him on the floor in immense pain and forcing Joe Wallis to award the fight to the champion.

The Sun agrees with *The Sydney Morning Herald's* account of the foul and also reported that Hugh McIntosh suggested a rule change after the fight. Fighters who were accidentally fouled would receive ten minutes to recover and only then would the bout be awarded to them if they couldn't continue. After the fight, Thornton was seen to "exchange kisses with three exuberant members of the fair sex"[1] on his way to the dressing room where he denied committing a foul. Two doctors examined Henneberry after the fight and confirmed he had suffered an injury, one of them stating that he would not have been able to continue even if he had been given a ten-minute respite.

McIntosh's syndicate 'The National Sporting Club of Australasia,' who promoted the bout, conducted an enquiry after the contest, interviewing Dr Sydney Jones, the ringside doctor, Joe Wallis and both contestants but determined that the foul wasn't deliberate and agreed to pay Thornton's share of the purse. They also stated that the board "will not tolerate foul fighting, and will take the gravest view of any breach of the rules which warrants consideration in the future."[2]

While Thornton made demands for a return with the champion, Henneberry weighed up offers to travel to England and fight the best middleweights there. The importation of heavyweights also left him without an opponent to face in Sydney as both Palmer and

Thornton had left the middleweight class for fights with the foreigners. While Hugh McIntosh had leased Sydney Stadium from Stadiums Ltd, he had no control of boxing in Melbourne. Dick Lean, chairman of Stadiums Ltd, made offers that were accepted for Henneberry to defend his middleweight title against Carroll at the reopening of Melbourne Stadium on 20 August.

Henneberry was known by reputation only in Victoria for his bouts with Palmer and had fought all of his bouts in Sydney. Despite this, the fight was expected to draw a large crowd for the Stadium's reopening and to keep Stadium Ltd in the boxing game in Australia.

> "Melbourne is dead keen to see Carroll in action again. Apart from the liking for the local boy, the knowledge that he can always be relied upon, and that Henneberry is a champion, is sufficient inducement for a roll-up."[3]

McIntosh and the N.S.C.A countered Stadium Ltd's Melbourne ploy by attempting to stage a bout between Stribling and Johnny Freeman at the Exhibition Building in Melbourne on 24 August but when Stribling injured his hand in a fifth round stoppage win over Jack Renault in Brisbane, the bout was cancelled.

With the fight billed as for the middleweight title, and both men fighting well under the middleweight limit for the entirety of their careers, no one expected the drama at the weigh-in. Henneberry reportedly checked his weight on the afternoon of the bout and was right on the limit of 11st-6lb. At some point after that members of Henneberry's camp informed Stadiums Ltd that the bout would only go ahead if his middleweight title was not at stake and Henneberry never officially weighed in, with his manager stating he was 11st-6.5lb on the evening of the fight.

Taking a similar attitude to when facing Critcher, Carroll agreed to the terms, and the bout took place. Carroll weighed in at 10st-11lb, closer to welterweight than middleweight. Unlike their first meeting, Carroll was ring fit and was confident he could keep up the effort he put forward during the early rounds of the first meeting for the duration of the contest. Henneberry this time was the one who was coming off an injury, and while he had fought in regional New South Wales, this was his first bout outside of the state.

Fred Henneberry and Jack Carroll
(National Library of Australia, nla.obj-148562750)

Similar to the first bout, Carroll started the better of the two. Henneberry applied constant pressure behind his high guard however Carroll only punched when the middleweight champion was in range to be hit and, worried about being caught late; he paced himself for the duration against the larger man. It was clear both men had learnt from their first contest, Henneberry waited until he cornered Carroll before he punched and Carroll fought sporadically and didn't waste unnecessary energy, which resulted in a slow opening round. Carroll opened up more in the second, and the difference in speed was startling. Henneberry barely landed a punch and returned to the corner with blood dripping from his nose.

The middleweight champion guarded closer in round three but Carroll was patient, and every time Henneberry left an opening Carroll landed with his left hand, which caused Henneberry's left eye to swell shut by the end of the round. The Victorian also showed tremendous skill when Henneberry moved him near the ropes, smothering his attacks and spinning out of danger. The fourth was Carroll's again after he landed three uppercuts that snapped Henneberry's head back. Despite the punishment, Henneberry continued to march forward, but he was thoroughly outboxed in rounds five, six and seven.

Way behind on points, Henneberry fought desperately in rounds eight and nine and had success landing his right hand to the body when he cornered Carroll. Carroll still scored with his left jab, but he was forced to trade more in these rounds, and Henneberry worked his body well with both hands in the ninth. The rally was short-lived, and Carroll reclaimed command in the tenth and Henneberry was out on his feet at the end of the eleventh. Henneberry took more punishment in the twelfth, and his right eye was cut and, after another dominating Carroll round in the thirteenth, both of Henneberry's eyes were swollen shut.

Despite his injuries, Henneberry continued to attack in round fourteen but was unable to land the punch to turn the tide. The two men touched gloves to start the final round, and while the crowd jeered Henneberry for rough tactics in the clinches, he fought a relatively clean fight. Henneberry attacked relentlessly in the final round but Carroll was punishing him with both hands as the final bell ended the contest, and the referee crowned Carroll, the winner on points.

Despite the official title not being on the line due to Henneberry weighing over the limit, Carroll claimed the title following the victory. His claim was recognised by the N.S.C.A, Leichhardt Stadium and other Sydney promoters. After the contest, Hugh McIntosh stated "The National Sporting Club of Australasia will now officially recognise Carroll as middleweight champion, even though the title was not involved. The old trick of a titleholder entering the ring half a pound over the limit will not work. It is as dead as a dodo. Carroll was under the weight limit. He defeated the holder in a contest of 15 three minute rounds. That is sufficient. He is the new champion."[4]

The victory effectively put Carroll at the top of both the welterweight and middleweight divisions and put him in a strong negotiating position for a fight with the recognised welterweight champion Bluey Jones. Henneberry was still officially the middleweight champion in future matchups, but the injuries sustained in this contest kept him out of action until October. While he would engage in rubber matches with both Carroll and Palmer in the future, Henneberry's name would forever be linked with another middleweight who was emerging from Queensland. Their bouts over the next twelve months would capture the imagination of Sydney fight fans.

RON RICHARDS

Randell William Richards was born on 8 May, 1910 at the Deebling Creek Aboriginal Mission near Ipswich, Queensland. Ron's father, Richard, was a fence builder, a skilled axeman and had a bare-knuckle boxer. Ron went to work with his father at the age of 14 and also became talented with the axe before he began boxing in Smally Higgins' boxing tents where he toured with a troupe of boxers around regional Queensland taking on all comers as an attraction during agricultural shows. Ron stood 5' 10½" tall, and his good looks and slick, counter-punching style helped him build up a solid fan base in Brisbane during his rise through the preliminaries in Brisbane.

Richards first recorded bouts seemed to take place on 28 April 1928. Richards fought twice that date; *The Queensland Times* described the first fight as "a good four-round preliminary, the result being a draw."[1] In his second bout, Richards knocked out A.Brock in the first round. His first career loss is believed to have occurred on 8 August at Brisbane Stadium when Norm Johnson stopped him in the first round of a six-round preliminary contest. It is likely these bouts weren't the only fights Richards had early in his career. Newspaper *The Brisbane Courier* list Richards' record as 23 wins from 26 contests with 20 KO wins in March 1932; however, there are no reports of these bouts taking place in newspapers.

Ron Richards
(National Library of Australia, nla.obj-148606605)

In his book 'Lords of the Ring,' Peter Corris states that Richards, like a lot of Australian boxers of the time, got his boxing start in Smalley Higgins' boxing tent in his teenage years. Tent boxing was a common attraction at agricultural shows throughout regional Australia in the 1920s. Professional boxers would sign with "tents" and travel around parts of regional Australia where they would take on all comers in contests, with the challenges coming from the audience. The challengers had the opportunity to make money by lasting the distance with the professionals, and many other

Australian champions also began their career in the tent. This likely explains why many of Richards' early career bouts are undocumented.

Ron Richards' next official bouts weren't recorded until 1932 when he met Jerry Symonds at Bohemia Stadium in South Brisbane. However, a fight on 6 February 1932 against a with a K. Briggs, a last-minute replacement for a fighter with the surname of Keeble, was recorded in *The Queensland Times*. Richards stopped him in the third round after being on top in every stanza. Richards would fight the majority of his bouts in 1932 at this stadium starting with the bout against Symonds on 24 February. Richards broke Symonds' nose in the first of a scheduled 10x2 minute rounds before dropping him early in the eighth round with, what would become his trademark, a right cross. Symonds corner threw in the towel after the knockdown, giving Richards a TKO win.

Newcastle light heavyweight Buxton Oliver, who had challenged for the NSW heavyweight title in November 1931, was billed as a big test for Richards. With knockout wins over New Zealand light heavyweight champion Fred Parker and NSW heavyweight champion, Ted Pickrang, Oliver carried knockout power in his hands. The bout took place at Bohemia Stadium and was the first recorded contest for Richards over 15x2 minute rounds. The pace was furious from the outset, but Richards was beating the heavier Oliver to the punch. In the third round, Richards put the Novocastrian down for a six-count with a right hand to the body. Oliver was game and battled back to win the fourth round and the two traded heavy punches in the fifth. Richards put Oliver through the ropes in the sixth round, Oliver returned and finished the round, but retired on his stool before the start of the seventh.

Richards was back in the ring three days later, knocking out Jim Morgan 30 seconds into the second round. April saw Richards fight another Newcastle fighter Wally Maher twice, both taking place at

Bohemia Stadium. Their first bout was controversial leading to a rematch the following week. Richards dropped Maher in the 2nd round and Maher, who was ready to rise at six, was counted out as he rose at nine and Richards declared the winner. Richards showed his superiority seven days later, blitzing through Maher again in two rounds but this time with no controversy.

Wins over the touring New Zealand middleweight champion Fred Parker (points) and Eddie Daniels (points) and Reg Hall (first round knockout) kept Richards busy through May and June. *The Referee* reported that Richards' first-round win over Reg Hall was his 20th win in a row:

> "Ron Richards, the Queensland colored middleweight, scored his 20th straight win when he knocked out Reg Hall, of Sydney, in the first round at Brisbane Stadium on Friday night. Richards, who is a great local favourite, is quickly gaining experience. He has gone from success to success." [2]

Ron would face the toughest test of his career next in Billy Richards, the veteran of 88 bouts. Billy was riding a seven-fight win streak since a stoppage loss to Jack Carroll in April 1931. Originally Ron Richards was to fight former Henneberry opponent Jimmy Pearce, but Pearce had injured his hand in a contest with Pat Appleton the week before leading to a Richards vs Richards bout. The fight, scheduled for 15x2 minute rounds, took place at Bohemia Stadium on 29 June 1932. Ron had a significant weight advantage, weighing in at 11st-3lb while Billy Richards was only 10st-5lb.

The smaller man Billy took the lead early on, outworking his larger opponent in close over the first eight rounds and making him miss when the two boxed from the outside. Billy was making Ron look amateurish in the first half of the fight, but a right hand to the jaw from Ron put Billy on the deck briefly in the ninth round. Ron's inexperience allowed Billy to survive and retake control of the bout by the 12th round. Ron's weight advantage took its toll in the last three rounds as he punished Billy, shaking him with his heavy right cross repeatedly.

The referee Joe Rivers announced the decision for Ron Richards at the end of the fifteen round contest, but according to *The Brisbane Courier*, many in the crowd felt the bout was close enough to be scored a draw. *The Queensland Times*, however, felt Richards showed his supremacy and deserved the decision:

> "The coloured youth's display against such an experienced gloveman further endorses the opinion that he is the finest middleweight produced in Queensland in the last decade."[3]

Billy Richards thought he won the contest and asked for a rematch the following week, which Ron accepted. The highly anticipated local bout would take place once again at the Bohemia Stadium on 6 July 1932. Unlike the first meeting this time it was Ron Richards who took the lead early on. Billy appeared slower than he was in their meeting the week before and allowed the younger and bigger man to control the tempo of the fight. Billy came back in the fourth and fifth rounds, hurting Ron badly with right-hand counter punches in both rounds. Ron unleashed his coveted right-hand and hurt Billy in the sixth round, but Billy's experience allowed him to survive and he slowed the pace during the next few rounds.

Ron had improved since the first fight and wasn't allowing Billy to outwork him in the clinches. His size and strength advantage wore Billy down heading into the final five rounds. Ron dominated rounds 11-14 with Billy using his experience to survive and conserve energy but seemed to be well behind heading into the final round. Billy took the fight to Ron in the fifteenth, but it appeared to be too little too late in the eyes of many spectators.

However, the referee thought different and awarded the decision to

Billy Richards, evening up the score between the two men at one apiece. The decision was unpopular with the crowd, and many newspapers thought the bout should have gone to the younger Ron Richards:

> "The coloured middleweight was extremely unlucky to lose the decision. In the opinion of this writer, Ron Richards won nine of the 15 rounds and two were even. It was Ron Richards' first set-back in Brisbane." [4]

With the win, Billy Richards headed south to Newcastle looking for a rematch with Jack Carroll, who had stopped him in 1930. Ron Richards was going to have to wait for the opportunity for a third fight, and instead, he fought former title contender Frank Vann. Vann had been very inconsistent since losing to Jack Haines in 1930, losing more than he won and he had not fought in six months before facing Richards. The bout was one-sided with Richards dropping Vann ten times before Vann wouldn't come out for the twelfth round. The following night, on 30 July, Jack Carroll stopped Billy Richards in their Newcastle bout which paved the way for a rematch between Carroll and Henneberry, as well as the third Richards vs Richards meeting, which took place two weeks later on 11 August 1932 in Brisbane. Ron Richards tipped the scales at 11st-4.5lb, while Billy again gave away weight coming in one stone lighter.

Both boxers felt each other out in a slow-paced first two rounds, in which Ron did most of the leading but the third round the fighters opened up and began trading with Ron getting the better of the action. Billy boxed cautiously in rounds five, six and seven but Ron dominated rounds eight through eleven and started to punish his smaller opponent. According to *The Brisbane Courier*, "it was only his coolness and exceptional toughness that kept him (Billy Richards) on his feet" during these rounds. [5] In round ten, Ron opened up Billy's left eye that had caused him to retire in the Jack Carroll fight two weeks before. Billy wouldn't go down without a fight, and he battled back in the final rounds, outboxing Ron in rounds twelve, thirteen and fourteen, but Ron Richards closed the show with a strong final round. One of the hardest punches of the fight landed after the final bell when Ron landed a right cross to Billy's jaw. Unlike the first two fights, there was no disputing this decision and Ron Richards gained superiority over his smaller, more experienced rival.

With the win over Billy Richards, Ron Richards earned his first title shot, against Queenslander Tommy Nivens, who according to newspapers held the Queensland heavyweight title. Records have Nivens as being inactive from 1930-1932 before the Richards fight. *The Brisbane Courier*, however, states that he held the Queensland Heavyweight title and had secured eleven wins recently while fighting in Sydney. Among those wins was a win over New Zealand middleweight champion Al McDonald and he had held American fighter Tony Tuzzolino, a previous opponent of both Carroll and Palmer, to a draw.[6]

The bout took place at the Bohemia Stadium on 19 August. Richards came in as a middleweight at 22st-5lb while Nivens had a weight advantage of over half a stone, tipping the scales at 12st. Richards boxed well from the opening bell but was having trouble catching up to Nivens, who was making Richards miss many of his blows by retreating out of range. In round two Richards landed a right cross to the chin of Nivens, which dropped him for the full count. Nivens recovered and, apparently still thinking the fight was on, threw a wild punch while in his corner which nearly hit one of his cornermen before again collapsing.

Richards never officially defended his Queensland Heavyweight title, but he stayed active through the rest of 1932. Richards scored a fifteen round decision win early in September over welterweight

Alby Roberts before agreeing to meet the touring Hawaiian light heavyweight Tony Gora. Gora had defeated Billy Richards in his last fight on 17 September, but before that, he had lost two more bouts, both to fellow touring Americans Clyde Chastain and Adolph Heintz. A "large attendance" witnessed Richards outbox a "sluggish" Gora over the 15x2 minute rounds,[7] with the only real trouble that Gora offered to Richards was in the fourteenth round when he surprised him with a hard right hand.

After the boring fight with Gora, Richards faced his toughest test in Pat Appleton. Appleton had mixed success since the draw with Henneberry, losing contests with Bob Thornton, Billy Richards and Jimmy Pearce, but was undefeated in his last three heading into the fight with Ron Richards. Always willing to travel, Appleton had fought his last three matches in three different states including his home state of Tasmania where he held Bob Thornton to a draw over fifteen rounds in a rematch of their February bout. This bout would be Richards' second headlining fight at Brisbane Stadium but would be the fourth different state that Appleton had fought in, in four bouts.

Despite suffering a cut eye from a fourth-round head-clash, Richards was too fast and aggressive for the Tasmanian, and when he kept Appleton on the outside, he dominated. Appleton had his moments in the middle rounds, scoring with body punches on the inside but Richards answered with uppercuts and the pace he set kept Appleton on the outside while his superior stamina allowed him to outwork his opponent. After dominating the final five rounds, Richards scored his most impressive win with a fifteen round decision in front of 1,500 spectators.

Richards completed his contract at Brisbane Stadium the three weeks later against veteran Jimmy Pearce. Pearce, just three weeks earlier, had lasted the 15 round distance in a rematch with middleweight champion Fred Henneberry in Henneberry's first contest since losing to Carroll in Melbourne. He could only last 61 seconds with Richards. When Pearce stepped in to work Richards' body, Richards replied with a short right hand that ended the contest. *The Referee* described it as "the prettiest punch seen for a long time in the Brisbane ring, and worthy of a champion."[8] This win confirmed that Richards was one of the top middleweights in the country, and would end the 12-year ring career of Jimmy Pearce.

Another fight with Billy Richards was scheduled for 11 November at Brisbane Stadium, but Ron withdrew with what was described as an "internal disorder"[9] and was set to take a brief holiday to Bundaberg, a city north of Brisbane in Queensland. The internal disorder and the "holiday" to Bundaberg was probably a cover, as Ron Richards fought on 12 November in Bundaberg. An attempt to try and move the bout with Billy Richards to Bundaberg, where it would draw a better crowd, was blocked by Brisbane Stadium, which left Ron matched with local fighter Billy Lees. Lees, who was coming off a win over Norm Johnson in a bout billed for the Queensland middleweight championship, was knocked out in the sixth round by Ron Richards. Richards is often referred to after this bout as the middleweight and heavyweight champion of Queensland. While the weights for this contest weren't reported in newspapers, this victory was likely the source of the middleweight championship claim.

Victories over Appleton, Pearce and Lees showed that Ron Richards was one of the top middleweights in the country and a few days after the win over Lees it was announced that Richards would make his Sydney debut, taking on Australian heavyweight champion Ambrose Palmer on 5 December at Sydney Stadium in a non-title fight. Palmer had taken a break following his loss to Young Stribling in October, but since his return, he had scored wins in October and November. His opponents in these return bouts, like Stribling, were American heavyweight imports who significantly outweighed him, however, they were not on the skill level that Stribling was on.

First up was Clyde Chastain on 24 October at Sydney Stadium. Born in Dallas, Texas, Chastain had campaigned modestly throughout the United States since his first recorded bout in 1927. In 1929 he lost back to back decisions to future welterweight world champions Jackie Fields and Raffaele Giordano, who boxed under the name Young Corbett III. In 1931 he lost on a cut to William 'Gorilla' Jones in an eliminator for the National Boxing Association middleweight title before moving up to light heavyweight where he lost to future world light heavyweight champion Bob Olin by split decision.

Since arriving in Australia in July, Chastain had defeated Tony Gora, Bob Thornton, Johnny Freeman and 'Tiger' Jack Payne, all in main events at Sydney Stadium. Three weeks before his bout with Palmer he had to settle for a draw with Adolph Heintz. With Henneberry and Carroll fighting in Melbourne and Palmer on the sidelines, the main drawcards in Sydney for the past few months had been the American heavyweight imports of Chastain, Heintz, Payne, Al Walker, and Frankie Wine. The return of Palmer was a huge boost for Sydney boxing fans, and 10,000 spectators filled the Stadium to see him do battle with Chastain. After a slow start, Palmer took over in the second round, and despite Chastain's half a stone weight advantage, he was never allowed back in the fight. Using his left jab, which Palmer scored a sixth-round knockdown with when he caught Chastain off-balance, and his "under-and-over left hook to the body and head,"[10] Palmer scored a wide unanimous decision over twelve rounds.

Two days after the Chastain contest *The Sydney Morning Herald* reported that Palmer would meet Johnny Freeman on 14 November at Sydney Stadium. Freeman was due to meet Young Stribling in Sydney on 29 October in what was going to be Stribling's last bout in Australia. 'The Georgia Peach' fought three weeks after defeating Palmer, but a lacklustre fifteen round decision win over Frankie Wine, in which the crowd departed the arena during the contest, prompted him to travel firstly to Brisbane, where he beat Jack Renault in five rounds, then Melbourne to face Freeman. Freeman had arrived in Australia in September but had not been successful, losing to Chastain in his debut before losing to Young Stribling in Melbourne on 22 September. Before arriving in Sydney, Freeman had fought Stribling in America, losing a decision, and had also fought future heavyweight championship contender Tony Galento.

Freeman didn't receive as much criticism as Stribling did for his role in the eighth round brawl. However ,this was possibly because he had already signed to fight Palmer, and bad press could influence the gate. Australia's 1908 Olympic boxing silver medallist and entrepreneur Reginald 'Snowy' Baker was appointed the referee in front of what was a solid crowd of 7,000 fans. Despite a one stone weight advantage and some underhanded tactics, Freeman couldn't do much with Palmer and had no answer for the Victorian's left hook. Freeman was out of the fight from the fifth round with only his size advantage allowing him to last the twelve rounds. While Palmer had the won the bout comfortably, the left eye that was damaged in the Young Stribling contest was opened up late in the fight.

Palmer returned to Melbourne following the victory over Freeman and trained for the Richards bout there, re-arriving in Sydney three days out from the contest. While the Australian heavyweight title was not on the line for this twelve round contest, Palmer had stated that he would put it on the line within a month should Richards defeat him. While Richards had not been seen by Sydney fans before, comparisons were being drawn to the first fight between Jack Haines and Ambrose Palmer as fans had not seen Palmer before he upset Sydney Stadium's star attraction in Haines. While

Palmer was the strong favourite, Richards' reputation as a knockout puncher had Sydney fight fans excited.

The afternoon weigh-in before the bout saw Palmer, who weighed in at 12st-0.5lb, with just under a 6lb weight advantage over Richards, who came in not much over the middleweight limit at 11st-8.5lb. While Richards could still make the middleweight division, Palmer had grown since losing the title to Henneberry 18 months ago, and while he had made the light heavyweight limit in all of his contests, most of his opponents had been heavyweights. Despite the weight disadvantage, Richards had shown that he had the power to knock out men larger than himself.

7,000 fans, including a number of players from the Australian and English cricket teams who were playing the first test match of the Ashes series in Sydney, were in attendance at Sydney Stadium to see what was advertised as a 12x2 minute round bout. Considering the contest was between a Victorian and a relatively unknown Queenslander over just two minute rounds, the fight produced a surprisingly large gate of approximately £700. Asked about the two-minute rounds at the fight, Hugh McIntosh stated that Palmer refused to fight over three minute rounds for the contest due to the cut on his left eye.

Palmer did enter the ring with plaster seen over his bad left eye, and he seemed to be guarding it throughout the contest. Richards started the better of the two and took the fight to the champion in the opening round, scoring with some clean right-hand punches while Palmer sat back and attempted to figure out his opponent. Palmer began to counter more in the second round, landing with short uppercuts to the head and left hands to the body in close but Richards still forced the pace and was having surprising success early on with his right hand.

Palmer found his range with the jab in the third round, snapping his head back with one in particular, and he began to score on the advancing Richards with his left hook while circling him. The Australian heavyweight champion also started working Richards' body with both hands in close after smothering but sometimes taking, his dangerous right-hand punches, but Richards scored often enough to keep the round even and seemed to have the lead after the first three rounds.

Richards followed his right hand up with left hooks in the fourth round but Palmer was reading the smaller man's attacks, and his defence was tightening with every round. Despite briefly falling through the ropes in this round, Palmer was beginning to take over, and his body punching was starting to slow Richards down. Rounds five and six were all Palmer as he effectively smothered Richards' work and concentrated on the Queensland champions body with both hands. Richards countered sporadically in these rounds but Palmer's size and body punching was wearing him down, and Palmer thoroughly outworked Richards.

Richards briefly staggered the champion in the seventh with a left hook-right hand combination to the chin which bloodied Palmer's mouth, but Palmer showed his experience and smothered Richards until his head had cleared and Richards was unable to take advantage. Rounds eight, nine and ten were all Palmer. Richards was unable to match the larger man up close ,and Palmer used his jab and superior defence to nullify Richards on the outside, and he imposed his will on the inside, making Richards wince when he landed to the body.

Palmer appeared to be coasting to an easy victory in the eleventh round when he got careless Richards landed a hard overhand right on the plaster above Palmer's left eye, re-opening the cut he suffered against Young Stribling. The wound bled profusely, and Richards came to life, but Palmer used clever defensive skills to survive the round. Richards threw everything at Palmer in the final round but was unable to score the knockout he needed and after some heated exchanges in the final round, the referee Joe Wallis awarded the decision to Palmer.

While the majority of the crowd agreed with the decision, Richards had made an impression on the Sydney fans, and a small number of his new supporters booed the decision. Most of the talk post-fight, however, was regarding Palmer's often injured left eye and how much time he would need off to let the injury fully heal.

> "It is now hoped that Palmer's eyesight will be considered, and the youthful champion allowed sufficient time to heal the soft skin and flesh above his oft-times lacerated eyebrows before another tempting money match is offered to him."[11]

Palmer's opinion of Richards following their bout was high. He stated that he thought Richards was the best middleweight in Australia and that he was greatly impressed with the punching power of the Queenslander. Addressing the two-minute rounds, Palmer stated that he didn't ask for two-minute rounds, but instead asked for an extra week to train for the bout. McIntosh wanted to keep the 9 December date and compromised by offering the bout over two-minute rounds, to which Palmer agreed. While Palmer was going to take a break from the ring to let his eyes heal, Richards was rumoured as the next opponent for the Australian middleweight champion Fred Henneberry in early 1933. This fight would be the first bout of a ten bout series that became the biggest rivalry in Australian boxing history.

FRED HENNEBERRY VS RON RICHARDS

Fred Henneberry had stayed active since his loss to Jack Carroll, fighting a twice in Newcastle in October. His first opponent in October was Jimmy Pearce, who proved more trouble in this contest than in their 1931 bout. Pearce again used his jab well in the early rounds but also found a home for his right hand which kept Henneberry at bay. Pearce seemed to have the lead at the halfway mark, and a frustrated Henneberry repeatedly hit the Novocastrian to the back of the head and after the bell. A furious rally in the championship rounds and a fifteenth round knockdown earned Henneberry a razor-thin decision, much to the dismay of the local crowd "who voiced their disapproval of the verdict."[1]

His next opponent was Al Bourke, who had been relatively inactive since his first bout with Henneberry, fighting only twice in 1932 with the last of those coming in June. Henneberry made the welterweight for the first time since his loss to Russ Critcher, coming in at 10st-3lb; almost one stone less than he had against Pearce three weeks earlier. Like Pearce, Bourke put up a much better fight than he had in his first bout with Henneberry. Bourke started fast and was in command of the contest through the first six rounds before Henneberry's fitness took over. Bourke rallied in the tenth but took heavy punishment in the last five rounds, and Henneberry had him out on his feet in the thirteenth, but Bourke held on to see the final bell, where Henneberry won the referee's decision. Al Bourke travelled to England the following year and would only fight once more in Australia, losing to Tommy King in 1935. While in England, British-born Bourke won the British Middleweight title with a fourth-round stoppage over George Gordon. He also challenged future light heavyweight title contender Jock McAvoy for the British Empire middleweight title but was defeated on points.

This fight would be the last time Henneberry would make the welterweight limit, and it was revealed after the contest that he had broken his left hand, which would require surgery, sidelining him until 1933. The wins over Carroll and Palmer had established Henneberry as one of the major drawcards at Sydney Stadium. However, the controversial ending against Thornton followed by the controversy around the weight limit and one-sided defeat to Carroll followed, plus the leasing of Sydney Stadium by Hugh McIntosh had effectively put Henneberry out of action in Sydney. Thornton had also claimed the title when Henneberry refused to give him a rematch, but he was held to a draw by Pat Appleton in a rematch and then lost three contests with American imports, so no one took his claim seriously.

The emergence of Richards as a contender who could fight at both middleweight and heavyweight allowed Henneberry back into the picture at Sydney Stadium. Hugh McIntosh opened the 1933 boxing season at Sydney Stadium by matching the Queensland heavyweight champion with Henneberry on 16 January. Henneberry's brother Bill accepted the fight on the condition that it was at the middleweight limit. It was a massive opportunity for Henneberry to re-establish himself as a star at Sydney Stadium and a lousy performance would likely relegate him to the smaller stadiums.

Less than a week out from the bout a dispute between Stadiums Ltd and the N.S.C.A, regarding the lease McIntosh's company had over the stadium threatened to cancel the contest. The fight was saved when an interim agreement was reached where Stadiums Ltd would promote the bout should the N.S.C.A lose the lease on the stadium. A few days after the contest it was announced that the N.S.C.A would cease staging bouts at Sydney Stadium, finishing Hugh D. McIntosh's business with the famous stadium that he built in 1908.

Henneberry impressed reporters during training in the week before the bout. In his last sparring session two days before the contest, Henneberry knocked out his sparring partner Royce McGrath, who had just defeated Alby Roberts at Leichhardt Stadium over twelve rounds four days earlier. McGrath, who also had wins over 'Bluey' Jones and Wally Hancock, was taken to the hospital and treated for a concussion which kept him out of action until later in the year. The form Henneberry was showing in the gym plus Richards' showing against Palmer in his Sydney debut had the Sydney fight fans looking forward to the bout.

The bout was scheduled for 12x3 minute rounds, which marked the first time Richards had fought three-minute rounds in his career. Despite the demands of the Henneberry camp for the fight to be strictly fought at the middleweight limit, Richards came in slightly over the limit (11st-6.5lb) however there were no issues with this reported in any accounts of the fight. Henneberry made the weight comfortably at 11st-3lb. While the sporting news in Australia the next day would focus on the infamous Bodyline Series and Harold Larwood's bouncer that struck Bill Oldfield in the head, the bout between Henneberry and Richards would go almost unreported but was one of the best domestic bouts seen in Australian boxing history.

Close to 6,000 were in attendance at Sydney Stadium as both men entered the ring. Richards had the advantage from the outside, where his fast hands and the deadly power in his right hand could be best utilised, and he attempted to keep the fight at a distance as the bout began. Henneberry immediately tried to smother Richards and work on the inside, where he could do his best work. Richards found a home for his right hand to the head early in the contest, but Henneberry took the punches and continued to press forward. Richards also landed the right to the body but couldn't discourage Henneberry's forward march. The first two minutes of the opening round was undoubtedly the Queenslander's, but Henneberry rallied in the final minute, landing hard right hands of his own that had some reporters scoring the opening round even.

The second round was all Richards. At the beginning of the stanza, he blinded Henneberry with his left jab and landed a beautiful sweeping right hand that momentarily stunned the man who had taken Palmer's middleweight title. Richards repeated the same move and had success again, following it up with a left rip to the body. When Henneberry attempted to smother Richards, Richards landed a hard uppercut and punished Henneberry with both hands as he followed up. Another right-hand counter hurt Henneberry badly as the round came to a close and, despite landing his own right-hand at the end of the round, Henneberry looked "in all kinds of bother"[2] as he returned to his corner.

Henneberry fought hard in the third round, picking off Richards' right hand with his left glove as he worked his way inside where he began a debilitating body attack. The fight shifted as Henneberry found Richards could not match him on the inside, and he snapped Richards head back with uppercuts while stifling his attempts to tie him up. Richards attempted to steal the round with a rally at the end, but Henneberry outpunched him in the exchanges. Henneberry poured it on again in the fourth, landing several rights behind the ear, and a left hook that shook Richards. The experience in the big bouts at the stadium and fighting three-minute rounds was beginning to show after the fourth. The pace of the fight caused Richards to breathe heavily, and when he fought back, he was wild with his punches, allowing Henneberry to slip or smother his attacks with ease.

While Richards was wild, he was still dangerous. One of these wild shots caught Henneberry high on the head early in the fifth and Richards landed a follow up right hand that forced Henneberry on the defensive. The Sydneysider used his experience and didn't allow Richards to land any more clean punches by returning to his tight guard. Henneberry boxed cautiously in the sixth, perhaps sensing that Richards would tire in the second half of the bout, and effectively used his jab and defence and while Richards forced the pace, he was still wild, allowing Henneberry to tie him up. Richards had a clear strength advantage in the clinches and while Henneberry was the much better in-fighter, Richards pushed him off well in this round and scored with his uppercut.

The seventh round was one of the most entertaining of the fight. Henneberry's cleaner punches game him the edge, and he hurt Richards with a right to the head early in the round before making him wince with a right-hand to the body. Richards threw heavy leather in return as Henneberry worked his body on the inside, but while he landed, he used vital stamina by loading up his shots and by trying to push Henneberry away. He came back in the eighth round, landing a right-hand that pierced Henneberry's guard. Henneberry was hurt and almost went down, but Richards lacked the energy to follow it up, and Henneberry continued to march forward and dig heavy shots into the midsection. The Queensland champion looked heavily fatigued in the ninth and tenth rounds, and his punches lacked the power they had in the early rounds.

Henneberry took more chances and noticeably outworked Richards in these rounds.

With the fight in the balance coming into the last two rounds Henneberry continued to attack, and a left hook landed flush on Richards' jaw, almost sending him to the canvas in the eleventh. Richards survived and fought back wildly, enough to keep Henneberry honest, and while Henneberry won the round, he had missed his chance to score a late knockout, and it would prove costly. The twelfth round was a wild affair, both men "fought like tigers,"[3] but Henneberry did the better work with his short punches on the inside. As the twelfth round came to a close, the decision was up in the air, and when referee Doug Barling ruled the contest a draw, the crowd cheered its approval.

Reporters had mixed receptions to the decision. Sydney newspaper *The Referee* and Melbourne's *The Sporting Globe* both reported the decision was a robbery and had Henneberry as the clear winner. Sydney's *The Sun* had the bout for Henneberry but a lot closer, scoring it six rounds to four with two even for the middleweight title claimant. *The Brisbane Courier* and Sydney's *Australian Worker* both had the bout a draw while Brisbane's *The Telegraph* scored the bout for Richards.

While the gate was a disappointing £380,[4] in the immediate days after the fight, there were talks of a rematch a fortnight later with the middleweight title on the line. Jack Carroll had returned to the welterweight division at the end of 1932 and had just signed to meet 'Bluey' Jones for the Australian welterweight title, giving Henneberry a chance to "reclaim" the title he had never officially lost in the ring due to his refusal to weigh-in for the return with Carroll. After the close of Sydney Stadium following the first bout, the rematch was to be held at Brisbane Stadium on 11 February however Henneberry's left hand, which was broken and had kept him out of the ring in the last few months of 1932, was swollen after the fight and this injury temporarily delayed any talks of a rematch.

After the withdrawal of Henneberry, Mike Marre, who had leased Brisbane Stadium, instead matched Richards with Bob Thornton, with the winner to meet Henneberry for the title in the following weeks. Thornton, like Henneberry, had found bouts hard to come by at first when Hugh McIntosh leased Sydney Stadium and was inactive for some months after the loss to Henneberry. He accepted a rematch in August with Pat Appleton in Appleton's hometown of Hobart in Tasmania. The bout was uneventful, the crowd counted the boxers out many times during the contest due to inactivity, and despite looking a clear winner, Thornton came away with only a draw.

With no middleweights in Sydney to fight after the takeover of Sydney Stadium by the N.S.C.A., Thornton fought at heavyweight against the Americans who were imported by McIntosh. Thornton was the first Australian to meet Clyde Chastain, giving away over a stone to Young Stribling's sparring partner. Despite putting up a courageous effort in which he "was still throwing punches at the end of 12 bitter sessions, "[5] Chastain was the clear winner on points.

Against 'Tiger' Jack Payne, another American fighter who had knocked out Australian heavyweight champion George Thompson just over two minutes into their 1926 Sydney Stadium bout, he gave away 1.5st, but lasted the twelve round distance. In his most recent fight, Thornton put up "another game display"[6] against Tony Gora, losing over 15x2 minute rounds at Leichhardt Stadium in November. A win over Ron Richards would potentially give Thornton his rematch with Fred Henneberry.

While the new promoter Mike Marre would have been pleased with the crowd at the re-opening of Brisbane Stadium, the fight was a poor contest and the decision by the referee, also Mike Marre, was equally poor. Richards, a renowned counter-puncher who prefers to sit back and look for openings for his vaunted right hand, had difficulty timing the unorthodox Thornton early in the contest and the opening rounds were slow. Both men looked to counter punch which resulted in few exchanges, but by the fifth round Richards was in control and landed his right hand whenever Thornton dared to attack, which wasn't very often. Thornton had his moments during the contest, especially in the late rounds, but had too much respect for Richards' power and Richards was the clear winner in at least ten of the rounds. The crowd counted both men out during the final round, but it seemed to be a clear victory to Richards. Many were shocked, however, when the referee declared the fight was a draw.

Despite the result, the bout did little to harm Richards' reputation, and talks of a rematch between Richards and Henneberry commenced immediately after the Thornton bout. Sydney Stadium had been closed after their first contest until the newly formed National Boxing Club (N.B.C) of Australia took over the lease of the stadium in late February. The man behind the N.B.C was Charles Lucas, who had managed the great Aboriginal boxer Jerry Jerome 20 years earlier and had brought many British boxers to Australia in the 1920s. Lucas had also been responsible for American promoter Tex Rickard's discovery of New Zealand heavyweight Tom Heeney, which had led to Heeney's title shot against Gene Tunney in 1928. The first big match that would be promoted by Lucas and the N.B.C was the rematch between Henneberry and Richards with the Australian title at stake.

The original date for the contest was 27 February, but it changed when Richards reportedly fell ill. However, a fight between Richards and New Zealander Harry Lister was scheduled for 4 March in Brisbane, which led to Charles Lucas contacting Richards' management for clarification. Richards' manager Pat O'Sullivan informed Lucas that the Richards-Thornton fight would have been called off due to Richards' illness if a replacement could be found, but when they received no answer regarding the bout with Lister, the Henneberry rematch was called off. Henneberry's hand, however, was still injured and he did not resume full training until 1 March which meant that he would not have been 100% against Richards if he could have fought at all.

Harry Lister, born in New Zealand, had fought for the New Zealand middleweight title in 1931 and had fought primarily in Western Australia since arriving in Australia until his most recent fights in Leichhardt and Newtown in Sydney. While he had now fought many times in Australia, Richards was a significant step up in class. Lister showed gameness in their fifteen round contest by lasting the distance, but his left eye was cut in the second round and closed by the seventh, and his nose and mouth dripped blood from the tremendous beating he was handed by the Queensland champion, who, despite slowing down in the late rounds, won a clear decision.

An agreement between Charles Lucas and Mike Marre, managers of Sydney and Brisbane Stadiums respectively, to trade boxers under contract for bouts was reached shortly after the Lister contest. Bobby Blay would travel to Brisbane to meet the winner of the Bobby Delaney vs Wally Hancock bout while Richards would return to Sydney to meet Henneberry on 20 March at Rushcutters Bay. The N.B.C further stated that they would not accept Carroll's claim as the middleweight champion and that they would recognise the winner of this bout as the middleweight champion of Australia.

"The biggest crowd since Palmer-Stribling"[7] was expected to be in attendance with many fans expecting a fight similar to the first exciting contest between the pair. Richards sparred with Wally Hancock in Brisbane before arriving back in Sydney six days out from the fight where he finished his preparations at Jack

Dunleavy's gym. Henneberry and his brother Bill were confident that after their first encounter that they had worked out how to defeat Richards, telling reporters that they would force the counter-puncher to lead rather than chasing him. Interviewed on the weekend before the Monday night contest, Richards told *The Sun* "Since I last fought Henneberry I and others have considered his style from every possible angle, and I am sure I have found a flaw in his defence, and it is on this on which I will concentrate."[8]

Both men were significantly lighter than in their first meeting at the 2 pm weigh-in, Henneberry this time having a slight weight advantage at 10st-13.75lb with Richards weighing 10st-13lb, almost half a stone lighter than he was just over two weeks ago against Lister. Queensland critics later questioned the weights of both men but in particular Richards, who had always fought right on or over the middleweight limit of 11st-6lb. The scales were reportedly tested by a State Weights and Scales Inspector half an hour before both men weighed in for the contest.

Joe Wallis was introduced as the referee, and he would play a significant role in the contest. Richards surprised many, including Henneberry, when he took the fight to Henneberry in the opening round, delivering long "one-two" combinations. The champion fought defensively but had trouble getting close to Richards where he could work and when he did Richards' hand speed advantage kept Henneberry's defence occupied, and he had little opportunity to punch back. Richards continued to lead with his one-two to the head in the second round but also countered in the second round with a right uppercut to the head or body when Henneberry lead. The first two rounds were easily the challenger's as Henneberry fought defensively and was often forced to clinch as Richards outpunched him in close.

Richards continued his success in round three, landing several right hands to the jaw and throwing long left hooks to the body but with little power behind them. Twice during the third round, Henneberry dropped his left hand and drew a right-hand lead from Richards which he countered with his own right. He failed to follow any of these up however, and Richards had the first three rounds in the bank. Henneberry took more chances in the fourth and started landing right-handed shots to Richards' body in close, but Richards still had success from the outside, landing his right hand over Henneberry's jab every time he tried to throw it. The fifth round was also for the challenger. Henneberry caught a lot of the punches on his arms and gloves but couldn't get himself into position to land, or even throw, any punches in return.

Midway through the sixth round Henneberry, coming out of a neutral corner, feinted a left lead and when Richards went to counter with his right hand, Henneberry beat him to the punch with his own right, which momentarily dazed the challenger. Henneberry followed it up with a left hook-right cross which landed on his retreating opponent and bounced Richards off the ropes. Richards fell into a clinch, and as Henneberry tried to pull his hands free to press his advantage, Richards landed a right of his own that made Henneberry's knees buckle, and the crowd roared their approval. Both men were still hurt as they traded punches for the remainder of the round. On two occasions during these exchanges, Richards landed borderline low punches on the champion that referee Wallis either didn't see or ignored. In an interview years later, Richards claimed that in the second fight that Henneberry began to tell him to "keep 'em up, black," when he landed these shots.[9] These comments turned the rivalry between the two men from competitive to personal.

Richards reassumed command early in the seventh round, landing a hard right uppercut on Henneberry's jaw as he tried to close the distance. This punch possibly hurt Henneberry as he stayed on the outside for the remainder of the round where Richards picked him off with jabs and right crosses. Richards landed two more punches around Henneberry's beltline which drew a complaint from the champion. Referee Joe Wallis ruled the punches were legal and told Henneberry to continue fighting. Henneberry worked his way inside more in the eighth round, landing several hard lefts to the body, but still took right hands from Richards. Another borderline punch that was ignored by the referee had Bill Henneberry arguing with Wallis in the corner at the end of round eight.

Richards still looked sharp in the ninth round, but Henneberry was having more success catching his punches on his forearms, and working his way in close, although he was still outscored. The referee finally warned Richards in this round, but for a rabbit punch rather than a low blow. Behind on points, Henneberry attempted to rally in the tenth round. After working his way in close, he landed a right hand around the back of Richards' left ear, which earned him a caution from Joe Wallis for rabbit punching. Henneberry exchanged words with Wallis then continued pressing forward at Richards, landing many hard body punches in the clinches. Richards' inexperience over the championship distance suddenly caught up with him, and he slowed down as Henneberry attacked relentlessly, having his best round of the bout.

The champion didn't let up in the eleventh round. Using his "smother" to take care of Richards' power from the outside, he had a clear advantage on the inside against the tiring Queenslander. A hard left hook hurt Richards just before the bell, and while Richards had a commanding lead, he had four rounds still to fight without much gas left in his tank. He tried to fight Henneberry off in round twelve, but Henneberry was too strong and continued to outwork Richards on the inside. Richards had little left as the 13th round started and Henneberry attacked. He forced Richards into a neutral corner with a series of punches before working his hands free as Richards tried to clinch. Richards lowered his head in an attempt to evade a right hand from Henneberry, and the punch landed to the back of Richards' head. Referee Joe Wallis stepped between the fighters and crowned Richards the winner by disqualification, and the new middleweight champion of Australia.

The crowd at first went silent as they comprehended what they saw before booing the decision of the referee. Fred Henneberry, who had won the title from Palmer on a foul, was stunned and while he didn't engage Wallis, his brother Bill lunged at the large referee. Fred restrained him and forced him to a neutral corner and then eventually out of the ring. Richards, the new Australian champion, was hurt by the punch and complained after the contest that he had been fouled numerous times by Henneberry, but many in the crowd felt that Wallis' call was premature. The Henneberry's were livid backstage, complaining bitterly about the low blows from Richards.

It was discovered after the contest that Richards had broken a finger on his right hand and a third fight would not be able to take place until at least Easter. Richards, who signed a three-fight contract with Sydney Stadium after winning the title, stated that he wanted to settle the issue with Henneberry before defending against any other challengers. Henneberry was also eager to prove he was superior to Richards after the controversial referee decisions in the first two bouts. The former champion was so keen to fight Richards that he told Charles Lucas that he wouldn't fight unless the opponent was Ron Richards.

The N.B.C was looking to capitalise on the success of the second fight and wired Richards to try and make the fight, but Richards' manager Pat O'Sullivan wasn't keen to make the fight straight away. Richards had put on weight in his time off while recovering from his hand injury and they wanted time for Richards to get back down to the middleweight limit if the title was going to be on the line. O'Sullivan criticised Henneberry's two title defences over a whole year during his reign as champion and told Lucas that if they wanted to fight for the title that Henneberry had to wait until

Richards could make the weight comfortably. They offered an above the limit fight in the meantime and also stated they were open to a rematch with Ambrose Palmer as an option if Lucas required Richards in the ring.

Henneberry took a physical labour job in the regional town of Temora, New South Wales while he waited for the opportunity to fight Richards again. He told Sydney Stadium that he was using the work to build his strength and stamina which would keep him fit until the third fight was scheduled, at which point he would begin his boxing training. Richards returned to the gym in mid-April and accepted a fight with Dealer Wells, a veteran from Wollongong who had a following in Brisbane after he knocked out Harry Lister just two weeks after Lister lasted the distance with Richards. Wells had returned to Wollongong where knocking out Jim Meighan on 8 April, before returning to Brisbane to finish his preparations to meet the Australian champion on 3 May. While Richards won the contest by a wide margin on points, he was far from his best form, and Wells made it a harder fight than it should have been. Wells briefly hurt Richards in round ten but otherwise lost decisively, taking severe punishment over the fifteen rounds.

Just before the Wells contest, Richards signed to meet Henneberry for a third time with the bout to take place on 29 May at Sydney Stadium.[10] The fight was eventually rescheduled for one week later to 5 June after Richards injured his arm in the fight with Wells. The new date also coincided with the King's Birthday public holiday, which meant there was a greater possibility of the bout attracting a large audience. The winner of the contest was to defend against Jack Carroll in what was set to be one of the most anticipated fights in Sydney for years. After his one-sided win over Henneberry in 1932, Carroll was confident he could take the middleweight title off either man.

Richards arrived from Brisbane for the bout on 25 May and

impressed members of the media in his workouts. Henneberry was also in good shape after spending a month in Temora chopping wood and carrying large bags of wool, and after the month off regular boxing training, he stated his troublesome left hand was back to full strength. Bill Henneberry insisted that Richards make the middleweight limit by 2 pm on the day of the fight and a $ £100 forfeit was agreed to in case either man came in over the middleweight limit. Ron's younger brother, Max, would make his Sydney debut on the undercard over ten rounds against Sydney bantamweight Dal Costa.

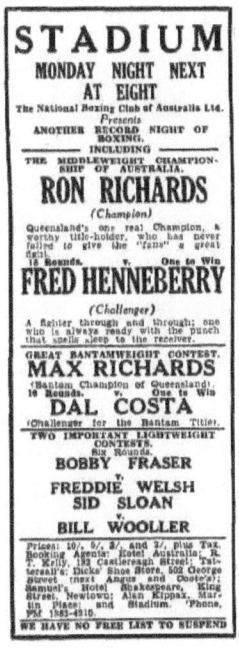

Less than a week from the fight a rumour circulated that Henneberry wouldn't fight unless someone other than Joe Wallis was the referee. Henneberry came out quickly to deny it. "Never has such a thought entered my mind," Henneberry told *The Sydney Sportsman*, " I get on well with Wallis, and though I still think he was wrong in ruling me out against Richards, I am certain that there was no malice behind the decision. These crazy rumours get me all hot under the collar."[11] This statement was a relief for Lucas, and when Richards weighed in comfortably under the limit (11st-5.5lb), it cleared the final obstacle for the fight.

As the crowd entered, Richards' younger brother Max was beaten in the final preliminary by Dal Costa, the corner stopping the fight due to a cut. While many expected a huge crowd, the weather discouraged many fans from attending, and a lesser crowd than the March rematch witnessed the third battle. Both men entered the ring shortly before 9 pm, and the fight started much the same as the first two did; Richards trying to keep Henneberry at a distance and Henneberry trying to close that distance. Richards was on his toes in the first round, using a jab that was mostly blocked but did allow Ron to set up his right hand and he landed two hard rights to Henneberry's body.

The defending champion had things his own way, but Henneberry landed a hard left hook towards the end of the round and followed it up with a flurry as Richards was on the ropes. Richards took the first round, but Henneberry was having more success early than he had in their last two fights. Henneberry started the second as he ended the first, pressing forward behind his "smother," looking for a way past Richards' jab and attempting to trap the champion in the corner. Richards had an answer when cornered early in this round, landing an uppercut and tying Henneberry off before spinning clear but it didn't face Henneberry. After some good bodywork, Henneberry again cornered Richards with a minute left in the round, feinted a left hook and landed a hard right on Richards' jaw. The champion went weak at the knees, and as he tried to clinch, Henneberry nailed him again and would have gone down if it weren't for the ropes. Henneberry attacked, but the bell saved Richards.

The champion's head had cleared as the third started and he clinched more as Henneberry got in close and fought with a more authoritative jab, using it to set up his right uppercut as he did in the first round. Henneberry kept coming forward and, despite losing the first half of the round, his persistence paid off and Richards finished the round defending on the ropes with Henneberry's body punching evening out Richards' better work early on. Richards' tactics weren't working so he abandoned the stick and move strategy and took the fight to the former champion in the fourth. The rally only lasted a minute, that's how long it took Henneberry to back Richards to the ropes again and continue his assault. A left hook staggered Richards again and Henneberry punished him with both hands for the remainder of the round. The time Henneberry had spent in Temora doing physical labour had shown to be worth it as his pace never looked like slowing up, and his punches seemed to be harder than they were in their last fight.

The fifth round was also one-sided, Richards couldn't find the punches to keep Henneberry off him, and Henneberry didn't look like slowing down. The crowd cheered Henneberry back to his corner as Richards looked disheartened on his stool before the sixth round. Richards again started the sixth well, taking the fight to Henneberry as he did in the fourth and landing a hard right hook to Henneberry's jaw that snapped his head sideways. The blow had little effect on the man from Albury, who took the fight to the champion again and the two men traded punches on the ropes. A minute into the round Henneberry's stamina took over, and he pummelled Richards from corner to corner for the remainder of the round. A right hand just before the bell bounced Richards into the ropes.

Richards got back on his toes to start the seventh but this only temporarily delayed Henneberry. A left hook to the body made Richards wince 30 seconds into the round, and Henneberry battered the midsection of the champion for the remainder of the seventh. Richards did land some counters, but Henneberry knew he lacked the power to hurt him at this stage and had abandoned his defence to encourage the Queenslander to open up, where unloaded hard punches into the openings Richards left. The champion was going through the motions to start the ninth, and Henneberry took command early, forcing Richards to the ropes with a barrage of punches. Richards tried in vain to use his feet to get away, but Henneberry wouldn't let up. A left hook and a right hand towards the end of the ninth dropped Richards face first to the canvas. He was up at five, and the bell saved him as Henneberry pounced.

The tenth was brutal, Henneberry dished out punishment for the duration and twice stepped back, expecting Richards to fall, before continuing to batter Richards when he continued to stand. A counter right hand from Richards landed late in the round, and he winced in pain, apparently injuring the hand. At the end of the round, Richards complained to his trainer about the injured hand. After a brief discussion, referee Joe Wallis was called to the corner and, after being told that the champion could not continue, Wallis awarded the fight to Henneberry on a technical knockout.

The ringside doctor examined Richards after the fight, and while he ruled out a break, he diagnosed Richards as having a blood clot between the muscles and the bone on his right hand. After the fight, Richards claimed to have hurt the hand in training for the bout and pointed to it as the excuse to explain the loss. The crowd applauded Richards as he left the ring, but many newspapers criticised Richards decision to stay on his stool and not finish the fight.

> " It must be confessed that Mr. Richards started off like a champion—even if he didn't finish like one. A champion doesn't quit. In the unwritten law of the prize-ring, there is only heroics. Only fighting fools indulged in such things. Mr Richards is not a fighting fool. He is an intelligent young man, who regards a combination of sick headache, pain in the tummy, sore knuckle, and the useless shedding of rich red blood with considerable distaste."[12]

The victory was a sweet one for Henneberry after the controversial ending to the second fight. He had fulfilled what he claimed he was on his way to doing in the second bout and had almost redeemed himself from his loss and his antics in the Carroll fight. The Henneberry-Richards battles were incredibly popular among Sydney fans, and the result paved the way for one a massive fight between two reigning Australian champions.

JACK CARROLL VS FRED HENNEBERRY III

After avenging the loss against Fred Henneberry, Carroll had a strong claim to being both the welterweight and middleweight champion of Australia. His claim of the welterweight title was because he had not lost under championship conditions while his claim to the middleweight title came from defeating Henneberry, who had purposely weighed in over the middleweight limit in order not to risk his title in the rematch with Carroll. While Stadiums Ltd named Carroll the middleweight champion after the Henneberry fight, the welterweight title had passed to Billy 'Bluey' Jones, after he had outpointed Russ Critcher three times in the space of five months. Jones, from Newcastle, NSW, was a veteran of the sport having turned professional in 1921, winning the Australian lightweight title in 1927 and again in 1930.

Jones had fought most of his career in his hometown Newcastle, but he had also fought in Sydney and Brisbane. Stadiums Ltd looked to continue building Carroll's popularity in Melbourne and cabled terms of an offer for Jones to face Carroll in Melbourne in

September 1932. Jones' trainer Tom Maguire turned down the offer as Jones had agreed to face the Canadian Tommy Fielding on that date in Newcastle. Pat McHugh, former Leichhardt stadium manager who now controlled a rival stadium in the Sydney suburb of Newtown after a dispute with shareholders at Leichhardt resulted in his termination, also tried to make arrangements to stage the Carroll-Jones welterweight title clash there. Meanwhile, McHugh's replacement at Leichhardt, Jack Hoult, organised for Carroll to return to Leichhardt to battle American middleweight Bert Sampson, with plans to stage a Carroll-Jones bout at Leichhardt three weeks later.

The Carroll-Sampson bout marked the re-opening of Leichhardt Stadium's Friday night fights. Sampson worked on a ship that was on its way from San Francisco to Sydney but the chief steward of the boat had been in contact with Hoult, and they had arranged for Sampson to meet either Carroll on 16 September. The American was little more than a preliminary fighter on the west coast of America, and his last recorded bout was more than a year ago. Sampson showed he was game but ultimately had no answer for the speed of Carroll. Rarely missing the target, Carroll's left hand opened cuts around both of Sampson's eyes, and the referee stopped the bout at the end of round eight.

With McIntosh's N.S.C.A promoting primarily heavyweight bouts, Carroll's services were in high demand as the premiere lighter man in Australian boxing. Following the match with Sampson on the 16th, Carroll returned to Melbourne to headline the first show at the smaller Fitzroy Stadium against Tommy Fielding on 23 September. After this bout, Carroll was to again return to Leichhardt to meet the popular lightweight fighter Alby Roberts on the 30th. McIntosh saw the potential in Carroll and was willing to sign the Victorian for bouts with Jones or Henneberry at Sydney Stadium, although Carroll wasn't keen to fight for the N.S.C.A.

after McIntosh had initially offered him only £50 for a fight with Bob Thornton.

Fielding had fought well recently, holding Australian champion 'Bluey' Jones to a draw in their rematch in Newcastle before knocking out another Newcastle fighter Wally Maher in his most recent bout. Carroll was guaranteed £80 for his fight at the newly renovated stadium, which could hold 2,000 spectators. The bout was a disappointing affair as Fielding came into the bout looking soft and ill-prepared for an opponent of Carroll's class. After a slow first three rounds which were controlled by Carroll the referee, former Australian middleweight champion Merv Williams, warned the men to fight harder in the fourth. The crowd counted both men out many in the next few rounds as Carroll continued to outbox the Canadian but seemed reluctant to take any risks. The referee called the fight off in the seventh round and declared it a "no fight."

Fitzroy Stadium management withheld the purses of both Carroll and Fielding for their lack of effort in the bout. Carroll returned to Leichhardt to battle Alby Roberts the following week, but Roberts' reputation for action had few worrying that they would witness a slow fight.

> "Whenever Aboriginal Alby Roberts battles there is never any danger of the referee thinking he is not trying, or that the other fellow (because Alby, by always boring in, makes him fight) is not doing his best, and that is why Leichhardt Stadium patrons are certain the fireworks will fly as soon as Jack Carroll and Roberts get going next Friday night"[1]

Roberts was a hard puncher from the northern New South Wales town of Lismore, and while he was at his best at lightweight, he carried his punch against larger men. Tragically, Roberts had killed Melbourne welterweight Bert McCarthy in their 1931 bout. Roberts also had a recent knockout win over Russ Critcher on his resume.

In his last fight three weeks ago, Roberts had lasted the fifteen round distance with Ron Richards.

Carroll's performance against Roberts quickly removed any stench that was attached to his name after the bout with Fielding, as the two men put on a show for the Leichhardt fans. Roberts took the fight to the Victorian throughout the fifteen rounds but was "outboxed and outfought" by the larger man. Both men traded punches in "hectic style" in a wild opening three rounds before Carroll began to use his superior footwork to make the smaller man miss wildly. Roberts, who was warned repeatedly for rabbit punching, looked stronger over the late rounds, but when Carroll "bombarded Roberts in the 15th round with a varied collection of punches," any doubt about the decision was removed. As Carroll and Roberts embraced at the end of the fifteenth round, referee Yank Pearl crowned Carroll, the winner.[2]

Re-injuring his troublesome left hand in the bout with Roberts, Carroll was forced to take a break following the fight. While there were again talks of a mega Victorian showdown between Carroll and Ambrose Palmer, who had returned to training after his loss to Stribling, Carroll refused to meet Palmer if Ambrose didn't make the middleweight limit. Palmer, however, had no intention of fighting at the middleweight limit again while Carroll had his eyes on cementing his claim as Australia's leading fighter at both middleweight and welterweight. Upon his return to the gym, Carroll told *The Labor Daily* that he wanted 'Bluey' Jones and the welterweight title first, and that he could find backing up to £500 for the fight.

The two men initially agreed to meet twice, with both bouts taking place in Jones' hometown of Newcastle. The first bout would take place over 15x2 minute rounds and the rematch at the welterweight limit over the championship distance with the title on the line. Shortly after this, Carroll was offered £200 guarantee for a bout with Ron Richards for the middleweight title at the Sydney Sports Ground. The contest was to be promoted by Charles Lucas, who planned to use his connections in Great Britain to stage quality international contests in Sydney. Jones fought a warm-up bout in the meantime, winning by disqualification over Alby Roberts, who repeatedly attempted to shove Jones over the ropes. Carroll was forced to withdraw from all scheduled bouts, however, when he injured his back during a workout, and he was ruled out until the new year.

The boxing landscape changed dramatically during the "off-season" at the end of 1932. Pat McHugh became the stadium manager in Melbourne and was keen to promote Carroll in his home city. McHugh had reopened boxing in Melbourne with a rematch between Ambrose Palmer and Johnny Freeman. Freeman put up a much better effort in the rematch with Palmer, dropping him twice in the eighth round (once through the ropes) but losing the decision. The new stadium manager was keen to bring championship boxing back to Melbourne, and with the debate among who the welterweight champion was having continued since Carroll's loss to Purdy in 1928, Pat McHugh secured the fight between 'Bluey' Jones and Carroll at Melbourne Stadium on 4 February for the Australian welterweight title.

The former champion looked sharp during his training, having recovered fully from the hand and back injuries that had kept him sidelined since his bout with Alby Roberts. Jones arrived just three days before the contest by express train from Sydney after completing his training in Newcastle. Carroll made the welterweight limit for the first time since his loss to Wally Hancock in 1931, weighing-in right on the 10st-7lb limit, 4lb more than the champion, who often fought at the lightweight limit even during his reign as welterweight champion.

Jones attacked at the bell while Carroll worked behind his jab, rarely missing the target and made the recognised champion miss. Jones was game early on, but by the fourth round, it was clear that Carroll was the superior boxer. The bout was one-sided, but Carroll continued to box cautiously, using his footwork and head movement to make Jones miss while Jones continued to bore in looking for a punch to negate the referee's scorecard. Carroll attacked more in the second half of the bout and showed that Jones was not in his class, countering his rushes with hard punches and finally ending matters in round ten with a right hand to the head followed by a left hook to the body that left Jones "squirming" on the canvas for the ten count. The victory was emphatic and left no questions as to who was Australia's best welterweight.

After the bout, Carroll's name was linked with both Henneberry and Richards as a viable option for new Sydney Stadium boss Charles Lucas who had replaced Hugh McIntosh and the N.S.C.A. at Sydney Stadium. Lucas immediately staged a rematch between Henneberry and Richards for the middleweight title, ignoring Carroll's claim to the title although stating that the winner of the bout would have to defend the title against Carroll. After the controversial ending in the Richards-Henneberry fight, a rematch was sort after limiting Carroll's options for an opponent. Wally Hancock emerged as a contender for Carroll's crown with a win over Bobby Delaney but lost the return by knockout in the third round. Carroll was eventually matched with 'Young' Cyril Pluto, a Western Australian fighter who was Melbourne for a fight with Reg O'Haire that fell through.

Pluto's best win was against the former Australian lightweight and welterweight champion Billy Grime in June 1932. Pluto left Perth for Sydney at the end of 1932 but then travelled to Melbourne after failing to get matched during two months in Sydney. After his fight with O'Haire fell through he took a huge leap up in class by taking on the Australian champion. The West Australian claimed to have had 70 professional contests for 60 wins, seven losses and three draws. Despite impressing with his toughness and conditioning, Carroll outclassed the young fighter after the fifth round. Although he started strong, the champion took his foot off the gas in the final rounds and coasted to an easy decision win.

The welterweight champion travelled to Sydney in mid-April after a short break from training following his latest win. Carroll stated he was willing to defend his title against Bobby Blay, a former lightweight title challenger who was known for his crowd-pleasing style. Blay would only fight Carroll if Carroll came in at a catch weight of 10st-4lb, 2lb under the welterweight limit, a weight Carroll was unable to make safely. Charles Lucas had promised to import a series of American and British fighters to challenge the likes of Carroll; however, these men wouldn't arrive until later in the year. With no welterweights in the country available to challenge Carroll and Henneberry and Richards still lined up to fight each other, Carroll was forced to stay on the sidelines. In May, Carroll told *The Sydney Sportsman* that he was "ready to meet the winner of Richards-Henneberry on June 19."[3]

After Henneberry stopped Richards in their third contest, talk in the newspapers quickly turned to the showdown with Carroll, who many still regarded as the real middleweight champion. Scheduled for 3 July, Carroll arrived in Sydney for the contest on 26 June and was showing good form during his gym workouts in Melbourne before departing for Sydney. While in Sydney, Carroll sparred Bob Thornton over four rounds, even standing and out-slugging the hard-punching middleweight during the fourth round. Unfortunately for Carroll, Henneberry withdrew from the fight less than a week from the contest after suffering from a series of boils on his head.

Brisbane Stadium offered Carroll a match with Ron Richards while Lucas was keen to match him with either Bobby Delaney or the winner of Bobby Blay's fight with Ernie Roderick, an Englishmen who was the first of Lucas' imports. Carroll turned down all opponents and chose to wait for Henneberry to recover. Roderick would draw his fight with Blay before losing to Delaney and Pluto in his last two bouts in Australia. Despite these losses, Roderick would go on to win the European welterweight and middleweight crowns as well as challenge Henry Armstrong for the world title, losing a fifteen round decision.

The Carroll-Henneberry rubber match was further delayed when Henneberry's boils continued to trouble him throughout July, and then again when Carroll's left hand was injured once again, putting him on the sidelines for another month.

Henneberry looked to a third fight with Ambrose Palmer, who was scheduled to meet Ron Richards in a rematch on 9 August, and stated he was willing to meet Palmer above the middleweight limit. Carroll indicated that he would be fit to fight Henneberry in September and the third fight was once again matched, this time for 18 September at Rushcutters Bay. Carroll re-arrived in Sydney on 2 September, earlier than usual to utilise the "dearth of suitable sparring partners" Sydney had to offer. The welterweight champion sparred again with Bob Thornton and also former opponent Alby Roberts to help him prepare for Henneberry's aggressive style.

Henneberry hired some smaller sparring partners to assist him in preparing for Carroll's speed advantage. His chief sparring partner was South African welterweight Barney Kieswetter, who had just started a lengthy tour of Australia and was coming off victories over Bobby Delaney and Alby Roberts. Henneberry's brother and trainer Bill told *The Sporting Globe* that, by his estimation, Keiswetter's speed was equal to that of Carroll. With the bout taking place on Monday evening, both fighters tapered off as the weekend approached. On Saturday morning, just two days before the fight, Carroll came down with the flu and was advised by a doctor to withdraw, but the welterweight champion ignored the advice and took the bout despite his ailment.

The agreement regarding the weight limit was that the fighters would meet at middleweight by 2 pm on the day of the fight. However no weights were printed outside the stadium; instead, the word "catchweights" was printed under both men. The two champions had come to an agreement that the fight would not be for the middleweight title and this likely affected the attendance, as many were expecting to see the Australian middleweight title on the line for the bout. An estimated 6,000, roughly half the seated capacity at Rushcutters Bay, were in attendance when both men entered the ring. Rumours were circulating before the bout that the former middleweight world champion Gorilla Jones was on his way to Australia and that the winner of this clash would get the first crack at the American.

Estimated to be about 7lb more than Carroll, Henneberry bore in at the opening bell in his typical fashion while Carroll flicked with his jab and ripped hard left hands to the middleweight champion's body and uppercuts to his head. Henneberry was aggressive with his intentions, but Carroll was clever in close, and Henneberry was unable to get his punches off, doing more wrestling than punching in the first round. The next two rounds went along like the first, Henneberry chasing Carroll "like a dog after a rat"[4] while Carroll used his jab and ripped punches on the inside before moving away again. The first three rounds were obviously for the welterweight king, but Henneberry did not look bothered and was planning on using his wrestling tactics to wear down the smaller man.

Henneberry had more success in round four and looked to have stunned Carroll with a pair of right hands towards the end of the round. Looking to press the advantage in the next round, Henneberry attacked, but Carroll staggered him with a left hook. Carroll then tore into Henneberry, and the two men traded heavy leather for the remainder of the fifth, with Carroll getting the better of the exchanges. Henneberry was wild in the sixth after referee Joe Wallis ignored his complaint of a low blow. He wrestled Carroll between the top two ropes drawing boos from the crowd when he hit Carroll as he attempted to untangle himself. Carroll also took the sixth with his cleaner punches in close. In round seven Carroll opened a cut over Henneberry's right eye with a jab and then made the larger man miss a series of punches while trapped on the ropes before tearing into him with both hands.

The boxing lesson continued in rounds eight and nine as Carroll knocked Henneberry off balance with a hard right hand and continued stifling his attacks up close. Henneberry kept charging forward, and the combination of this and Carroll's flu began to take its toll on the smaller man towards the end of round nine. Well behind on points, Henneberry started his rally in the tenth after landing a right hand on Carroll as he moved away. The Victorian had made similar punches miss all night, but was beginning to slow and the blow that surprised both him and Henneberry when it landed. Carroll staggered, and Henneberry attacked with the ferocity he had become famous for and it was only Carroll's ability to ride with the punches that kept him standing. The welterweight champion, now bleeding from his left ear, rallied in the last 30 seconds of the tenth and the crowd went wild as he landed numerous hard blows on Henneberry at the end of the round.

A pair of right hands landed for Carroll to open the eleventh round and one of them opened a second cut over Henneberry's left eye. Henneberry attacked wildly and was easily picked off by Carroll for the remainder of the round. A barrage of shots for Henneberry was his best moment in the twelfth round, but he was otherwise outboxed by Carroll, who was punching with speed despite his fatigue. The thirteenth round, the one that was so unlucky for Carroll in the pair's first meeting, nearly spelt the end for Henneberry this time, Carroll made him wince with a body shot early in the round and let both hands go as he targeted the middleweight champions body with "a blizzard of leather."[5] Two more lefts downstairs almost dropped Henneberry later in the round but he grit his teeth and fought through the pain until the bell saved him.

Likely needing a knockout in the final two rounds, Henneberry attacked, and Carroll's effort in the previous round had drained him again. A right hand from Henneberry landed on the top of Carroll's head, sending him on unsteady legs towards the ropes. The middleweight king again tore into the smaller man but couldn't find the right distance to get off punches with his full power as he smothered his own work and allowed Carroll to tie him up. By the final round, Carroll had recovered, and he used his jab to full effect, bloodying Henneberry's mouth and outpointing him easily. At the end of the fifteenth, the crowd cheered as Wallis rightfully crowned Carroll, the winner on points.

Henneberry complained after the fight that Carroll's jab had often landed with the open glove and that the referee shouldn't have allowed him to hit with a part of the glove that wasn't the knuckle. The bout did little to harm the 22-year-old middleweight champion's reputation, and many were looking forward to a fierce battle between Henneberry and Gorilla Jones before the end of the year. Jones would not come to Australia, but Henneberry would get his chance before the end of 1933 with former world welterweight title challenger Dave Shade, who was one of many Americans about to fight for the N.B.C on Australian soil.

Carroll returned to Melbourne triumphant but was advised to rest for at least one week so he could fully recover from the flu. The offers poured in for Carroll after the victory with Brisbane Stadium wanting to match him with Ron Richards, Leichhardt guaranteeing £125 if he would meet Kieswetter and Sydney Stadium looking to match Carroll with former world junior lightweight champion Tod

Morgan, who had outpointed Bobby Blay in his Sydney debut. Morgan was ringside for the Carroll-Henneberry bout and stated he was impressed by both and described Carroll as "a real star" of the ring.[6] Carroll would accept the Morgan fight, and, after proving his supremacy in Australia, it would be his chance to show that he was one of the best welterweights in the world.

THE AMERICAN INVASION

Charles Lucas had successfully negotiated with Tod Morgan, former world junior lightweight champion, to travel to Sydney to boost the lightweight ranks in Australia. Morgan was born Albert Pilkington in Dungeness, Washington. As a child, he was often sick, and his father had hopes of him becoming a jockey prior to his health issues. Thinking that the drier climate of the California mountains would be beneficial to his son's health, the family relocated to the town of Eureka in 1920. Morgan began boxing to help with his health problems, and he was a natural at the sport, turning professional before the end of 1920 and fighting in main events in 1921. He won numerous titles on the West Coast and unsuccessfully campaigned for a shot at featherweight champion Kid Kaplan in 1925 before challenging Mike Ballerino for the junior lightweight world championship.

Morgan won the junior lightweight title with a 10th round stoppage and made 19 defences of the title over the next four years before losing the title to Benny Bass in 1929. The division wasn't recognised in Australia, and upon his arrival in Australia, many estimated that he had outgrown the lightweight division. Morgan scaled 10st-4lb, 9lb above the lightweight limit, for his debut against Bobby Blay. The American was "unquestionably world class" against Blay,[1] punishing the fan favourite over fifteen rounds with his left hook and sending Blay into retirement in the process. Morgan fought again, one week after Carroll's victory over Henneberry, taking on former British featherweight champion Nel Tarleton. In front of 11,000 spectators at Sydney Stadium, Morgan dropped Tarleton for a nine-count in both the first and seventh round as well as scoring a knockdown at the end of the fourth, but a tremendous display by Tarleton in the second half of the fight earned him a draw.

Both of Morgan's bouts had taken place at Sydney Stadium, and it was the perfect venue for Morgan to test Carroll. Morgan liked the prospects of boxing in Australia so much that after the fight with Tarleton he made arrangements to extend his trip. After recovering from the flu in Melbourne, Carroll returned to Sydney on 29 September to prepare for the bout with Morgan, scheduled for 9 October. The bout was fought at a catch-weight of 10st-7lb, and Carroll was under contract to make that weight or forfeit £150. Morgan boxed daily with Russ Critcher while Carroll again used Bob Thornton and Alby Roberts as his chief sparring partners. With both Carroll and Morgan drawing large crowds for their training sessions, a huge attendance was expected for the bout. The quality of boxing in the recent matchups involving both men had many Sydneysiders anticipating a great contest.

The 27-year-old Carroll not only made the 10st-7lb catch-weight but came in comfortably under the welterweight limit, weighing 10st-6.25lb at the 2 pm weigh-in. Morgan was 65.4, and while he was vastly more experienced, having more career wins than Carroll had total fights, he was shorter, older and lighter than the Australian champion. Official measurements before the fight listed Carroll at 5'7 tall with a one inch reach advantage over the 5'6 Morgan. Upon entering the ring, it was clear that Carroll was much taller than that and as the fight began it was clear he had the greater reach of the two men. Sydney Stadium was a sell-out, and the 12,000 in attendance were treated to a world-class boxing exhibition.

Tod Morgan - ex world Jnr. lightweight champion
(National Library of Australia, nla.obj-148612108)

Carroll pawed with his jab to open the first round while Morgan tried to close the distance and the opening round consisted of much holding and wrestling but very little punching. In the second round Carroll began to fire in close and, while Morgan still wrestled more than he punched, Carroll showed that he had the quicker hands of the two men and took the second round with his short left hooks in close. The American had more success in the third round, landing a few shots to Carroll's right side before Carroll cut loose with both hands. While he didn't have Morgan in trouble, Morgan had no answer for the Victorian's speed. Morgan tried unsuccessfully to punch with Carroll in the fourth round and occasionally landed to the body, but Carroll's speed was still on display. An uppercut opened a cut under Morgan's chin in the fourth, and a jab opened a cut on the bridge of his nose in the fifth.

Morgan continued to march forward and try to turn the tide, but Carroll would have none of it and used his foot-speed to keep Morgan on the end of his punches and unloaded with barrages whenever he closed the distance, before spinning out of trouble. The former world champion tried to hold Carroll in place and hit with his free hand, mostly to the body, but Carroll continued to blast him with both hands before dancing away, opening another cut on Morgan's left cheek in the sixth. Carroll was so dominant that the crowd were beginning to lose interest in the bout. As the rounds ticked by, Carroll continued to win them and build a lead on points that could only be reversed with a knockout. Morgan landed with a solid right hand in the ninth, but Carroll still did more than enough to take the round. The crowd began to grow quiet in rounds ten and eleven as Carroll's boxing exhibition continued. The American continued to look for the punch to end matters in rounds twelve and thirteen but couldn't find the Australian welterweight champion until the fourteenth.

With many in the crowd losing interest as Carroll won round after round in similar fashion, no one expected Morgan to finish as strongly as he did. About two minutes into the fourteenth round, the American caught Carroll with a left hook to the point of the chin as Carroll attempted to spin away from the corner as he had done effortlessly earlier. Carroll staggered after the blow landed and Morgan threw everything at him as the Australian champion covered up and held on until his head cleared. The crowd suddenly came to life as Morgan tried to end the fight, but the previous thirteen rounds of punishment had taken their toll on him, and Carroll was able to survive the round. The American won the last round as Carroll boxed mostly defensively to avoid a repeat of the fourteenth, and as the final bell sounded, Carroll grinned at Morgan as referee Joe Wallis declared him the winner.

Despite the one-sided nature of the first thirteen rounds, the crowd "stayed behind for fully 10 minutes to cheer the fighters"[2] after a thrilling final two rounds. The gate had totalled £1,000, securing a career-high payday for Carroll of £250. Morgan was treated for his facial wounds after the bout while Carroll suffered a ruptured blood vessel in his groin that had swollen up during the contest. The injury forced Carroll to withdraw from a match with another American, Al Trulmans, who had just arrived in Sydney. Trulmans was to travel to Melbourne to meet Carroll on the night of the Caulfield Cup, but due to Carroll's injury, Trulmans faced Ron Richards on the same date in Sydney. Carroll's bout with Trulmans was rescheduled for 4 November, just under two weeks after Trulmans would meet Richards.

After outpointing Johnny Freeman in Brisbane, Richards had fought Ambrose Palmer in a rematch on 9 August at Brisbane Stadium. Palmer was well over a stone heavier than Richards, and when Richards suffered a bad cut over Richards left eye in the opening rounds, he never had a chance:

> "It was evident from the opening rounds that Richards was to receive severe punishment. Palmer, crashing his left to the body and head with force and precision, sustained a relentless attack and was well ahead on points when the bout was stopped."[3]

Richards had bounced back well from his second loss to Palmer, outpointing Harry Lister for a second time at Brisbane Stadium. Trulmans, who resided in San Diego, was a small middleweight who was more to Richards' size than Palmer or Freeman. The 22-year-old Trulmans had worked his way up as a preliminary fighter on the west coast of America. In 1932 and 1933, he had headlined many shows in his hometown of San Diego, including a ten round loss to former world welterweight champion Young Jack Thompson.

Displaying what was described as his best performance in Sydney so far in his career, Richards outpointed Trulmans over 15 rounds. Richards landed his potent right-hand counter early into the contest, staggering Trulmans with the blow. The punch landed numerous times throughout the fight for the Queensland middleweight and heavyweight champion but every time he stung Trulmans, the American came back ferociously. The last round was the best round of the fight. Trulmans hurt Richards early in the final stanza with a left hook before Richards staggered him with a right moments later and the two continued to battle away until the closing bell. The crowd cheered the decision by Joe Wallis but, despite the loss, Trulmans performance proved that he belonged in the ring with Carroll.

West Melbourne Stadium, under Stadiums Ltd, had suspended its boxing season back in March, with Pat McHugh unable to compete against Sydney in his bid to bring quality opponents to Melbourne for bouts. The three major boxing attractions in Melbourne before the closing (Palmer-Freeman, Carroll-Jones and Freeman-Payne) earned a combined gate of £1,000. With little money available in Melbourne, both Palmer and Carroll had travelled north to take fights in Sydney and Brisbane for better pay. With Carroll and Palmer fighting interstate, there wasn't another boxer in Victoria who could draw similar crowds leaving Stadiums Ltd no choice but to lease Melbourne Stadium to the N.B.C, who sent Charles Lucas to Melbourne as manager, while Mike Marre replaced Lucas at Sydney Stadium. Within 12 months of their creation, the N.B.C had control of all three major boxing stadiums in Australia.

The National Boxing Club of Australia re-opened West Melbourne Stadium with 'Young' Llew Edwards vs Nel Tarleton on 16 September. The bout drew 6,000 spectators for a £600 gate, and the

Melbourne fans witnessed a beautiful boxing exhibition by Tarleton, who "had the comfortable margin of 10 winning rounds"[4] according to the press. Former world heavyweight title challenger Bill Lang, who was the referee, saw differently and awarded the decision to the home fighter Edwards. Lang stated that he gave two rounds to Edwards because Tarleton had failed to break clean, which tipped the scoring in favour of the hometown fighter eight rounds to seven. Tarleton, who had impressed the Melbourne fans with his boxing skills, travelled to Sydney after the fight to meet Tod Morgan.

West Melbourne Stadium was forced to temporarily close again in October after huge winds damaged the roof. The second big fight to take place under the N.B.C's control of the Stadium would be Carroll's match with Trulmans on 4 November. The American travelled down to Melbourne following his loss to Richards, which had taken place just two weeks after his voyage from America and many were expecting him to be in better condition for the Carroll bout. The middleweight Trulmans, who weighed 11st-2lb against Richards, was under contract to make 11st at 2 pm on the day of the fight with Carroll or else pay a £50 forfeit. When Trulmans hit the scales, he had put on more weight since the bout with Richards, weighing in at 11st-2.5lb, well over the agreed limit. Carroll was almost half a stone lighter at 10st-11lb.

Trulmans' weight advantage gave him little help against Carroll, and after some good exchanges on the inside in the first two rounds, the Australian champion dominated from round three with his left jab. Trulmans repeatedly tried to bring the fight to the inside where he could use his weight advantage but was kept off balance by Carroll's feints, and when he managed to close the distance, Carroll outpunched him on the inside. The crowd grew restless during the middle rounds as Carroll outboxed Trulmans but only did enough to win the rounds. Trulmans displayed his iron chin in the thirteenth round, taking Carroll's left hook flush on the chin and walking through it and came back in round fourteen, briefly stunning Carroll with a right hand. The fifteenth round was uneventful as Carroll boxed cautiously behind his jab to protect his lead and won the bout comfortably on points.

There were plenty of offers for Carroll following the wins over Morgan and Trulmans. Leichhardt Stadium was keen to match Carroll with the South African fighter Barney Kieswetter, who was undefeated since his January loss to Russ Critcher, offering a £250 purse for the bout. Another American fighter, Lee Paige, was to make his Australian debut one week after Carroll's bout with Trulmans, taking on Bobby Delaney with the winner of that fight making for a solid matchup with Carroll in Melbourne. Ron Richards was Sydney Stadium's preferred choice as Carroll's opponent, with Richards even stating he would meet Carroll at a catch weight. Kieswetter was ruled out when he broke his jaw in a twelve round draw with Sydney middleweight Herb Coady, and after Delaney knocked out Paige, he was matched with Al Trulmans and then Ron Richards bouts at Brisbane Stadium.

Carroll's next move was put on hold until after the result of the upcoming bout between Fred Henneberry and Dave Shade. The arrival of the American Dave Shade early in November was another exciting addition to the Australian boxing scene. Shade, born in 1902, had been a professional since 1918 and had fought well over 200 bouts. Shade had fought two world welterweight champions; boxing two draws with Jack Britton in 1921 and 1922 before losing a highly disputed split decision to Mickey Walker in 1925 at Yankee Stadium. Shade and Walker had previously split a pair of fights in 1921 and, after the third bout with Walker, Shade moved to middleweight. Walker also jumped to the middleweight class, taking the middleweight crown from Tiger Flowers in 1926. Despite being ranked among the best middleweights in the world since 1926, Shade had never received another title shot after his loss to Walker.

After arriving in early November, Shade was matched with Ambrose Palmer with the bout to take place on 27 November at Sydney Stadium. The American was an immediate hit among the Australian public, arriving off the boat with a walking stick and a cigar, he stated he would be in shape to meet Palmer in three weeks. Setting up his training at Harry Stone's gym in the Sydney suburb of Newtown, Shade had a wide variety of sparring partners from bantamweight through to heavyweight to work with as he prepared for Palmer. Like Carroll, Shade used ex Australian middleweight champion Bob Thornton as his chief sparring partner in the days leading up to the bout, drawing large crowds to his daily workouts.

The bout was a massive opportunity for Palmer with the N.B.C cabling an offer to Maxie Rosenbloom, world light heavyweight champion, to come to Sydney to defend his title against Palmer should the Australian be victorious against Shade. Charles Lucas left for the United States days before the Palmer-Shade bout, looking to bring more Americans to Australia for fights and he was to meet with Rosenbloom during his trip. Rosenbloom had twice defeated Shade in 1926, winning both bouts on points and although Palmer was now fighting in the division above, Shade would provide a stern test for the young Australian. Palmer scaled 12st for the bout while Shade was well under the middleweight limit at 11st-4.5lb.

A crowd of over 10,000 cheered both men as they entered the ring for the fifteen round bout, but they later counted both men out as they grew restless with both fighters' technical approach and, at the end of the contest, they vehemently booed the decision. The bout was, by all accounts, a highly skilled boxing match. Palmer was the aggressor while Shade showed solid defensive skills throughout the contest and countered the Australian well, with both men having trouble landing their punches. Shade, who complained about a number of low blows during the contest, used his head movement in particular to trouble Palmer. Palmer's best weapon was his left hook, and he was able to defend many of Shade's leads, having most of his trouble when Shade countered him. Palmer badly cut Shade's lip in round thirteen, but Shade's best two rounds were the last two of the bout. The American's effort and skills won over the crowd, but not the referee Joe Wallis, who crowned Palmer, the winner.

Sydney newspaper *The Referee* agreed with Wallis' decision and felt that the crowd scored the bout on who they enjoyed seeing more, rather than who was more effective:

> "The 15 rounds were mostly kept from being one-sided in Palmer's favor by the superlative ring-smartness of Shade and his habit of drawing attention to his own work. The crowd knew who had won the points; it cheered and at odd times created mild pandemoniums, and had once or twice joined in a chorus that started from the "outers" in counting the fight out. The contest mostly bored, occasionally thrilled and sometimes educated. But whatever it was, Palmer won it."[5]

Despite the loss, Shade became more popular after the bout due to the skill level he displayed as well as his antics. Palmer told *The Sydney Sportsman* that Shade had talked to him throughout the entire contest. When the crowd counted the fighters out in the eighth round, Shade asked Palmer "what's wrong with those guys? Do they want us to decapitate each other?"[6]

After the bout, Shade was complimentary of Palmer, although he stated that he would need at least another two years of fighting in America before he was ready to meet Rosenbloom. The American went back into training for the bout with Henneberry, scheduled first for 18 December at Sydney Stadium, but then delayed for Boxing Day after the cut Shade suffered to his lip against Palmer became septic. Carroll was hopeful of a bout with Shade should he beat Henneberry, who was not a weight division larger than him like Palmer. For Henneberry, this was a huge opportunity to bounce back from the loss to Carroll and show that he was among the best middleweights in the world. Both men impressed in their training displays in the weeks before the bout and another solid attendance was expected at Rushcutters Bay.

Both men made the middleweight limit comfortably, and a crowd of approximately 10,000 witnessed the bout. Henneberry pushed the pace in the early rounds, but Shade was able to counter him successfully and nullify Henneberry on the inside, where the majority of the fight took place. The bout began to heat up in rounds four and five, but Shade remained on top, his ability to walk Henneberry onto his counter punches being the difference early. Henneberry had more success in rounds six and seven, forcing Shade to the ropes with a hard right hand and drawing blood from his mouth but Shade remained very much in the contest, laughing off Henneberry's best punches and making many of his shots hit only air. Shade targeted Henneberry's body in round eight, landing many right hands to the midsection, which brought back a number of low blows from Henneberry.

Shade continued outboxing Henneberry in rounds nine and ten, continually making the Australian champion miss and spinning himself out of the corner when Henneberry worked him there but Henneberry continued to force the action against his slippery opponent. Henneberry's dirty tactics came out again in the eleventh round, a number of head-butts causing swelling around Shade's right cheek but referee Joe Wallis ignored Shade's appeals. Shade used his jab to keep Henneberry off in round twelve, but Henneberry's youth and strength began to take their toll in round thirteen. The Australian champion landed several hard blows in the thirteenth and fourteenth but never had Shade in trouble as Shade ducked under many of his punches and used all his experience to weather the storm. Shade, despite his fatigue, boxed on even terms in the final round and despite winning the contest clearly, the crowd booed the decision against the hometown fighter.

Henneberry seemed to have no issue with the decision after the bout, congratulating his opponent after referee Wallis' decision. Despite the loss, many felt that Henneberry would learn a lot from being in the ring with such an experienced ring man. Shade praised Henneberry after the bout, calling him a "tiger" and said that after "a year of continuous, hard fighting against first-class men should see him fit to fight in any company."[7] One week before the contest, Ambrose Palmer stopped overmatched Western Sydney heavyweight Alec Stanton in four rounds at Leichhardt Stadium. The bout angered N.B.C management, worried that Palmer may injure himself, either physically or as a drawcard, if he performed poorly in the fight, but the brief feud was settled before the Stanton bout and arrangements were made for Palmer to face Shade in a rematch in the new year.

Bobby Delaney emerged as the top contender for Carroll's welterweight championship two weeks before the Shade-Henneberry clash, with a surprising 15 round decision over Ron Richards in Brisbane. Delaney, who also outpointed Al Trulmans in Brisbane the week before, was too fast for Richards and outworked the larger man in eleven of the fifteen rounds. Any talk of a match with Carroll ended when Delaney became seriously ill a week after the bout, again leaving Carroll without an opponent. Leichhardt Stadium tried to capitalise by offering Carroll a guarantee of £225 for three contests, which Carroll turned down as he had told the N.B.C he would defend against Delaney when Delaney was fit. The bout between Carroll and Delaney, however, would never take place as Delaney priced himself out of it, and instead fought Barney Kieswetter on 10 February.

Palmer's 1934 campaign would open with a rematch against Dave Shade on 15 January at Sydney Stadium. Should he prove victorious in the rematch with Shade, Palmer was considering a trip to England to face the British Empire heavyweight champion Len Harvey, who defeated Shade in 1930 by razor-thin decision at London's Royal Albert Hall. The Australian champion arrived back in Sydney one week out from the rematch, finishing his training at Jack Dunleavy's gym. Shade returned to Newtown at Harry Stone's gym, where he appeared to be in even better condition than he was for the Henneberry bout and his confidence was high, telling *The Daily Telegraph* that he was "certain of wiping off that first defeat" to Palmer.[8]

For the third time in under two months, more than 10,000 spectators packed into Sydney Stadium to see Shade, who weighed in lighter for the rematch at 11st-3.5lb. Palmer was slightly heavier than last time, weighing 10lb more than the American. The size difference showed early in the contest as Palmer was able to bully Shade to the ropes where he unloaded with hard punches to the head and body, landing with surprising ease. The Australian continued his fast start in round two, scoring with a hard left hook as Shade went on the defensive, attempting to weather the storm of the younger, larger man. Shade opened his offence in the third round, landing a hard left to Palmer's head but the Australian roared back, and the two men traded punches until the bell with the crowd on their feet.

Shade's defence and counter-punching skills were in full effect in round four as he made Palmer miss and drove him back into the ropes with hard counter-punches. The pace of the fight finally backed off in round five although Palmer landed the best punch of the round, scoring with a left hook to Shade's chin. The Australian started the sixth round well, scoring with a series of clean punches before Shade countered with a left hook. Palmer drove Shade back to the corner and, after stepping to his right, threw a wild left to the body which landed well below Shade's belt and dropped the American to the canvas in a heap. For the fourth time in his professional career, Ambrose Palmer was disqualified for a low blow. For the second time in as many fights between the two men, the crowd booed referee Wallis' decision as many felt Palmer was on his way to a knockout win.

Many fans were keen to see a third fight between Palmer and Shade, but Palmer took a break from training following the loss, paving the way for Shade to rematch Henneberry at Sydney Stadium on 29 January. After this bout, Shade was to meet Jack Carroll on 12 February; however, bad luck would again rob Carroll of his chance to show his talent against a world class opponent. The Henneberry-Shade rematch drew a poor attendance, with many Sydney fans not willing to watch Shade again after the ending of the bout with Palmer. Shade was reported to have become discouraged after seeing the dismal turnout, which was about half of what it had been for his previous Sydney contests and after he suffered a hand injury sometime in the fight, this lead to an uninspired performance. Henneberry, however, was eager to gain revenge on Shade and he put on the best performance of his career.

After Shade did the better work in the first two rounds, Henneberry took the fight to the veteran, using a double and triple jab to back Shade to the ropes where he unloaded with both hands. Shade defended well and landed the harder punches but Henneberry was the busier fighter, and his work-rate began to take its toll on Shade in the second half of the fight. A hard right hand at the start of round eight signalled the turning of the tide as the 22-year-old Australian continually backed Shade to the ropes where he mauled the American. Shade rallied in rounds ten and fourteen, but with one good hand, and an opponent nine years his junior, he could not find the punches to back Henneberry off him. Shade was credited for his "superb ring generalship," and his ability to make Henneberry "miss like a drunken sailor" throughout the bout, but Henneberry's aggression entitled him to Joe Wallis' decision.[9]

After the bout Shade told the N.B.C that his hand injury would require six weeks to heal and that he had no intention of remaining in Australia during that time, cancelling the proposed bout with Carroll. Shade earned more than £1,500 in his four bouts in Australia, while both Ambrose Palmer and Fred Henneberry entered the world rankings for their performances against the highly ranked American. The fights with Henneberry and Palmer were among the last in Shade's career, and after fighting a number of times in his adopted hometown of Pittsfield, Massachusetts at the end of 1934 and early in 1935, he retired to run a cafe. Shade is regarded as one of the greatest boxers to have never won a world title.

The N.B.C. had also bolstered its roster with another North American fighter, Canadian Billy Townsend, who arrived in Sydney just before the New Year and had begun training at 'Slam' Sullivan's gym in Sydney. Townsend had scored a win over Tod Morgan in 1931 and had been in the ring with lightweight greats Benny Leonard and Tony Canzoneri, although he lost both bouts. Townsend was expected to give Carroll a tough test and was billed by the Sydney newspapers as a "K.O. puncher."[10] His Australian debut would come against Australia's lightweight champion, Jimmy Kelso, on 22 January. The Canadian's debut drew 10,000 fans at Sydney Stadium, and after a fast-paced bout, a low blow from the foreigner floored Kelso, leaving him unable to continue at which point referee Wallis awarded the fight to Kelso on a foul. Ringside Doctor Sydney Jones examined Kelso after the bout and agreed that the foul had left him in no position to continue.

Carroll had been recovering from a cut on his arm which had kept him out of the gym. His wife, Doreen, had given birth to their second daughter, Elaine during his hiatus from the ring. The welterweight champion had been staying in shape by running with a greyhound he had purchased named "Endeavor Boy" while waiting for a suitable opponent. Jimmy Kelso and Billy Townsend fought a rematch on 5 February in front of another crowd of 10,000 fans at Sydney Stadium. Townsend started the bout well, hurting Kelso in the opening minute but the Australian lightweight champion battled back, outpunching the Canadian on the inside throughout the middle rounds before seeing off a rally from Townsend to take the decision. With two losses in his first two bouts in Australia, Townsend was not considered viable for Carroll, who signed to fight middleweight Jack O'Brien at the end of February at West Melbourne Stadium. This bout also wouldn't take place as days later Carroll's father passed away after an extended illness and Carroll took time off training to mourn.

A thumb injury delayed Carroll's attempts to resume training in March. The opponent for Carroll upon his return was still not clear as Delaney and Kieswetter split a pair of bouts in February and March, with Delaney first knocking Kieswetter out in the third round and then again knocking him out one month later only to be disqualified for a low blow. Another American import, Ralph Lenny, arrived in March and was matched with Billy Townsend for his first encounter on Australian soil, taking place on 19 March at Sydney Stadium with the winner to fight Jack Carroll at the end of March.[11] The media were hyping Lenny as a future world champion, stating that he was a "perfect scientific fighting machine" and that he had only lost four bouts "in the early part of his career" out of 153.[12]

Despite the reported ability of Lenny, he had no answer for the aggression of Townsend, and it was one-way traffic from the third round onwards. Townsend, who suffered nasty cuts to his lips and nose early in the bout, hurt Lenny with his left hook numerous times in the third and continued to hurt him with punches from both hands as the bout continued into the middle rounds. Lenny showed flashes of his skill, using his jab and his defence to outpoint the Canadian for periods of the fight, but Townsend would eventually catch him with one of his heavier punches. Lenny was in serious trouble in the ninth round, and Townsend dropped him in the tenth, at which point his trainer stepped through the ropes to end the contest giving Townsend his first win on Australian soil. While the bout only drew a live gate of £350, it secured Townsend a date with Carroll.

Although there is evidence to the contrary, Bill Ahearn, who had replaced Pat McHugh as manager of West Melbourne Stadium, claimed years later that he had to persuade Carroll to come out of retirement to fight Townsend. He contended that Carroll had quit boxing to work at the slaughterhouse full-time during his layoff between the Trulmans and Townsend fights, although newspaper evidence suggests that Carroll had actively sought fights and was training during this period. Ahearn claims, however, that Carroll was fed up by Sydney Stadium overlooking him for big fights and had quit the game because he was broke. Ahearn went to Bill O'Brien's barbershop, where he offered Carroll a fight with Townsend at West Melbourne Stadium and gave Carroll an advance of £10 to secure the match.

The proposed March date had to be pushed back until 21 April due to the injuries to Townsend's face he suffered against Lenny. Townsend resumed his training in Sydney before travelling to Melbourne for the bout, arriving on 16 April with his former opponent Jimmy Kelso, who was now his sparring partner. Carroll looked in excellent shape in his workouts with trainer Bill O'Brien and, despite almost six months out of the ring, few thought the Australian champion would have trouble with the Canadian. At the 2 pm weigh-in, Carroll made the agreed weight limit of 10st-7lb, coming in a quarter of a pound under, while Townsend was well under at 10st-2lb.

Townsend was not intimidated by Carroll's reputation, and he came straight at the Carroll in front of 5,000 of his local supporters, sinking in hard left hands to Carroll's midsection. Carroll boxed defensively, looking for openings and while he never looked in serious trouble against the aggression of the Canadian, he was forced to use every ounce of his ring generalship to avoid Townsend's early onslaught. The crowd cheered in the third round as Carroll took the fight to Townsend and the two men traded punches, with Carroll getting the better of the exchanges. The Australian's left rip was his primary weapon, and he countered Townsend's body attack with his own blows to the midsection and the body shots took their effect early in the fourth round as Carroll began to pull away.

By the fifth round, Carroll was in command. Townsend threw very little as Carroll was either occupying the Canadian's gloves with his blistering flurries or not in range to be hit. From time to time Carroll let Townsend open up, and he slipped or parried the shots and responded with "a machine-gun burst of flying leather"[13] that immediately put Townsend on the back foot. Rounds seven and eight were one-sided as Townsend could offer little in return against Carroll's brilliance. At the end of the eighth, Townsend's left eye was gashed, and his face was badly bruised up, and after 50 seconds of the ninth round had passed, referee Bill Lang decided he had seen enough and declared Carroll, the winner by technical knockout.

It was a forceful display from Carroll after six months out of the ring, showing that he had lost none of the speed or skill that had made him famous. The arrival of another American also helped clean up the clutter of contenders who were all clamouring for a bout with Carroll after his absence. Ranked number three in the world lightweight rankings, Wesley Ramey had arrived in Australia in February and, outside of Dave Shade, was the most well-credentialed American import yet. Despite only turning professional in 1929, Ramey had fought 92 times, winning 74, and had been ranked inside the top ten lightweights in the world since 1930. In April 1933, Ramey, weighing slightly over the lightweight limit, outpointed reigning world lightweight champion Tony Canzoneri in a non-title match and was currently ranked number two contender in the world behind Canzoneri and the new champion Barney Ross.

Ramey spent some time training and acclimatising to the conditions in Sydney before he accepted his first fight. After Jimmy Kelso's two wins over Billy Townsend, he was matched with Ramey for the American's Australian debut as Ramey would be a good test of the popular Australian's ability on the world stage. Like Shade, the American Ramey's training sessions were a popular attraction and also like Shade, Ramey proved to be a good draw for the N.B.C with £1,200 worth of paying customers attending his debut at Rushcutters Bay. Kelso was game, but Ramey was in another league, and he never allowed the shorter Australian inside where he was effective, using his jab and footwork from the outside before smothering the Australian on the inside for the full fifteen rounds to take an easy decision win.

While many were impressed with Ramey's skill, his safety-first approach didn't win him any new fans among the Australian audience. Ramey was matched for his second Australian bout with Bobby Delaney, who had recovered from the illness that had cancelled a highly anticipated match with Carroll in January. Delaney's fights with Kieswetter, combined with his wins over Ron Richards, Al Trulmans and Lee Paige at the end of 1933, placed him as the logical local contender for Carroll's welterweight crown. Delaney was matched with Ramey for 31 March, three weeks after Ramey's debut win over Kelso and during the Easter long weekend. It would be Delaney's first bout in Sydney since his impressive stoppage over the highly touted Paige and many Sydney fans were eager to see if the popular Queenslander could upset Ramey.

A poor showing by Ambrose Palmer at Rushcutters Bay a few days before the bout against American Marty Sampson, combined with

Ramey's cautious effort with Kelso affected the crowd, but 9,000 paying spectators were keen to see how Delaney handled the highly ranked American. Ramey showed his versatility and rather than boxing Delaney on the back foot as he did Kelso, he kept the dangerous punching Australian on the back foot for the duration of the contest. Delaney's vaunted right hand was barely thrown as Ramey kept him off balance for the entire fifteen rounds. The bout lacked any thrills and Ramey was correctly given the decision after a slow fifteen rounds. It would be the last time Delaney appeared at Sydney Stadium, and as the once popular fighter thanked the crowd after the bout, he was greeted with silence. Delaney retired from the ring after outpointing Alby Roberts at Brisbane Stadium in June and took a job as the new manager of Brisbane Stadium.

With Ramey not making the lightweight limit for either of his bouts with Delaney or Kelso and few other options available for him, the N.B.C. put forward an offer for him to meet Carroll at the welterweight limit. Ramey at first wanted Carroll to make 10st-4lb but after Carroll's trainer Bill O'Brien rejected this, Ramey agreed to Carroll making the welterweight limit of 10st-6lb or posting a £50 forfeit. Despite just nine one-sided rounds in the ring in the last six months, Carroll displayed his incredible speed in training, boxing with his old rival Charlie Purdy in the days leading up to the bout with Ramey. Ramey kept his gym sessions closed, and after his different tactics against Kelso and Delaney, many were wondering what tactics he would employ against a larger man who could also match him for speed.

Carroll spent two hours in a Turkish bath on the morning of the fight to shed the final 3lb and avoid paying the £50 forfeit. He made the weight, coming in at 10st-5.75lb while Ramey was closer to the lightweight limit that the welterweight limit, weighing 9st-10.5lb. Another poor showing by Ambrose Palmer, this time in his second fight with the American Roy Williams, whom he outpointed on both occasions, which occurred one week before the Carroll-Ramey bout was thought to have possibly hurt the takings for the big welterweight clash. The promoters were delighted when fans began lining up hours before the contest was due to take place and an estimated 14,000 witnessed Carroll's bout with the third best lightweight in the world. It was the largest crowd at Rushcutters Bay since Palmer battled Young Stribling.

The size difference between the two men was startling, but the surprising part of the fight was the advantage Carroll also held in speed. After the two men sparred for half of the first round, Ramey landed the first meaningful punch. Feinting with his jab, he hooked around Carroll's guard and landed the punch cleanly, which brought Carroll into action, and he backed the American to the ropes with his jab and the two men traded for the remainder of the round. Although Ramey landed some solid counter punches, Carroll getting the better of the action. Ramey dealt with Carroll's left jab well in the second session and took the round with a pair of solid uppercuts that landed within moments of each other. Carroll again attacked furiously after being hit with the blows, but Ramey countered better in the second and made Carroll miss with many of his punches.

Both men exhibited a high skill level for much of the third, and there was little to separate them as each man put on a clinic of defensive techniques. With 20 seconds remaining in the round, Ramey attempted to move away from Carroll as he advanced, but Carroll timed his backpedal perfectly, throwing a huge left hook from his waist that caught the American on the jaw and dropped him heavily to the canvas. Ramey was on his knees by the count of three but wisely did not rise until the count of nine and the bell sounded before Carroll could press his advantage. Sensing he couldn't outbox the larger and quicker man, Ramey attacked at the start of the fourth, sinking in a hard left to Carroll's body but Carroll had him in trouble again before the end of the round, only Ramey's defensive ability saving him from a second trip to the canvas.

Ramey continued to attack in the next few rounds, but with each passing round, Carroll stifled his rally sooner. By round eight Ramey's legs were tired, and he knew he couldn't move around the larger man anymore, so he took the fight to the Australian champion. Carroll sensed Ramey was fading and toyed with him, pushing aside his best blows with ease and allowing the American to take the eighth round, knowing that he had nothing left for the remaining seven. Carroll measured Ramey for the first half of the ninth round before he unleashed with both hands, cutting both of Ramey's eyes and breaking his nose as he battered him from one side of the ring to the other. At the end of the ninth round, referee Wallis checked on Ramey but the American was game, and he answered the bell for the tenth. Wallis came to his rescue after the first barrage landed and crowned Carroll, the winner by technical knockout.

Ramey was disappointed with the loss, but his effort against a man just as good, but much larger, was well received by the Australian fans. The Carroll bout was Ramey's last in Australia, and while the American made excellent money for his three fights down under, he decided to visit South Africa, using the time during the voyage to allow his broken nose to heal. The loss to Carroll started Ramey on a form slide that led to him being removed from the world top ten, although he returned to his previous form in 1935. Ramey challenged for the junior welterweight title late in his career, losing to Canada's Max Berger. in 181 career contests, he was only stopped four times.

The win had many Australians believing that Carroll was capable of winning the world championship should he be given the chance. Despite the size difference, Carroll showed his speed was level with any man in the world, and the wins over Ramey and Townsend, as well as his wins over the other Americans Morgan and Trulmans, proved that he was among the best in the world. Earning £350 for his bout with Ramey, Carroll had also cemented himself as one of the N.B.C's best drawcards despite being out of the ring for the first half of 1934. With Henneberry and Richards due to meet for the fourth time in a few weeks, and many other American challengers on their way to Australia, the 27-year-old Carroll had plenty of opponents to keep him busy over the remainder of the year.

JACK CARROLL VS RON RICHARDS

After almost stopping Ambrose Palmer in their first meeting, and then capturing the Australian middleweight title from Fred Henneberry, Ron Richards' prospects had looked as promising as any fighter in Australia until stoppage losses to Henneberry and Palmer derailed his career. The Queensland middleweight and heavyweight champion's form was very sporadic after the Palmer fight; he looked good in outpointing Harry Lister and the American Al Trulmans but, after dropping Bobby Delaney in the second round of their December contest, he was outhustled by the smaller man after the third round, and went on to lose a decision.

The inconsistent form continued for Richards into 1934, and his two January bouts with Barney Kieswetter were evidence of this. On 20 January, Richards was again beaten to the punch by a smaller man for ten rounds until Kieswetter claimed a foul in the tenth and, after examination by the ringside doctor, the South African won the fight on a foul. In the rematch nine days later, Richards' aggression kept Kieswetter "on the run for three-quarters of the fight," [1] but the bout was ruled a draw, a decision that was very unpopular with the Brisbane fans. In the next seven weeks, Richards showed good form by scoring knockout wins over Tommy Fielding, Tommy Nivens and the New South Wales heavyweight champion Jock McDonald. His winning streak was brought to an end when he was outpointed by Jack O'Brien in Townsville one month later.

Following his loss to Dave Shade in January, Ambrose Palmer spent £200 and made his way for England by boat, with the hope of fighting the British heavyweight champion Len Harvey. Palmer's boat headed west and stopped at Fremantle in Western Australia, where Palmer received an offer of £900 for three fights from Jack Munro if he returned to Sydney. Munro, a former manager of Sydney Stadium, was acting purely as guarantor and the bouts would take place under the N.B.C. banner but with Munro ensuring Palmer would be paid £300 for each match. Meanwhile, the N.B.C had organised fights for Palmer; he was to meet the Americans Marty Sampson and Roy Williams, but after he left, Fred Henneberry stepped in to take these bouts. With Palmer back in the picture, Lucas told Henneberry that Palmer would get preference against both opponents.

Henneberry responded by calling for a third fight with Palmer, but the bout could not be made after Henneberry wanted Palmer to make the middleweight limit. Palmer turned this down and instead fought Sampson and Williams twice for his three big-money bouts, winning each contest on points but turning in a disappointing performance on each occasion. Henneberry, angered by the favouritism shown to Palmer, headed north to Brisbane where he agreed to defend his middleweight title against the winner of the upcoming rematch between Ron Richards and Jack O'Brien at Brisbane Stadium on 7 May. Richards scored two more stoppage wins over Jock McDonald in between the bouts with O'Brien, both coming in round eleven.

Richards almost wiped out O'Brien's previous victory in the first round when he badly hurt the Victorian with a right hand to the jaw. O'Brien was in trouble again in the second round after Richards dropped him with a left hook to the midsection, but O'Brien boxed his way out of trouble and came back in the middle rounds, cutting Richards' left eye and taking command through the second half of the fight. The bout was highly entertaining, but O'Brien's superior defence and conditioning gave him the edge down the stretch, and he won the referee's decision, and the right to face Henneberry in May.

Despite his wins over Richards, who had three tremendous battles with Henneberry, O'Brien was no match for the Australian middleweight champion. Henneberry attacked from the opening bell and never allowed O'Brien into the fight, winning every round and slowly draining the challenger of his stamina with his two-fisted attack. The challenger was on his last legs in the 12th round when he shot a right hand below Henneberry's beltline, and referee Fred Craig disqualified him.[2] On the same night in Townsville, North Queensland, Ron Richards faced Bob Thornton, who was undefeated in 1934 with three wins. Richards was the aggressor throughout the first ten rounds and only Thornton's "clever defensive work" kept him in the fight. Thornton rallied in the final rounds but was "punished heavily" in the final round. Richards was the clear winner on points.[3]

After the bout, Brisbane Stadium's new director, Bobby Delaney, announced that Richards and Henneberry would fight for a fourth time on 26 May. The bout would be fought over two-minute rounds without the Australian title on the line.[4] It was to have taken place on the 19th, but Richards requested another week due to an arm injury he suffered in the rematch with Thornton. Henneberry refused to stay idle and took two fights in the interim, both in New South Wales and neither at Sydney Stadium. First up was Alby Roberts who, after being dropped in the seventh round, only lasted the distance because of his constant holding. Fred's second bout, just days before the Richards clash, was at Leichhardt Stadium against the British lightweight George Thompson. Thompson was dropped in the first round and battered until the referee Jack Haines stopped the bout.

The middleweight champion arrived in Brisbane one day after his bout with Thompson. Richards, meanwhile, had been training a hectic seven day per week schedule at Brisbane Stadium, giving exhibitions each day for two weeks leading up to the bout. Even without the middleweight title on the line, there was a lot at stake for both men. With both men having one win apiece in their three previous contests there was bragging rights as well as a £100 side bet on the bout. A win in this bout would also increase the chances of securing a big money fight against one of the many foreign fighters currently fighting in Australia.

In front of a sold-out Brisbane Stadium, Henneberry and Richards once again put on a show. Henneberry suffered a cut early in the first round of the fight, but otherwise had the better of the opening sessions by using his ever improving defence to avoid Richards' powerful blows and take the fight to the inside, where he held the advantage. Richards worked his body in these early rounds but Henneberry built an early lead by continually keeping him off balance with his jab and Richards was unable to land his right hand with any consistency. At the start of the sixth, Henneberry looked to be taking over, but Richards ended the round with his best moment of the fight so far, catching Henneberry with a series of left hooks as he came inside before having the better of the inside work. Richards continued Henneberry on the inside in the seventh, where he outpunched the Australian champion.

Henneberry came back well in the eighth and ninth round and used both hands to punish Richards on the inside, but Richards opened his cut eye with another jab, and the blood continued to flow for the remainder of the fight. Richards scored well with right hands to the body in the tenth and surprised Henneberry with his conditioning as he matched the champion punch for punch in round eleven. The referee warned Henneberry, who was showing visible signs of frustration, for using his forearm in the twelfth and Richards landed some heavy right hands from the outside towards the end of the round. The Queenslander's conditioning finally began to wilt in the thirteenth, and Henneberry threw everything at him in the final three rounds. Although he was tiring, Richards fought back gamely, but Henneberry's early lead and his strong finish gave him the decision.

Despite losing the fight, Richards' efforts were praised afterwards as Henneberry had proven he was world class and Richards showed that he was still competitive with him. Pat O'Sullivan, Richards' manager, challenged Henneberry to a rematch immediately after the fight but with the title on the line, stating that Richards would be victorious over three-minute rounds. Henneberry's rift with the N.B.C. continued, however, and despite the N.B.C. telling him he had to defend his title, Henneberry refused to fight at any stadium run by them. Richards, meanwhile, agreed to a rematch with Jack O'Brien at the end of June to stay in shape for the title fight.

Held in Mackay, Queensland on 27 June during 'Carnival Week', the third bout between Ron Richards and Jack O-Brien fight was a wild affair with both fighters fighting exchanging punches after the bell in many rounds. Richards put O'Brien down for an eight count in the fifth round. The seconds of both men entered the ring during a brawl at the end of the seventh round, with O'Brien taking blows from one of Richards' corner-men. The police restored order before Richards pressed the advantage in the next round, punching O'Brien threw the ropes early in the eighth and into the ringside seats. O'Brien beat the count and came back for more and the two men traded punches for the remainder of the round. The fight continued to be wild into the later rounds, with Richards forcing the issue and O'Brien showing skilful defence. Despite Richards scoring two knockdowns, after 15 rounds the bout was declared a draw which was met by hoots from the crowd.

Meanwhile, Jack Carroll had resumed training after the bout with Ramey but, with his dominance over the local welterweight division, there were few attractive opponents for him. Without an opponent in his weight class, and with Ron Richards looking for a way to place pressure on Henneberry to defend his title against him, Richards and Carroll agreed to face each other at Sydney Stadium on 23 July. The bout was to take place in Melbourne initially, but the N.B.C. again decided to suspend operations in Melbourne due to their inability to consistently stage quality fights there. By the end of July, the N.B.C. announced that they would permanently close West Melbourne Stadium, which would be once again run by Dick Lean and Stadiums Ltd, who announced their re-entry into boxing in September.

The bout between Carroll and Richards was billed as a middleweight elimination bout, with the winner to meet Henneberry for the Australian championship. While Carroll was the heavy favourite in this fight based on his form against world class opposition, Richards was the larger man, and he had proven that his punching power was capable of knocking out men larger than himself. A catch-weight of 11st was agreed to for the bout and, despite Richards having fought at heavyweight during his career, his recent weights were close to this weight. Richards had even shown that he was strong at this weight, having weighed in under the proposed catch-weight for his recent knockout wins with McDonald, Fielding and Nivens.

Arriving more than two weeks before the bout, Richards trained hard at Jack Dunleavy's gym. The catch-weight proved not to be an issue when Richards weighed in 2lb under the agreed weight almost one week before the date of the fight. *The Sydney Sportsman* reported that Richards was in tremendous shape for the bout, to which Richards replied: "I will need it all on Monday night, if I beat Carroll it will not be an accident."[5]

Carroll arrived in Sydney one week later, sparring again with Bob Thornton and Charlie Purdy. The incentives for Carroll were high as Brisbane Stadium, now run by recently retired Bobby Delaney, had offered him another fight with Henneberry on 8 August, during 'Exhibition Week,' which guaranteed to add to what would already be a big money fight. Henneberry's dispute with Charles Lucas had continued as he had signed to meet Harry Lister at Leichhardt Stadium to stay fit for the big bout at Brisbane Stadium in a month. With Ambrose Palmer taking a short break from boxing so he could play Australian Rules Football, the announcement of the Carroll-Henneberry bout outside of the N.B.C's umbrella meant that, after the Carroll-Richards bout, Lucas did not have control of any of Australia's three biggest drawcards.

At the official weigh-in on the day of the fight, Richards surprised many when he not only made the weight comfortably but weighed less than the welterweight Carroll. More surprises came on the evening of the fight when Richards removed his robe before the start of the bout. The Queensland middleweight and heavyweight champion did not look his strong self as he was noticeably thinner in the face and legs. Carroll also noticed Richards' weak appearance, and uncharacteristically attacked the naturally larger man at the opening bell. While Richards was never in any trouble, the speed and ferocity of Carroll's attack took him by surprise, and he spent much of the opening round retreating.

Carroll again attacked in the second round, having similar success and Richards was too busy moving out of harm's way to mount any counter-attack. While no serious damage was inflicted in the opening two rounds, they were rounds in favour of the Victorian.

Early in the third, Richards planted his feet and landed a hard right hand to Carroll's jaw, which gained the respect of the Australian welterweight champion and forced him to revert to his usual tactics. Richards continued his success early in the fourth, landing another hard right hand to Carroll's jaw but Carroll's jab bloodied Richards' mouth and nose in this session, and he landed a hard left hook to the jaw of the Queenslander, his best punch of the fight.

After a scrappy fifth round in which neither fighter gained a significant edge, the turning point of the fight came in the sixth. During a clinch, Carroll suffered a badly gashed left eye that was either caused by a head-clash or a Richards right uppercut. At the end of the round, referee Joe Wallis checked the cut but ruled it wasn't significant enough to warrant stopping the contest. The wound was cleaned up by Bill O'Brien during the minute's rest before the start of round seven, but Carroll, sensing the fight could be stopped if the injury worsened, attacked at the beginning of the eighth in an effort to end the fight. Richards also sensed a chance to finish the bout but was quickly forced to retreat as he had no answer for Carroll's hand-speed.

Carroll battered Richards in round eight, often switching stances to get more leverage on his powerful left hook and the Queenslander could do little more than cover up and try to give himself room. The pasting continued in round nine as Carroll landed a sweeping right hook that staggered Richards. Richards fought back more in this round, but his legs were weakening. He could do little to stop the onslaught, and he was on the verge of going down as the bell sounded to end the ninth. It was now Richards whose facial injuries were in danger of causing the bout to be stopped as his lip was badly damaged, his nose gushing blood and his eyes beginning to swell from the repeated blows that Carroll was landing.

Richards tried to turn the tide in round ten but it was his final stand, and his blows were wild. Carroll shot out his jab and used his faster feet before continuing his attack as Richards slowed in the second half of the round. After a slow round eleven, the welterweight champion attacked in the twelfth and Richards offered little in return. The swelling around Richards' eyes continued to grow into the thirteenth round, as did the one-sided nature of the contest. Referee Wallis examined Richards at the end of the thirteenth round and convinced Richards to surrender, giving Carroll a technical knockout victory.

While many criticised the catch weight after the bout, suggesting that Richards coming down to the 11st limit was to blame for the loss, it was perhaps Richards' overtraining that left him in such a bad way. Richards had proven in his previous bouts during 1934 that he was capable to making the weight and performing well there and the fact that he was at the weight a week before the contest suggests that it should not have played a factor. In both his bout with Carroll and the fourth contest with Henneberry, Richards had trained longer than usual for the contest, and his performance had suffered during the second half of the fight.

Despite the loss, Richards only required a couple of stitches to his lip after the bout, and he was back in the ring less than three weeks later. Weighing almost a stone heavier than in his match with Carroll, Richards knocked out heavyweight Son Tealy 25 seconds into the fourth round with a right to the jaw. Carroll, meanwhile, was forced to withdraw from the bout with Henneberry due to his badly cut eye, leaving Henneberry without an opponent for Exhibition Week. Henneberry, who outpointed Harry Lister a few days later, didn't reconcile with Lucas and the N.B.C. and returned to Brisbane where he would battle Ron Richards two more times in 1934.

The fifth battle between Henneberry and Richards took place on 25 August at Brisbane Stadium. The fight once again sold out despite Henneberry's title still not being on the line. Richards, who weighed in over the middleweight limit, started well, winning the first round easily with a pair of clean right hands and a hard left hook just before the bell. In the second round, Richards attacked and continued to find a home for his right cross, one of which made Henneberry's legs buckle. Henneberry tried to smother Richards' attacks but had trouble getting past the Queenslander's jab. The middleweight champion had more success in round three, working Richards' body on the inside but Richards evened the round with his right hand in the final minute.

The bout was shaping up to be another electrifying encounter when it ended suddenly in the fourth round. The two men were trading blows in the fourth when Henneberry landed a low punch that was obviously a foul. Richards briefly sank to one knee, and his corner complained, but the appeal was turned down by the referee, who told the fighters to continue. Sensing Richards was vulnerable, Henneberry attacked and, after another flurry of blows, Richards sank to the canvas from a left hook that was again below the belt before Henneberry landed a right hand to Richards while he was on one knee. The referee called the doctor in to examine Richards while he was down. Richards' father, who was working Ron's corner, briefly entered the ring and was involved in a shouting match with Henneberry, before he was removed. After consultation with the doctor, the referee awarded Richards the fight on a foul in the fourth round.

While few argued with the decision to disqualify Henneberry for his indiscretions, some purists believed that Richards could have been disqualified for the actions of his father entering the ring during the round. Henneberry also did not seem to have any issue with the disqualification. Both men now had two wins apiece in their five-fight series, with both of Richards' wins coming by way of disqualification. The sixth fight would not take place straight away, however, as Henneberry returned to Sydney, looking to be matched with Ambrose Palmer upon Palmer's return from New Zealand.

Henneberry was so keen to fight Palmer that he and his brother sat down with the N.B.C. in September and settled their differences, announcing that he would fight again at Sydney Stadium. Palmer, however, told the N.B.C. that he was not interested in bouts with Henneberry or any other local fighter.

Richards, meanwhile, won bouts at the smaller Bohemia Stadium in September and October over Al Rex and Jimmy Richardson respectively. Bobby Delaney's brief stint as manager of Brisbane Stadium came to an end when he got the itch to fight again, and Charlie Bonham replaced him. Bonham wanted to start his tenure as Brisbane Stadium manager off on the right foot and, after negotiating with Charles Lucas, signed Henneberry for two fights, the first of which would be Ron Richards on 10 November. The bout would once again not involve the Australian middleweight title, although Richards' manager Pat O'Sullivan stated they would claim the title with a second victory in a row over Henneberry. The bout would also be fought under the "no foul" rule, under which a boxer could only be disqualified for a foul that was ruled intentional.

Henneberry was noticeably sharper in the sixth bout compared to the fifth, and he set a furious pace from the outset, using his jab to off balance Richards and set up his inside attacks. Richards gave ground and used a pawing jab to give himself enough distance to land his right hand, which he did land occasionally, but Henneberry's smothering tactics never allowed Richards to get more than one off at a time. Richards' cleaner shots gave him the edge in the first rounds but Henneberry's defence was excellent, and he caught a lot of Richards' blows on his arms and rolled under the Queenslanders counter right hands. Henneberry beat Richards to the punch in the third with a hard right, which forced Richards on the defensive but Richards boxed well off the ropes and was never in serious trouble.

The champion's improved defence was effective in lowering Richards' output, which allowed Henneberry to win the next few rounds with his two-handed flurries on the inside. Richards attacked in the seventh, sensing he was behind on the cards, but Henneberry focused on his defence and gave away the round before he resumed his attack in the eighth, drawing Richards' leads before hammering him on the inside with both hands. Richards could do little but hold and wait for the referee to separate the fighters once Henneberry got past his right. The crowd booed the Australian champion in the ninth when he pushed Richards threw the ropes and then struck him as he tried to untangle himself.

By the tenth round, Henneberry had the timing on Richards' right hand, and while Richards was able to land the punch sporadically, Henneberry had a commanding lead heading into the twelfth. After a small section of the crowd began started a ten count on the boxers during a slow start to the twelfth round, it spurred both men into action. The two men traded punches over the next round and a half, and while Richards punched more on the inside and held less, Henneberry still held the advantage. Richards showed signs of weakening in the fourteenth as Henneberry was able to push him to the floor during a clinch. The champion saw off one final rally from Richards in the last round, and the referee crowned Henneberry the winner on points at the end of the fifteenth.

Richards' manager Pat O'Sullivan was still adamant that Richards would defeat Henneberry over the championship distance of 15x3 minute rounds and offered a £100 side bet if he would put the title on the line. Henneberry turned this down as he had an agreement to meet Jack O'Brien the following week again in Brisbane and then had his sights set on Palmer in Sydney. Both men had reportedly shown marked improvement in their second series of fights, and with Richards just 24 years old and Henneberry a year younger, both men still had bright futures ahead of them. Henneberry would stop O'Brien a week later, this time in the 13th round, before returning to Sydney to try and lure Palmer into the ring for the third time.

For Richards, 1934 had been a disappointing year with losses to Carroll, Henneberry and O'Brien he had learnt a lot of lessons that would benefit him in the years to come. He ended the year by scoring a one-sided eighth-round knockout over O'Brien, and the dominance over a man who had beaten him twice and drawn with him earlier in the year displayed how much he had improved. O'Brien was never in the fight and Richards dropped him in the first round before punishing him until "a terrific two-handed attack"[6] put him down again at the end of the eighth. The bell saved O'Brien, and his corner was unable to revive him during the rest period. The win showed that Richards was still improving despite some hard losses in his career and the 24-year-old would become one of Australia's greatest draw-cards.

CLIMBING THE WORLD RANKINGS

After the cancellation of the proposed fourth bout between Jack Carroll and Fred Henneberry in early August, Carroll agreed to meet Tod Morgan in a rematch on 27 August. Morgan had been successful since the loss to Carroll, although he had been fighting men much smaller. After splitting a three-fight series with Australia's lightweight champion Jimmy Kelso (Morgan won the first, Kelso the second and the third bout was a draw) in October and November of 1933, Morgan put an exclamation mark on the series with an eighth-round knockout in July. He followed these wins with a first round knockout over the Welsh boxer Tommy John and a decision over top Australian lightweight contender Herb Bishop.

Carroll returned to Melbourne after the Richards bout, going back to work at his brother's slaughterhouse while his eye healed up. He resumed light training in early August before travelling to Sydney the week before the bout where he completed his preparations at Paul Harbulot's gym with his usual sparring partners of Purdy and Thornton. While Morgan was a heavy underdog due to the size difference between the two men, the N.B.C anticipated a large crowd with many hoping to see a repeat of their classic ten months earlier. Both men showed they were in tremendous shape for the contest, sparring up to ten rounds a day with various sparring partners. The Australian champion weighed in well under the welterweight limit at 10st-6lb, carrying a significant weight advantage over Morgan, who was under 10st at the weigh-in on the afternoon of the bout.

Commercially the bout was a huge success with a sell-out crowd witnessing the contest. However, the fight was nearly called off just moments before it was due to start. An argument between Morgan and the N.B.C. over money that Morgan believed was owed to him from previous bouts, was not settled until right before the fight was due to start. Morgan had lost his temper during the argument, and he fought emotionally as the contest began, uncharacteristically attacking moments after the opening bell. He missed with a wild left hook, which was countered by a hook from Carroll, who then took the fight to Morgan before Morgan clipped him with a wild right hand. The two men traded heavily, and on relatively even terms for the remainder of the round until Morgan sunk an accidental low blow into Carroll's protective shield moments before the end of the first. The punch dropped Carroll to his knees, and he remained there as the bell ended the first round.

Referee Joe Wallis spoke to him as he was down and, eventually, Carroll's seconds assisted him to his corner. After a brief interval, Bill O'Brien called over referee Wallis to instruct him that Carroll's groin protector had been broken and one was fetched from backstage to replace it. After a five minute interval, the second round finally started, and Morgan continued to fight wildly. Despite having Carroll trapped on the ropes or in the corner for most of the second round, Morgan missed most of his punches and returned to his corner at the end of the second with a severely cut lip and a bloody nose. Morgan, still wild, landed his left hook a number of times to Carroll's jaw in the third, but Carroll established his jab in the fourth, opening a cut over Morgan's left eye and winning the round.

With Morgan unable to deal with Carroll's jab, the bout grew incredibly one-sided from round five onwards. Morgan continued to fire away, especially in the clinches, but Carroll landed with tremendous speed and accuracy and never looked in any danger. Morgan was punished by Carroll's jab from the outside and assaulted at close quarters with punches from both hands. In the eighth round, it looked like Morgan wouldn't last the distance, but the smaller man kept on attacking and taking punishment. By the ninth, the ring resembled an abattoir before Carroll opened another cut, this time over the right eye, in round ten. Morgan barely escaped the eleventh, with the crowd cheering his ability to absorb the punishment as Carroll teed off with both hands.

After another one-sided round in the twelfth in which Morgan's blood showered the pressmen in the front row, Carroll work-rate finally slowed down, as the physicality of the contest began to take its toll. Boxing cautiously, Carroll coasted through the final three rounds and won an easy points decision. The crowd gave Morgan a standing ovation after the bout, and although the American's face was a mess, he told reporters afterwards that he could have boxed another ten rounds. Quoted after the fight, Carroll said that Morgan was "a wonderful little fighter" and he was "sorry to punish him."[1] With an estimated 12,000 in attendance, the bout was a nice payday for both men, and with Morgan at the end of his contract, it proved an incentive for the American to stay in Australia.

With few options to match against Carroll, Lucas looked to match him again with Ambrose Palmer, who was on his way back from New Zealand after a pair of decision wins. This matchup brought criticism for Lucas and the N.B.C. with many wanting to see both men in with world class opponents from the weight division they fought in, rather than each other. Lucas shot back at this criticism, stating that due to Carroll's supremacy over Henneberry after Henneberry had fought on even terms with Palmer, he was a strong chance of defeating the larger man. Palmer, however, publically turned down the fight, stating that he wouldn't risk a potential world title shot against a smaller man:

> "You can take it from me that I have no intention of fighting Jack Carroll. Yes, we might draw a big 'gate' but you must remember that in such a fight I would have everything to lose and nothing to gain. People would expect me to beat Carroll - probably, to knock him out inside half a dozen rounds, for I would have an advantage in weight of at least a stone, and a corresponding advantage in strength. What good would it do for me to merely beat him on points? Carroll is a clever, shifty fellow. Nobody knows better than I do what he is capable of. Suppose he got a decision over me. Would 750, or even 1,000 compensate me for my loss of prestige? It would not."[2]

After suffering from influenza in September, Carroll was sidelined from training, which delayed his return to the ring, but by the end of the month, he was back in the gym. The N.B.C. announced that they were importing Jack Portney, a welterweight from Baltimore who was the last man to defeat Wesley Ramey before Ramey's trip to Australia, and Carroll was to be first in line to meet Portney. The bout with Portney was to take place on 29 October in Rushcutters Bay;[3] however, Carroll indicated that he wouldn't be ready for Portney by the end of October and Herb Bishop got the first fight with Portney. The bout with Portney would be delayed further after Sydney welterweight Billy Martin issued Carroll a challenge for his welterweight title, which Carroll accepted.

Billy Martin had fought all over Australia since turning professional in 1930, and he had not lost since dropping a decision to Cyril Pluto in October 1933. The 20-year-old Martin had twice avenged the loss to Pluto in 1934, and also had a win over the Queensland fan-favourite Reg Hickey. In Martin's last bout, he had claimed the "junior welterweight championship of Australia" with a seventh-round stoppage over Jack Fitzgerald in Fitzroy, although the weight class and the title weren't taken seriously outside of Fitzroy. It was the first time Carroll had defended the title since winning it from Bluey Jones in 1933, and many expected the fast punching Martin to cause the now 28-year-old champion some difficulty.

The bout proved too big of a jump up in class for the young challenger, and it was a dull affair for the paying audience of £400. Martin took the fight to the champion in the first round before Carroll landed with both hands to the body, stinging the younger man. Martin fought defensively after this and allowed Carroll to do all the leading. In the fourth round, Martin had his best moment of the fight when he landed hard right to Carroll's jaw, but Carroll fought back and had re-established control by the end of the round. The remainder of the fight was dull as Carroll was the only man fighting and could do little to bring the challenger out of his shell. At times, when Martin fought back at the start of a round, he looked good, but every time he opened up, Carroll answered and sent Martin back on the defensive. Martin lasted the fifteen rounds, but Carroll was the easy winner on points.

With many still interested in a fight between Carroll and Ambrose Palmer, Carroll added to the hype when he called out the Australian heavyweight champion after his win over Martin:

> *"Please tell Palmer that I am the logical contender for the light-heavyweight title. I have beaten on Richards and Henneberry much more convincingly that Palmer did. Tell him, too, that I have always been ready to give away weight, and also that he is*

afraid to engage me in a real fight, as I look far too dangerous for his liking."[4]

Jack Portney, meanwhile, had opened his Australian campaign with three bouts in as many weeks. Portney lived up to his reputation in his debut against Bishop, scoring three knockdowns in the eighth round on his way to a comfortable fifteen round decision win. Portney's southpaw stance confused Bishop, who had annexed the lightweight championship from Jimmy Kelso with a 13th round knockout in September, and the Australian was never able to get going during the contest with many wondering how he survived the fifteen rounds. The American also fought the following week, stopping Sydney welterweight Alf Blatch in the seventh round. With Carroll facing Martin on 19 November, Portney signed to fight Tod Morgan on 12 November.

Despite Morgan being more experienced than the Australians who had battled the left-handed Portney, the southpaw stance also confused him, and Portney had a strong start to the bout. Regularly scoring with his left hand to the body and head, Portney opened a cut on Morgan's forehead and over his right eye. The blood spurred Morgan on, and he rallied back in the second half of the bout, forcing Portney to hold on numerous times. Referee Joe Wallis repeatedly warned Portney for holding, and it wound up costing him the fight. Despite getting the better of the early parts of the round, Portney faded under Morgan's relentless assault in the later rounds and this, combined with the repeated warnings for holding, allowed Morgan to even up the bout, and referee Joe Wallis ruled the fight a draw at the end of the fifteenth.

Carroll was matched with Portney after his win over Martin, with the bout set to take place on 3 December at Sydney Stadium, but when Carroll injured his right hand in training, it postponed the fight until 17 December. Portney faced Morgan in a rematch on 3 December to stay fit for the big bout with Carroll, but when Carroll then injured his knee on the day of the Morgan-Portney rematch, the fight was cancelled, as the knee injury would keep Carroll out of action until mid-January. Portney learnt from his first encounter with Morgan and avoided the inside exchanges by using his superior footwork to earn a close decision over the aggressive Morgan. After the bout, Portney announced that he would return to America but was keen to return to Australia in the new year to face Carroll.

The Australian welterweight scene was about to gain another world-class operator with the arrival of Willard Brown, who was ranked number eight in the world after knockouts over world junior welterweight champion Battling Shaw and experienced New Yorker, Joe Glick. He had since split a three-fight series with the top five welterweight Eddie Wolfe, and the August edition of 'Ring Magazine' started that "If Willard Brown isn't the welterweight champion of the world within the next year or so, it will be because he doesn't get a crack at the title."[5] With over 100 recorded fights on his record and being a natural welterweight, Brown was the most credentialed opponent to fight in Australia during Carroll's professional career thus far.

The 21-year-old Brown arrived with his wife on New Year's Day and was immediately in the gym, impressing Sydney's reporters. With Carroll's knee still injured, Brown was matched with Jimmy Kelso for his first fight in Australia, with the contest set for 21 January. Kelso, who had been knocked out by Tod Morgan and Herb Bishop in his previous two matches, was no match for the world-rated Brown. Brown picked him apart with ease, putting Kelso down and through the ropes in the third round with a left hook before a right hand to the jaw dropped him to the canvas face-first for the count in the fifth. Kelso, who retired after the bout, was unable to leave the ring for several minutes after the knockout. It was an emphatic victory for Brown as Kelso had previously upset import Billy Townsend and proved durable against both Tod Morgan and Nel Tarleton.

Tod Morgan, who had bounced back from the loss to Portney with a knockout over the Brisbane Stadium star Reg Hickey in Hickey's Sydney debut, was the next opponent for Brown. Morgan once again considered leaving Sydney after his first bout with Portney but decided to extend his trip, earning large purses in his rematch with Portney and in the fight with Hickey. Brown was proving quite popular among the Australian fans, with large crowds flocking to his training sessions at Sammy Hart's gym in George Street in Sydney. Despite a match between two Americans, the N.B.C. were so confident of a large crowd that they raised ticket prices by as much as 50% for the contest.

While the ticket prices affected the crowd, the bout drew approximately 10,000 paying customers to the stadium in Rushcutters Bay. After Brown removed his robe before the start of the fight, a series of boils were apparent on his right arm and shoulder. Despite the obvious handicap, Brown controlled the early rounds with his jab and footwork, never allowing Morgan to work when he came in close. Brown landed numerous left rips to Morgan's midsection, but most of the action up close was spoiled as both men wrestled more than punched in the clinches. After the first five rounds, Morgan was way behind on points and didn't look like he was in the fight as Brown was having no trouble avoiding his slow punches.

In the sixth, Brown went on the defensive and Morgan worked his way back into the fight, taking the round with his aggression but was met by a barrage of punches to open round seven. For the first minute of the seventh Brown was in total command before he landed a low blow and was penalised. Morgan rallied in the second half of the round, and his aggression began to unsettle Brown. Morgan stunned Brown with a hard right hand at the end of the seventh and continued to build momentum in the eighth as Brown fought mostly on the defensive for the entire round. Brown was weakening in the ninth round, and Morgan continued to eat into his early lead, taking the tenth with his aggression, but Brown's ability to smother Morgan's blows kept him out of trouble. The bout had somewhat evened up after Brown's early lead, and Morgan seemed to be the stronger of the two men.

Brown won the eleventh with a brilliant display of counter punching, out-manoeuvring the former world champion in close and landing solid left hooks to Morgan's jaw. The first half of the twelfth round was also Brown's as he continued to have success with his left hook. Suddenly Brown tired, and the crowd cheered as Morgan attacked viciously, taking the second half of the round as Brown held on. With the crowd going wild, Morgan hurt Brown with a left hook in the thirteenth and battered the world rated American for the duration of the round. Boxing smartly in the last two rounds, Brown was able to stifle a lot of Morgan's attacks and fight the final two rounds on even terms, and at the end of the final round, referee Joe Wallis gave Willard Brown the decision based on his work in the early rounds.

The Sydney crowd had gotten behind Morgan during his rally in the second half of the contest and, despite many of the later rounds being close, they booed the decision. Some of the newspapers agreed with the crowd's display. *The Sun* thought that Morgan won eleven of the fifteen rounds, scoring a number of the early rounds to him for his aggression. *The Referee* also thought that Morgan "had a small margin in his favour at the end" while *The Labor Daily* reported that Brown told Morgan that he should have won the decision. *The Sydney Morning Herald*, however scored the fight for Brown while *The Daily Telegraph* also agreed with referee Wallis, stating that "sometimes the crowd is wrong, last night the crowd was definitely and unmistakably wrong."[6]

After the bout, it was revealed that Brown should not have been fighting as he had the boil on his right shoulder lanced just the night before. The wound was so well treated, however, that Brown decided to go through with the battle and, after spending a few days in the Blue Mountains, he returned to training. Brown disputed the reports that he had told Morgan he lost the bout:

> "I did not speak to Morgan. In fact, I have made it a practice never to discuss a referee's decision. If it is against me, I accept it without any complaint. If it is in my favour, I try to take it in the right sporting spirit, but I would like to assure the public that I never made any comment to Morgan or anyone else. I would like to say, however, that I regard Morgan as a grand little fighter. If he would like to meet me again he has only to say the word."[7]

The rematch wouldn't eventuate and Morgan, after two years in Australia, decided to head home to America at the end of February. On the weekend before his departure, Morgan was part of a fishing party who caught a tiger shark, measured at just over 13 feet long (around 4m).

With the rematch against Morgan off the table, Brown turned his interests to Jack Carroll, who had advised the N.B.C. that he would be ready to fight on 4 March. Brown decided to keep busy before this date, and he accepted a fight with the hard-punching American Bobby Wilson just two weeks after his bout with Morgan. The punching power that Wilson had shown in his training exhibitions had many predicting that he would knock Carroll out if the two were to meet. The southpaw Wilson, from Washington DC, had won 33 recorded bouts in his career, with 29 coming by way of knockout, although the Australian newspapers listed the number of his knockout wins at 47 from 72 total fights. The contest between Wilson and Brown had one of the most remarkable starts of any fight ever fought in Australia.

From the opening bell, it was all Willard Brown as he repeatedly stung Bobby Wilson with right hands for the first two and a half minutes of the opening round. With just 15 seconds remaining in the round, Wilson uncorked a huge left hook which left Brown on the canvas. Brown beat the count, but Wilson met him immediately with a right hand that put him down and through the ropes. The bout appeared over but the bell sounded to end the first round, and Brown's seconds helped him to his corner. Wilson went in for the kill after Brown's corner spent the minute between rounds reviving him and put him down for the third time with a left hand. Brown was up at eight, but was down from the next punch, although this time just for the count of three. Another left buckled Brown's knees but Brown then met Wilson's next onslaught with a right hand, which backed the southpaw off and from there he was able to smother Wilson's efforts. With one minute remaining in the round, Brown began his own rally as he hammered Wilson with right hands to the jaw at the bell.

Despite suffering four heavy knockdowns, Brown took the fight to Wilson in the third round, and Wilson struggled to keep the pace with the man who he had in such desperate trouble just minutes earlier. After being thoroughly outboxed in the third and fourth rounds, Wilson looked dejected in his corner before the start of the fifth. He was always dangerous with the power he possessed, and many in the crowd held their breath for Brown every time Wilson let his hands go. Brown, however, had recovered and he was in complete control for the remainder of the fight, and although Wilson had his moments in rounds six, nine and thirteen, Brown had his measure and punished Wilson for the rest of the contest. The Sydney fans, who hooted Brown after he was given the decision over Tod Morgan two weeks earlier, wildly cheered as he was crowned the winner after the near disaster in round one.

The bout proved a prosperous one for Jack Carroll as he now had two opponents who the public was interested in seeing him fight. The scheduled 4 March bout with Willard Brown would go ahead, and two weeks later, Carroll would meet Bobby Wilson, provided he didn't suffer any injuries against Brown. Carroll had remained in

Melbourne while he regained his fitness after the knee injury he suffered in December, arriving back in Sydney one week before the first of his two bouts with the Americans. Any doubts over Carroll's fitness or his speed after the knee injury were quickly put to rest when Carroll showed his excellent form in the gym.

Regardless of Brown's reputation in America and his world ranking, Carroll was the heavy betting favourite among the Sydney fans. With interest shown in both men's daily workouts, the Carroll-Brown bout was shaping up to be another sell-out for the N.B.C., who once again raised the price of admission to "pre-depression prices" to maximise the gate. Before the bout, both men had agreed to fight at the welterweight limit "take or give a pound," and Carroll scaled slightly over the welterweight limit, giving him a 4lb weight advantage over the American who came in at 10st-3.5lb. The bout drew more than £2,000 paying spectators with approximately 12,000 in attendance at Sydney Stadium to see how Carroll fared against a true world class welterweight, and the crowd roared as he climbed through the ropes.

The American appeared confident as the bell sounded to start the fight and he immediately rushed at the taller Carroll, landing with a left to the body. Carroll tried to establish his jab, but Brown had success with his jab and used it to work his way inside where he attempted to use his left hook to the body. Carroll was able to smother Brown's efforts in close but looked slow with his responses and couldn't find the target until the second round, which he opened with a hard jab to Brown's chin. Brown acknowledged the blow then took the fight back to Carroll, landing his left downstairs again. The jab was working better for Carroll during this round, but Brown was intelligent and made many of Carroll's leads miss, countering one with a hard right hand near the bell to end the second round.

The Australian champion opened the third round at a faster pace, tearing into Brown, landing a left hook off his jab before following up with a series of short left hands on the inside. The fight continued at close quarters in this round, and Carroll drew first blood, opening a cut over Brown's right eye with a left hand on the inside. Brown used his jab effectively to keep Carroll from pressing the advantage but Carroll was beginning to warm up after a slow start, and it took all of Brown's defensive skill to avoid Carroll's jab for the remainder of the round. The American continued his body attack in the fourth, apparently hoping to slow Carroll down in the later rounds. Carroll's defence was tight, and he caught many of the blows on his elbow while scoring with his jab, but Brown took the round with a big right hand before the bell. Carroll took the punch well, but Brown was encouraged by his success with the right, and he continued to throw it in the fifth. Many of these right hands sailed over Carroll's left shoulder, but Brown won the round, and after five rounds of fighting, he had a small lead.

Brown looked to build on his lead in the sixth and drove Carroll into the ropes with a hard right hand to the body early in the round and then looked to follow up on the inside. Carroll exploded, driving Brown back to the ropes with a flurry of punches which took the American by surprise and he was forced to clinch. Carroll continued with his success, landing his jab at long range and unloading with both hands on the inside. Brown never looked in trouble, but he had no answer for Carroll's speed, and at the end of the sixth his nose was bloodied, and his right eye was gushing blood. A second cut was opened over Brown's left eye in the next round as Carroll continued to spear him with the jab and out-punch him on the inside. At the end of the seventh, Brown had cuts over both eyes that were bleeding, blood from his nose and swollen lips.

After another one-sided round in the eighth, Brown showed his courage by firing his jab to open the ninth and digging in hard body shots as Carroll attempted to use his superior hand speed on the inside. The Australian champion returned to his jab and took the honours in the round, but Brown remained dangerous and continued to fire his hard right hand but was unable to hit the elusive Carroll with the blow. The tenth round started fast, and Carroll was getting the better of the exchanges on the inside until Brown landed a short right flush on Carroll's jaw, briefly stunning him. Carroll responded with a seemingly unending barrage of punches that drove Brown to the ropes where he continued to punish the American for the remainder of the round.

Sensing the finish was in sight, Carroll opened the eleventh with another barrage of blows which forced Brown to clinch. A short right hand brought more blood from Brown's nose, and his face was a mask of blood. All Brown could do was tie Carroll up and wait for referee Wallis to separate the two men, where Carroll continued his assault. A left hook and a right to the body put Brown down briefly in round twelve as the thrashing continued. Brown remained upright for the remainder of the twelfth, but Carroll continued to punish him both at long range and on the inside. At the end of round twelve, the bout was finally stopped by referee Wallis due to the damage around Willard Brown's eyes.

Both men earned close to £500 for the bout, but the victory had finally cemented Carroll among the world's elite welterweights. Brown was in awe of Carroll after the fight, and he crossed to the Australian's corner after the bout and was heard to say to the man who had just whipped him "you're a wonderful fighter."[8] Afterwards, Brown told reporters that Carroll "was a beauty" before he was taken to the Stadium doctor to have his injuries examined.[9] Carroll was unmarked after the bout and his bout with Bobby Wilson, set for two weeks later, would go ahead. With Jack Portney also on his way back to Australia and eager to face Carroll, the Australian champion would be kept busy with hard fights for the early part of 1935.

With the Americans now ranking Carroll in their world rankings, Charles Lucas was talking about bringing the world welterweight champion, Jimmy McClarnin, to Sydney to defend his title against Carroll. McLarnin was in his second reign as world champion after regaining the title from the brilliant Barney Ross in September, just months after Ross had defeated him. 'The Belfast Spider' first won the title with a first round stoppage over the Italian-born champion Raffaele Giordano, who fought under the ring name 'Young Corbett III' in May 1933 before he surrendered the title in his first defence to Ross, who had also won the world lightweight and junior welterweight championships. Both bouts between Ross and McLarnin were savage, and it was likely that the two men would fight a third time, with both New York and Chicago angling for the rubber match between the two popular fighters. Regardless, the N.B.C. cabled McLarnin an offer of £5,000 to come to Australia and face Carroll.

"Australia is pretty far away," [10] was McLarnin's reported response and his manager Charles Foster told the American press that he was yet to receive an offer for McLarnin to travel to Australia, stating that the next bout for his world champion was likely to be in New York. Meanwhile, Carroll had the hard-punching southpaw Bobby Wilson to deal with, and he returned to the gym days after stopping Willard Brown. Stylistically, the bout was viewed as a much harder test for Carroll despite Wilson's loss to Brown, as many felt that the only way to defeat the fast and clever Carroll was by knocking him out and Wilson had proved his punching power. Wilson shared this opinion in an interview with *The Daily Telegraph*:

> "I am going to take a chance with Carroll. I can take any punishment Carroll can give me., He will not hurt me. I have never been knocked out in my life therefore I will take an unlimited amount of chances to score the punch that I reckon will win the fight. I regard Carroll as a great boxer, I studied

every move he made in his fight with Willard Brown, and I am satisfied that it will take a puncher rather than a boxer to defeat him."[11]

Carroll responded the next day, saying he welcomed Wilson's tactics to take the fight to him and that he shouldn't underestimate his ability to punch:

"I invite Bobby Wilson to walk in as much as he likes next Monday night. Those tactics will suit me, and I expect to cut Wilson up a good deal. He also has to hit me before knocking me out. If he can, I shall be the first to congratulate him. Nearly every time I fight it is said that my punching does not hurt yet I have stopped the majority of my opponents in the last few years."[12]

Wilson, slightly heavier than Carroll, attacked throughout but his claims that he would take "unlimited chances" proved false. Wilson had no answer for Carroll's jab, which snapped the American's head back in every round, and he was quickly reduced to a punching bag. Carroll was always cautious of the American's power, but he rarely lost an exchange during the bout. His clean punching opened a cut over Wilson's left eye in round three and another cut over his right eye in the eighth. Carroll suffered a graze to his right cheek in the eleventh round from a head-clash, but his rapid-fire blows were taking their toll on Wilson and the bout grew more and more one-sided as it entered the final rounds. With both his eyes bleeding profusely and Carroll in total command, Wallis stopped the fight at the end of round thirteen.

With Henneberry and Palmer already ranked inside the top ten in the world, and now Carroll established as one of the world's leading welterweights, N.B.C. manager Charles Lucas saw an opportunity to break the mould of Australian boxing. Attendances were limited at Sydney Stadium, and the world champions in

America were unlikely to fight for 25% of the gate at the Rushcutters Bay stadium. Lucas resigned as manager of the National Boxing Club and began negotiations to lease the Sydney Sports Ground. He planned to stage five contests each year with only big international fights staged at the arena, which could hold at least 30,000 spectators. Lucas was to leave for America in July to try and lure the welterweight champion of the world to Australia to face Carroll.

The new N.B.C. boss was Jack Munro, a former Sydney boxing manager who promoted Les Darcy's first bout in Sydney in 1914, and he was quick to put together an upcoming schedule at Rushcutters Bay. Just days after his win over Wilson, Jack Carroll agreed to meet the American Jack Portney, who had first come to Australia to fight Carroll before injuries kept him out of the ring.

Jack Carroll and Jack Portney before their April 1935 bout
(National Library of Australia, nla.obj-148615407)

Portney arrived for his second trip to Australia on 22 March, reportedly looking in excellent shape. He had managed to squeeze in a fight during his time back in America, winning a ten round decision over Jimmy Jones. Portney told reporters that a contest with

Carroll was his reason for returning and that he was going to make the most of his chance with the Australian star.

While training at 'Slam' Sullivan's gym, Portney knocked out several sparring partners at the gym, and due to the ferocity in which he trained, Sullivan was forced to pay several boxers from other gyms to do rounds with Portney.[13] Carroll had his own trouble finding suitable sparring partners to prepare for the left-handed Portney, and many were predicting the southpaw stance to trouble the Australian champion. The bout promised another excellent attendance and Munro predicted that the attendance would be larger than in Carroll's bout with Willard Brown. Both men comfortably made the welterweight limit, but Carroll was the heavier man by more than 3lb.

As predicted, Portney's southpaw stance confused Carroll as the bout began. Portney's game plan consisted of crouching low to negate Carroll's height and reach advantage and smothering the Australian's leads but, on the occasions when Carroll anticipated his rushes, he launched lead left hands to the head and body from the southpaw stance. The plan worked brilliantly in the first two rounds as Portney landed hard left crosses that set Carroll back on his heels, and the crowd were cheering against their champion. Unsure how to lead against both the southpaw stance and his low crouching opponent Carroll looked flustered as Portney won the first two rounds. Carroll focused on his defence in the third round, blocking Portney's blows with his forearms, but was still unable to land anything significant on the southpaw.

Portney was gaining in confidence and began mixing in his right hook, but Carroll was slowly working his way into the contest and started backing Portney into the ropes, despite not throwing or landing much of significance. The fourth round saw both men holding more than punching but Carroll's ability to catch Portney's leads was bringing him back into the fight, and he began punching more on the inside. The fifth round was the first in which Carroll started to show dominance, and he was able to back Portney into the ropes and began landing short punches, bloodying the imports nose. The jab was finally evident for the Australian champion in round six and Portney began to show signs of fatigue due to the physicality of the fight, and he had lost a lot of the speed that he had a few rounds earlier.

Due to both Carroll's confusion in dealing with a southpaw opponent and Portney's fatigue, the fight became very messy and was marred with a lot of holding. From round seven onwards, Carroll took control, but he was unable to show his brilliant speed against the awkward tactics of Portney. Joe Wallis was forced to work overtime, continually breaking the fighters as Carroll was looking to do his best work in the clinches and Portney looked for respite, rather than risk fighting in the range where Carroll operated at his best. While the crowd never booed or hooted the fighters, the early cheers for Portney died down by the tenth round as Carroll began to go to work. All the fighting in the second half of the fight was by Carroll, who often switched to southpaw himself to try and land cleaner blows. By the final round, Carroll had overcome Portney's early advantage and built himself a comfortable lead. Portney threw everything at Carroll in the final round but was unable to score a knockout, and Carroll won the decision, and the crowd of 14,000 agreed.

Portney was disappointed after the bout but gave Carroll credit, stating that he didn't expect the wiry Australian to be so strong in the clinches. "That chap is as strong as a heavyweight," Portney said to reporters in his dressing room after the fight. "He's smart and hard to land on in close. You keep trying to put him where you know you can pin him with a punch but he dances away, and what is worse, he keeps punching." [14] The American also stated that he didn't expect to run into someone so brilliant in Australia and said that Carroll was talented enough to be fighting at Madison Square Garden rather than in Australia.

Carroll took a break from training after the bout, returning to Melbourne after having spent over two months in Sydney. In the three bouts he fought so far in 1935, Carroll had earned more than £1,000. Speaking to reporters after arriving back in Melbourne, Carroll talked about the difficulty Portney's style presented and his troubles getting suitable sparring for the bout:

> "Portney is decidedly awkward, for in addition to being a southpaw, he keeps away well, but when he does come in he is strong enough to force a man to the ropes or off balance. Still, I was able to have a good innings at times at close quarters. One of my difficulties was the absence of southpaws in Sydney so that I could not get any preparation along that line. This I found some trouble for a few rounds, but after that I was able to manage him better."[15]

Carroll returned to his job in the slaughterhouse after a brief holiday with his wife and daughters in country Victoria, but the success of his recent fights had made him a star in his home city. Many more passersby were paying attention to the Australian champion as he went about his day in the Victorian capital despite it being almost a year to the date since Carroll's last bout in Melbourne. Many in Melbourne were keen to see their champion in action again, especially considering his recent success over the international opponents. However, with Stadiums Ltd back in charge in Melbourne and Charles Lucas looking to bring the winner of the upcoming third bout between Jimmy McLarnin and Barney Ross to Sydney to fight Carroll, it was unlikely for Carroll's next fight to be anywhere but Sydney.

After his holiday, Carroll returned to training at Bill O'Brien's gym while waiting on Munro's choice of his next opponent. The winner of the upcoming bout between Willard Brown and Jack Portney at Sydney Stadium was likely to gain a rematch with Carroll as their prize. The contest was horribly one-sided as Portney scored three knockdowns in the opening round and reopened the cut above Brown's left eye that caused the stoppage against Carroll. Brown tried to battle back, but Portney repeatedly found openings in his defence and thoroughly thrashed Brown through the first five rounds. Joe Wallis inspected Brown's eyes before the start of the sixth but allowed the fight to continue, but after the bout continued in its one-sided manner, he stopped it early in round six.

With news out of New York that Ross had regained the welterweight title from McLarnin, it left the potential for Carroll's title shot up in the air as Charles Lucas had only spoken with the McLarnin camp thus far. With the title fight temporarily off the table, Carroll and his team looked to stay busy and with Portney's victory over Brown, he was the logical choice for the Australian champion's next fight. Worried that the dull nature of his first bout with Portney would affect the crowd and his purse in the rematch, Carroll demanded a £300 guarantee for a rematch with the southpaw. The N.B.C agreed, and Carroll arrived in Sydney two weeks ahead of the rematch and stated he was prepared to stay in Sydney provided Jack Munro could match him in bouts no more than three weeks apart. Upon arriving in Sydney, Carroll had to drop almost a stone to make the agreed weight limit of "welterweight give or take a pound," his recent financial success and break from training to blame for his increase in weight.

The rematch was a messier affair than the first fight, and Carroll's demand for a guaranteed purse ended up doubling his earnings as the bout drew only an average attendance. Portney, who weighed in slightly heavier than in the first bout, kept to his game-plan in the first fight of either smothering Carroll or firing lead lefts and then tying up the Australian and Carroll still had trouble with Portney's crouching, southpaw style. Portney again had the better of the first few rounds, landing a hard left hand in the third and Carroll showed his frustration, often switching to southpaw to try and get past Portney's lead arm. The first five rounds were dull, with a lot of holding and Portney seeming to have the edge with his cleaner blows before the bout came to life in the sixth.

Midway through a slow round, Portney drove Carroll back in a clinch after missing a barrage of punches and Carroll emerged from the exchange with cuts on his right eyebrow and cheek as the result of a head-clash. Portney opened up and took advantage of Carroll's injury and won the round with a series of left hands before the bell. Carroll's eye continued to swell between rounds, and while he fared better in the seventh, his eye was almost swollen shut by the end of the round. The American continued to hold in the eighth and ninth, and while Carroll was doing all of the scoring, his eye was closed completely at the end of nine. Referee Wallis examined Carroll's eye before the start of round ten but allowed the fight to continue. Sensing the fight may be stopped, Carroll had his best round so far, opening up on Portney and winning the round comfortably with a series of two-handed rallies.

Despite the drastic drop to make the weight limit in training, Carroll's fitness was as good as ever, and he continued to unload with both hands in the later rounds of the bout. Portney used his "third glove" many times in the next two rounds, ramming his head into Carroll in the clinches as Carroll continued to outscore him easily. At the end of twelve rounds, the fight seemed to be in the balance as Portney had taken a number of the early rounds and Carroll had come on in the last few since the injury. The final three rounds were, by far, the best of the fight. Carroll landed many more blows, but Portney landed the harder shots. A left hand from Portney in the fourteenth briefly shook Carroll, but the Australian champion, according to most accounts, won the final three rounds and did enough to earn the decision. Referee Joe Wallis, however, couldn't separate the two men and ruled the bout a draw after fifteen rounds.

The Daily Telegraph wrote that "Portney looked the winner" in the bout stating "a decided majority was in favor of Portney, who subjected Carroll to more punishment than at any other time in his career."[16] *The Sydney Morning Herald* also agreed with this, writing that "Portney established a lead in the early rounds and seemed to retain it."[17] *The Labor Daily* wrote that they thought Carroll "won comfortably" due to his superior aggression and defence.[18] *The Referee* was confused how Wallis managed to give Portney a draw due to his tactics of "rush, punch, grab and clinch, and there hold on like a limpet; or to flounder against Carroll and hold him against the ropes with his body, at the same time boring him with the crown of his head."[19] *The Sydney Sportsman* and Melbourne newspaper *The Sporting Globe* also scored the bout in favour of Carroll.

Talks of a third fight between Portney and Carroll quickly fizzled out as Carroll demanded £500 to fight the awkward southpaw a third time. Portney offered a "winner take all" basis for the third fight, but this was turned down by Bill O'Brien, who told Portney's Australian manager Sammy Hart that Portney's head-butting tactics cost him a third fight. Two weeks after the draw with Carroll, Portney fought fellow American southpaw Harry Devine, stopping him in ten rounds. Portney had planned to stay in Australia and continue to press for a third fight with Carroll until he received news from America that his wife had fallen ill. After speaking with the N.B.C., he was released from his contract and left Australia on 24 July. Portney boxed professionally for three more years, with his only losses coming to the formidable African-American fighters Cocoa Kid and Holman Williams.

After having the wounds to his eyes treated post-fight, Carroll stated that he would be ready to fight again in two weeks, and the following Monday after the Portney-Devine clash, Carroll headlined at Sydney Stadium against another American, Tommy Jones. Tommy Jones was one of the newest importations by the N.B.C. and although he did not have the reputation of Ramey, Brown or Portney, the 18-year-old American impressed reporters during his initial workouts after arriving in Sydney. Jones, born in Worcester, Massachusetts, learned to box in the army, with Australian media reporting that he "won an army championship at age 16" before turning professional. While records since put Jones' record closer to 70 career bouts with 42 wins, newspapers in Australia reported that he had 46 career fights for 42 wins. The sparring sessions between Jones and another American import Tommy King, who had just drawn with Fred Henneberry over fifteen rounds, showed Jones was a tidy boxer with a solid left hook.

The Australian champion had kept his weight down and was sitting around the welterweight limit well before the day of the fight. In sparring sessions with Alf Blatch, Denny Reilly and amateur champion Fred Inskip, Carroll displayed the speed and timing that he had taken him to the top of Australian boxing. Charles Lucas, meanwhile, had finalised his agreement to lease the Sydney Sports Ground and with neither Palmer or Carroll under exclusive contract to the N.B.C., Lucas stated he was interested in both men. Under Lucas' scheme, the boxers would draw a percentage of the "gate," and after other expenses were paid for, the rest of the money would be donated to various hospitals. While he proposed to have Palmer open his season in a bout with Len Harvey for the Empire title, Lucas also stated that he was in advanced negotiations with a "world-famous welterweight" to face Carroll later in the year.

Both Carroll and Jones weighed in at the welterweight limit for their bout on 8 July. Despite Carroll's bouts with Portney being frustrating to watch, Carroll once again drew a massive crowd at Rushcutters Bay with only an epidemic of influenza in Sydney preventing a sold-out crowd. The 18-year-old Jones started fast, which was expected for a fighter of his experience level, but his early success surprised many. The first round was fought at a high pace and on somewhat even terms with Carroll landing well with his jab but Jones able to close the distance and force Carroll into many exchanges. The second round was fought almost entirely at close quarters as Carroll invited his younger opponent on the inside and was surprised at the composure Jones showed in there. Jones placed many short left hooks on Carroll's jaw and picked his punches with the patience of a veteran rather than an 18-year-old. After two rounds, Jones had a clear lead in the scoring.

Starting round three behind his jab, Carroll stepped up his work rate, and while Jones continued to impress on the inside, the Australian welterweight champion dictated where the fight was fought. Whenever Jones close the distance, Carroll unloaded briefly before spinning Jones and returning to his jab. Jones returned to his corner at the end of the third with blood from his lips and was on the end of a one-sided lacing in rounds four and five. Sensing he was overpowering the younger fighter, Carroll took the fight to Jones on the inside in round six and was easily outpunching the American until Jones timed a right cross, which landed squarely on his jaw, which first sent Carroll to the ropes before he fell on his back. Carroll was up at the count of two and boxed cautiously for the remainder of the round.

Despite the knockdown, Carroll took the fight to the American again in rounds seven and eight. Jones remained dangerous but was only able to land occasionally, and at the end of the eighth, his right eye was beginning to swell. Carroll walked into another right hand in the ninth round that briefly stunned him but otherwise controlled the pace of the round, and he continued to outbox and outpunch Jones in the tenth and eleventh as the tempo began to slow. With a huge lead on points, Carroll coasted through the final four rounds, and although he continued to target the American's swollen eye, managing to swell it "as big as a balloon" by the final bell,[20] Carroll chose to play it safe and won a clear decision after fifteen rounds.

The reason Carroll had not pushed the pace in the final rounds was that he had suffered a muscle strain in his side sometime around the ninth round. The injury turned out not to be serious, only keeping Carroll out of the gym for a week but after returning to training, Carroll injured his wrist, which would keep him out of the ring for longer. "I was getting into some good money, but it's all in the game," Carroll told Melbourne newspaper *The Herald* after he returned to Melbourne following the cancellation of a proposed rematch with Willard Brown on 29 July, which was to mark the re-opening of West Melbourne Stadium under Stadiums Ltd. Carroll shot down rumours that the wrist injury may end his career, stating that he would be ready to fight again in just a few weeks and that he intended to continue boxing "for at least another two years."[21]

At the end of July, Charles Lucas announced that the first show he would hold at the Sydney Sports Ground would see Carroll matched with the Dutch fighter Bep van Klaveren, who was the number two contender for Barney Ross' world welterweight championship. Lucas had been in negotiations with Van Klaveren's manager Jim Caffery, and an agreement was reached for the 1928 Olympic gold medallist to fight Carroll, and then up to two more bouts, with the Carroll fight taking place on the last Tuesday in November. Carroll had taken close to a month off training to fully recover from the injuries he suffered in the fight with Jones but was keen to fight before his big fight with Van Klaveren so he would be match fit. With Willard Brown returning to America, the N.B.C. matched Carroll with their newest importation Paul Schaefer on 16 September.

The Canadian born Schaeffer arrived in Australia on 22 August after fighting in the United Kingdom for the last two years. In December 1934, Schaeffer knocked out the 250 fight veteran Billy

Bird in three rounds and then in January he knocked out the British welterweight champion Pat Butler, also in three rounds. Although some members of the Australian media reported that Schaeffer had won his last 13 bouts by knockout, he had, in fact, won nine of his last ten with seven knockouts. Carroll showed good form in his workouts with Bill O'Brien in Melbourne before he travelled to Sydney to complete his training. *The Labor Daily* reported that Carroll was "in fine form and much fresher than Sydney fight fans have seen him since the Willard Brown engagement."[22]

Schaefer started the fight confidently, but it didn't take long for the fans in attendance to realise they were witnessing a mismatch. Carroll landed with everything he threw at long range, easily slipped the foreigners blows and out-manoeuvred Schaefer on the inside, landing many hard body punches in the first three rounds. In the fourth, Carroll stepped up his offence and landed a series of solid hooks and uppercuts in close. The fifth was horribly one-sided, and Schaeffer was out on his feet at the end of the round as he had no answer to Carroll's hand speed. The one-way traffic continued early into the sixth and, after Schaeffer took a barrage of unanswered blows, referee Joe Wallis stepped between the two men and stopped the bout, ruling a no contest as he felt Schaeffer wasn't trying his best. Carroll looked on in shock as Wallis immediately left the ring while Schaeffer's seconds assisted their badly beaten fighter.

The crowd booed the decision, and many stayed in the arena long after the bout was stopped, hoping to hear an explanation of what had happened. Wallis was interviewed by *The Daily Telegraph* after the bout and defended his actions because he felt Schaeffer wasn't doing his best. When the reporter asked Wallis if he thought his decision also penalised Carroll, Wallis stated that he "completely exonerates Carroll and I will report to management that he should be paid his money."[23] Carroll was paid his money a day later; however, the N.B.C. defended Wallis' ruling, citing a clause in the contract stating that the referee had the right to call no contest if he felt a contestant "is not endeavouring to win the contest."[24] Schaeffer wasn't paid for his part in the no-contest, and he returned to the United Kingdom after the bout.

The "no contest" result had serious ramifications politically in Sydney boxing. With Charles Lucas looking to promote richer fights at Sydney Sports Ground and the N.B.C. running out of fresh opponents for Carroll to face, the Schaeffer bout marked the last time Jack Carroll would fight at Sydney Stadium in his career. Two days after the no contest with Schaefer, Carroll signed a contract to meet van Klaveren at the Sydney Sports Ground. With world welterweight champion Barney Ross reportedly after a £15,000 guarantee to defend his title against Carroll in Australia, a win over the man recognised in New York as the best fighter in the world behind Ross and McLarnin would put Carroll in a much stronger position to negotiate a title shot.

JACK CARROLL VS BEP VAN KLAVEREN

Lambertus "Bep" Steenhorst was born in Rotterdam on 26 September, 1907 but took the surname of his stepfather when his mother remarried when he was eight years old. Bep attended primary school but left when he took a job as a butcher's assistant as a teenager and began boxing around this time but did not start to compete until he was 16. In 1926, van Klaveren won the Dutch flyweight title and the following year he moved up to featherweight, winning the national title there as well.

After winning the national featherweight title again in 1928, Bep qualified for the Olympics in Amsterdam. He defeated four men in as many days, including climbing off the deck to outpoint American Harry Devine in the semi-final, to win Olympic gold, making him a national hero. As of today, van Klaveren remains the only Dutchman to achieve this feat and the former butcher's boy was presented to the Dutch Queen Wilhelmina. Bep won the national featherweight title again in 1929 and turned professional shortly after, beginning as a lightweight in the paid ranks.

Despite his popularity at home, Bep often fought overseas, fighting in the United Kingdom, South Africa and Germany in his first two years as a professional. After just three years as a pro, Bep won the European lightweight championship from the ten-year veteran Harry Corbett, winning a fifteen round decision in Bristol. He defended the title twice before losing it in July 1932 in his hometown against the Italian Cleto Locatelli on points. Bep had been struggling to boil himself down to the lightweight limit by the time he fought Locatelli, and he decided to make a move to the welterweight division as well as moving to America to try and establish himself as a contender for the world title.

Making his American debut in November 1932, van Klaveren "won every round" against the Brooklyn lightweight Paolo Villa at the smaller St Nicholas Arena in New York. After two more wins at St Nicholas Arena, van Klaveren outpointed the number one welterweight contender Baby Joe Gans over eight rounds in his Madison Square Garden debut. After this win, van Klaveren entered the top ten welterweights in the world, being ranked #10 in the February 1933 edition of Ring magazine. He won two more decisions before he was matched for his first headlining show at the Polo Grounds in New York against the former world title challenger Billy Petrolle.

Petrolle had been a contender on the east coast for many years and had defeated three future world champions Jack 'Kid' Berg, Tony Canzoneri, Battling Battalino and Jimmy McLarnin. Although he was coming off back-to-back losses to Barney Ross and Tony Canzoneri, the latter for the world lightweight title in November 1932, Petrolle was still a top contender in the ultra-competitive lightweight and welterweight divisions. Bep was fighting on relatively even terms, with some reporters giving him the lead, before he suffered a cut over his right eye, forcing the bout to be stopped after four rounds. Despite the loss, Bep continued to climb the world rankings with wins in his next six contests, including a decision over Petrolle's younger brother Frankie, before he relocated to the west coast in 1934.

Now ranked #2 contender in the world for McLarnin's world title, van Klaveren fought #3 contender, Ceferino Garcia, from the Philippines, in his Los Angeles debut. Garcia had fought all over America since arriving in 1932 and had won 22 from his last 24 contests since losing to the Mexican Kid Azteca in July 1933. Garcia's wins included a tenth round knockout over Meyer Grace and a ten round decision over Baby Joe Gans. The bout was closely contested over the first eight rounds before Garcia finished the stronger, earning a narrow decision with *The Los Angeles Times* scoring the bout 6-4 in his favour.

Bep reversed the decision five weeks later, with a clear-cut ten round decision with welterweight king McLarnin in attendance for the bout:

> "Jimmy McLarnin, welterweight champion of the world, must have seen a pretty good contender for his crown last night as he sat in a third row seat at the Hollywood Legion Stadium. The gentleman in question was Bep Van Klaveren, Holland's contribution to the fistic art. McLarnin must have been quite interested as he watched Van Klaveren outpoint Ceferino Garcia before a packed house while the crowd marvelled at the speed, grace and boxing ability of the Dutchman. And if McLarnin is looking for a worthy opponent in the near future, Van Klaveren is the man. Or so he appeared last night. It was a clear cut victory for the boy from the country of dykes. There was absolutely no doubt of Van Klaveren's superiority last night. A stinging left jab and brilliant infighting made awarding the decision little trouble for George Blake. At no time was Garcia in the running with the possible exception of the last two rounds."[1]

Looking to secure his world title shot, Bep travelled to San Francisco to battle the former world champion Young Corbett III, who had surrendered his title to McLarnin in 1933 by first round knockout. Corbett, who lived in nearby Fresno and fought much of his career in San Francisco, had outpointed former world welterweight and middleweight champion Mickey Walker in his most recent bout and had won three in a row since losing the title, although he had left the welterweight division with aspirations to fight for the middleweight title. A win over a former champion would put van Klaveren in line for a title shot. Bep forced the fight throughout, dropping Corbett in the first round and winning over Corbett's fans throughout the ten round bout but Corbett was given the ten round decision, and the San Francisco crowd booed the verdict. In a rematch, fought four weeks later, Corbett was the clear winner.

The back to back losses against a man with over 130 professional fights did little harm to van Klaveren's status as one of the world's elite welterweights. After marrying Margarite Olivera, a former Hollywood actress and the daughter of a banker, Bep bounced back with a ten rounds decision over Los Angeles welterweight Carlos Salomon before being matched with the number one contender for the world championship Kid Azteca. Azteca, from Mexico City, had only lost twice in his last 27 bouts which included two wins over Ceferino Garcia in 1933, a fourth-round knockout over Meyer Grace and decision wins over Baby Joe Gans, Eddie Wolfe, Cocoa Kid and Izzy Jannazzo. The bout with the Dutchman was Azteca's first in America in close to 12 months, and the two would square off on 24 May at the Legion Stadium in Hollywood, four days before Ross and McLarnin would fight for the third time.

The 1928 Olympic champion put on a clinic in winning a one-sided ten round decision. *The Los Angeles Examiner* reported that Bep "made the Mexican look silly," continually making him miss his blows before tearing in to "drop six or seven stinging wallops" on Azteca.[2] Azteca reportedly only won one of the ten rounds against the Dutchman, and the decision was well received by the Los Angeles crowd, who were mostly there to see the popular Mexican fighter. The win put van Klaveren in line to meet Barney Ross for the world championship, but the offer to travel down under and take on a little known Australian contender for 25% of the live gate on 26 November would prove too tempting for the Dutchman.

Bep returned to Holland and was making plans to travel to Sydney after fighting for the European title when Jack Munro announced that Bep would meet Carroll at Sydney Stadium on an N.B.C. promotion rather than on Lucas' promotion at Sydney Sports Ground. Lucas made contact with van Klaveren by phone and then sent him money for his trip to secure his services, telling *The Sun* that "despite whatever announcements have been made, the public can rest assured that Bep van Klaveren will fight Jack Carroll at the Sports Ground."[3] The European title fight was off, and van Klaveren set sail for Australia, arriving in Fremantle on 12 November on the Oronsay. The bout with Carroll was scheduled for 10 December, giving van Klaveren almost a month to get himself in shape after his long voyage.

Jack Carroll, meanwhile, had been enjoying his life away from the ring since the controversial fight with Paul Schaefer. Carroll turned down offers from the N.B.C. to meet the Americans Mark Hough and Tony Rock, choosing to wait for van Klaveren to arrive before he fought again. The decision to turn down these bouts was likely due to the many changes in Carroll's life since the no contest with Schaefer. The money he had made from the bouts earlier in the year had allowed Carroll to purchase a new home in the Melbourne suburb of Moonee Ponds as well as a new car and his wife Dorothy had just given birth to their third child, Donald. The Australian champion had continued to work in the abattoir during this time, but after the birth of his son, he resumed light training for the biggest fight of his career.

Bep arrived in Sydney on 21 November after a brief stop in Melbourne, where he and Carroll met and posed for photos. Upon his arrival in Sydney Bep spoke to the media, explaining that he was unable to train on the boat due to the hot weather and that he would begin training that weekend. He also stated that he had not heard of Carroll while he was in America, but he figured the Australian must be a good boxer due to his ranking. After making arrangements to train in Coogee, Bep visited Coogee Beach in Sydney's Eastern Suburbs and was swimming in the unprotected part of the beach when people on the beach spotted a nine-foot shark swimming nearby. After hearing the shouts from the beach, Bep swam quickly to shore and watched in amazement as the shark swam by. The van Klaveren's soon left the beach after his wife was ordered off for her inappropriate swimming costume.

The sharks weren't the only thing troubling van Klaveren. After a week of training, he told reporters that he had been fighting the local mosquitoes every night until the early hours of the morning. "If Jack Carroll can sting as much as your mosquitoes, I'm in for a great time," joked Bep to reporters attending his training sessions.[4] The Dutchman was reportedly a little heavy but otherwise, his condition was described as fit as he began his training and his two-handed assaults on the heavy bag were particularly impressive. Carroll arrived in Sydney at the end of November and began his training on Oxford Street in Sydney, and the displays in the gym from both men had many calling the bout the most important and anticipated since the Tommy Burns-Jack Johnson heavyweight title clash on Boxing Day in 1908. Just days before the fight, however, van Klaveren injured his ankle forcing a brief postponement.

The new date of the bout was, coincidentally, 26 December; 27 years to the day since the Burns-Johnson heavyweight title bout. The delay only caused more anticipation for the contest, and up to 500 spectators were present to watch both men train leading up to the new date. Bep was confident and told Sydney newspapermen that he planned a "whirlwind" attack and hoped to knock Carroll out by round ten. The ankle injury did little to slow down van Klaveren, who was often seen vigorously running around Sydney's eastern beaches each morning with his stepfather riding his bicycle close behind. Although the Australian champion was upset that he would miss Christmas dinner with his family in their new home, the delay in the fight did not affect his training. Carroll's trainer Bill O'Brien was confident that Carroll would be the victor, stating his fighter was as good as he was when he twice beat Fred Henneberry.

Jack Carroll and Bep van Klaveren
posing for an advertisement in 1935
(*National Library of Australia, nla.obj-148524292*)

Carroll and van Klaveren both gave public training exhibitions at Sydney's Capitol Theatre on 23 December as their final open workouts. Regardless of van Klaveren's reputation, Carroll was the favourite in the betting with many believing it would take a knockout puncher to end Carroll's world title aspirations and with Bep having scored only nine knockouts in his career, the punters were expecting Carroll to outpoint the Olympic champion. The speed and high punch out that both boxers had shown in their training exhibitions had many anticipating a world class fight, and with an Australian lightweight title fight as the main undercard, Charles Lucas' venture promised to draw a huge crowd.

The first bit of pre-fight drama was when van Klaveren weighed more than 2lb over the agreed catch-weight of 10st-9lb, weighing 10st-11lb-2oz on the afternoon of the bout. The fight would go ahead, and Carroll collected a £50 fine from van Klaveren's purse. The last bit of drama was the unexpected rain storm that hit Sydney at 8 pm on the evening of the bout, which was held in an open-air arena. Despite the weather conditions, 25,000 eager fans braved the elements to see the Australian champion and the world's #2 contender square off in the pouring rain. Referee Harald Baker called both men to the ring, and despite being the lighter man (Carroll weighed 10st-8lb-20z), Carroll was taller and significantly larger than his opponent.

Living up to his nickname of 'The Dutch Windmill,' van Klaveren immediately tore into Carroll, who was forced back to the ropes after the first flurry. Carroll kept his cool and calmly tied Bep up before spinning back to centre ring, but van Klaveren was soon after him again. Both men displayed their hand speed with short bursts in the first round, which was fought at close quarters and on very even terms. The rain continued to pour in the second round, and van Klaveren looked unsteady and unsure on his feet, but he continued to press forward and force the fight. Carroll was more reserved and was taking his time, happy to give up the second round while he contemplated his tactics. Bep slipped as he came in early in the third round and the sudden skidding of his feet brought both men's heads together, opening a cut over van Klaveren's right eye, which enraged the Dutchman. He muscled Carroll into a neutral corner where he recklessly attacked, and while his aggression gave him the round and the early lead, his blows were ineffective.

The Australian champion was more active in round three, and rather than just tying up his opponent, he began to time Bep's rushes, landing short combinations before stifling the counters with his superior wrestling. The rain was starting to ruin van Klaveren's tactics and with Carroll establishing his left hand, 'The Dutch Windmill' lowered his output as he was unsure how to work his way to the inside. Carroll used his jab and footwork well throughout the middle rounds, dictating the range by landing hard, clean jabs from the outside and smothering van Klaveren up close. Bep would explode with both hands on occasion, but Carroll dominated the fight from rounds five through to the end of round eleven. *The Argus* reported that "the rounds needed little description" due to Carroll's dominance and that he "won so easily he amazed even his greatest admirers."[5]

With four rounds remaining, van Klaveren needed a knockout. He opened round twelve desperately, and the fury of his assault caught Carroll off guard. In the first minute of the round, it looked as though Carroll was in serious trouble as van Klaveren battered him with heavy right hands as he slid along the ropes. After Carroll worked his way out of danger, he landed a series of hard jabs that made Bep's damaged right eye swell, and he used his steadier feet to make the Dutchman miss. The rally brought the crowd to their feet, but once Carroll regained control, he never let van Klaveren back into the fight. The final three rounds were one-sided, and while van Klaveren fought more effectively than in the middle rounds in his desperation to score a knockout, Carroll was too clever and won the rounds easily and was awarded the decision of referee Baker to the cheers of the rain-drenched Sydney fans.

Speaking to reporters after the bout, van Klaveren blamed the rain, his five-month layoff and the referee for his loss and denied that Carroll was a better boxer than himself. He dismissed the Australian's power and said that if he fought with the "holding and hitting" style in America, he would be penalised repeatedly. Bep's stepfather was forced to return to Holland after the bout to look after his younger kids, but Bep stayed in the country and was keen for a rematch. Carroll dismissed Bep's claim that the rain was the cause of Bep's poor performance, stating that he also had to fight through it. "I am very sorry that he got all of it (the rain) and I had none," Carroll sarcastically told reporters after the bout before further stating that van Klaveren was probably the best man he had fought.[6]

The live gate was £4,522 and, despite the rain, Carroll took home just under £1,000 with the bout producing the third largest live gate in Australian boxing history behind the Johnson-Burns and Palmer-Stribling contests. The contest was well received by the crowd, who shielded themselves from the rain with anything they could find including old newspapers and empty potato sacks collected from nearby rubbish bins. After the fight, Charles Lucas told *The Sun* that there would have been many more in the crowd, but traffic proved to be an issue, and many were unable to get to the arena. Lucas also said it was his intention to have Barney Ross defend his title against Carroll in Sydney at Easter.

Jack Carroll was eager to see his family after the fight, and he was on the express train to Melbourne on the morning after the fight. In Melbourne, he was met by his wife and kids, a number of reporters as well as a large crowd of supporters when he arrived at Spencer Street Station. The Australian champion was quick to depart, leaving his trainer to answer questions about his future. O'Brien told reporters that they had received many offers from overseas, but they weren't going to rush into any decision and that Carroll had no intention of fighting overseas in the next six months. While Carroll was on the express train from Sydney, Stadiums Ltd chairman Dick Lean was on the express train to Sydney to negotiate the rematch, which he was looking to stage at West Melbourne Stadium. Bep, however, was not keen to travel to Melbourne for the rematch.

"If my eye is all right I want to fight him again in Sydney in about five weeks. I don't want the match in Melbourne. I like the crowds here."[7]

Carroll took a brief break from training, but stated that he was keen for the rematch, provided van Klaveren made the agreed weight limit. Lucas had no intention of allowing Dick Lean and Stadiums Ltd to host the fight at West Melbourne Stadium, which only could only hold 12,000 fans. With van Klaveren also preferring Sydney, the rematch was announced by the Sydney Sports Ground promoters, with the fight taking place on 11 February. Despite the announcement, both Dick Lean and Jack Munro were still trying to coax Carroll into fighting at either West Melbourne or Sydney Stadium. In a statement to *The Sporting Globe*, Carroll stated he would only fight for Lucas in the near future:

"As I have said before, I will not consider any proposition until I have completed my pat with Mr Lucas. I have not signed an agreement, but I promised Mr Lucas that I would fight for him so long as he would provide opponents, and I shall honour that promise by meeting van Klaveren on February 11 and even to the extent of a third meeting if necessary. Then, if there are more contests offering I shall take them; if not, I am prepared to consider offers from other promoters."[8]

Carroll also stated that it would take a world title opportunity to get him to leave Australia. Lucas had been in talks with New York and their recognised world middleweight champion Eddie Risko in regards to a tour of Australia, with Carroll and Henneberry the likely opponents. These talks quickly died off, however, when Risko demanded 33% of the gate and Carroll stated he wouldn't fight up a weight division for any less than 25%.

Bep van Klaveren's camp, meanwhile, had somewhat fallen apart.

With his father leaving shortly after the first fight, his wife had grown homesick and had convinced Bep that he should also leave. Bep asked to be released from his contract but Lucas refused, and when the van Klaveren's attempted to leave anyway, Lucas was granted a writ for breach of contract, and both Bep and his wife were detained by a sheriff's officer while on board a ship that was minutes away from departing Australia. The bail totalled £822 for both of the van Klaveren's, which meant that Bep would lose almost the entire purse that he earned from the first bout with Carroll if he left without fighting the rematch. Lucas and van Klaveren had a meeting days after Bep was released on bail where they settled all their differences with van Klaveren stating that he had misunderstood his obligations to Lucas.

The preparation for the rematch was much more to Carroll's liking as he was able to spend most of his time at home with his family and he did not leave for Sydney until just over a week before the rematch. After arriving in Sydney, Carroll learnt that New York had sent an offer of £3,000 for him to travel there and meet Risko for his middleweight title. Carroll was delighted with the offer, telling reporters that he was likely to accept it if he defeated van Klaveren again in February. His opponent was reportedly looking in even better shape than he did for the first fight and, without the seven-month layoff that Bep blamed his loss on in the first fight, 'The Dutch Windmill' was confident that he would reverse the loss this time around. Dave Smith, the former trainer of Les Darcy, visited van Klaveren in camp, with his advice to the Dutchman being to make Carroll come to him rather than pursuing the Australian champ.

In order to stop the rain affecting the match, Lucas arranged to have the ring covered by a temporary roof. A rare public weigh-in was held at the David Jones menswear store on Elizabeth Street in Sydney. Bep van Klaveren made weight coming in 2lb lighter than the first fight, weighing in at the agreed limit of 10st-9lb with

Carroll weighing in at 10st-8lb. The weather conditions looked threatening on the evening of the fight, but the rain stayed away. Commercially the bout wasn't as successful as the first meeting, but Carroll and van Klaveren still entered the ring at the Sydney Sports Ground in front of 20,000 spectators.

Bep employed Dave Smith's strategy early in the fight and sat off Carroll in the first round before attempting to counter the Australian champion's leads with body punches. While van Klaveren had success to the body in the first, Carroll's jab and long-range assaults were landing enough to at least give him an equal share in the first round and, in the second round, Carroll's jab rarely missed its mark. Employing his own body assault, Carroll landed several hard left rips to van Klaveren's midsection in the second, and his jab drew blood from his opponent's mouth in a one-sided second round. Bep abandoned his counter-punching strategy in the third and landed with his right early but couldn't keep up with the Australian's work rate and by the end of another one-sided third round, van Klaveren was visibly bleeding from inside his mouth and had a nasty cut over his right eye.

The one-sided manner of the bout continued, and while van Klaveren was able to stage one or two strong rallies in each of the next three rounds, Carroll won each round with a clear margin. The pace continued to be high, and both men were bloody by the fifth round as Carroll sported two small cuts, one over each eye, and van Klaveren's was badly cut both above and below his right eye. Carroll was in command in the seventh and eighth, cleverly blocking the Dutchman's leads he scored with hard jabs that snapped van Klaveren's head back and landed a number of clean right uppercuts to his chin whenever Bep got past his jab. The pace of the contest got to both men by the ninth round, but Carroll's hard left jab and superior defence continued to add to his lead.

Carroll got his second wind in the eleventh and inflicted further damage to van Klaveren's right eye. Bep landed a hard right hand in the round twelve, which briefly shook Carroll but the Australian was soon back in command, and van Klaveren's right eye was a bloody mess. Referee Harald Baker checked on van Klaveren's condition at the end of the thirteenth but despite the pasting that he was receiving, the Dutchman would not give in, and he continued to look for the punch to end the fight. Carroll continued boxing smartly, using his jab to damage the right eye further while tying Bep up in close and not allowing him to get any offence started. The crowd gave van Klaveren a standing ovation at the end of the fight, and even though it was a stretch to score one round in his favour, the import's ability to take the punishment dished out by the brilliant Carroll earned the respect of the crowd.

The victory for Carroll was vindication after many agreed that the rain was the cause of van Klaveren's first loss to the Australian champion. The win also firmly established Carroll as the top contender for the world welterweight title. The receipts for the bout saw Carroll, who turned 30 just days before, earn £573 for his one-sided win. The bout also raised £300 for local hospital charities. Unlike the first fight, van Klaveren had nothing but praise for Carroll after the one-sided rematch. "He is very good; very clever and awkward," van Klaveren told *The Sporting Globe*. "I have never fought anyone like him before, and there is no one in America like him."[9] The Dutchman's face was a mess after the bout, and he was advised by doctors not to fight for at least six weeks. Bep had no intention of waiting six weeks to fight again, and Lucas released him from his contract, ending his tour of Australia.

Charles Lucas put forward an offer to Fred Henneberry after the bout, guaranteeing both men £1,000 if they would fight each other for the Australian middleweight title at Sydney Sports Ground. Henneberry, however, was due to meet Ambrose Palmer for the third time in just over three weeks and the N.B.C. wasn't going to let one of their best drawcards fight on a rival promotion. Carroll told *The Labor Daily* that he was willing to travel to America, but not for the next four months and only to face Barney Ross for the world's welterweight championship. As well as his offer to Henneberry, Lucas had cabled an £8,000 offer, plus travel expenses, if Ross would come to Australia and face Carroll.

Barney Ross, born Beryl Rosofsky on 23 December 1909, has one of the most remarkable personal stories in the history of boxing. His family relocated to Chicago when Beryl was just 18 months old, where his father began operating a grocery store. His father had wanted Beryl to become a rabbi but Beryl idolised the local gangsters, and while he kept up his studies at home, he gambled and shoplifted with other youths when he was away from his father's eyes. One of his childhood friends was a boy two years younger than him named Jacob Rubenstein, who would later become known as Jack Ruby.

When he was 14, his father was killed during a robbery and his family was split apart. His mother had a nervous breakdown, and his brothers and sisters were placed in an orphanage. Beryl was determined to bring his family back together and went to work for local gangsters, including Al Capone before he began boxing as an amateur. Fighting as often as five times a week, 'Barney Ross' would sell the trophies he won as an amateur in the hopes of earning enough money to bring his family back together. He won the Chicago Golden Gloves in 1929 before he turned professional, where he won 36 from his first 40 professional fights.

After wins over Frankie and Billy Petrolle, Ross challenged world lightweight and junior lightweight champion Tony Canzoneri for both titles in Chicago, winning a razor-thin decision over ten rounds in June 1933. Canzoneri bitterly disputed the decision and a rematch was fought six months later, with Ross winning another decision that could have gone either way. The money Ross earned from winning the championship allowed him to set his mother up in an apartment that was also big enough to house his brothers and sisters. Ross vacated his lightweight title before he challenged Jimmy McLarnin in 1934 for the world welterweight championship.

In front of 60,000 fans at Madison Square Garden, Ross outboxed McLarnin to win the fifteen round decision and his third world title. The win was special for the Jewish population as McLarnin had a reputation for defeating Jewish boxers. In the rematch less than four months later, McLarnin added to this reputation, winning the title back from Ross over fifteen rounds. The third fight, held at the Polo Grounds in New York on 28 May 1935, saw Ross win the title back from McLarnin in another fifteen round decision exactly one year after he first won the title from McLarnin. In twelve months the two had fought one of the greatest trilogies in boxing history.

As one of the most popular boxers in the world, there was little incentive for Ross to travel to another country and risk his title and his reputation against a dangerous, and relatively unknown challenger in Jack Carroll. Lucas was confident he could come up with the money to entice Ross to Australia, provided he did not have to donate a large percentage of the profits to charity, which was one of the terms of the lease of the Sydney Sports Ground.

> "The fight could be organised for Easter Monday night, provided we were freed from the present high percentage allocated for charity. I could secure Ross for £8,000, and I have backers for that amount, but I could not take the risk unless the percentage to charity was changed to a donation."[10]

Carroll took a two-week break from training while he waited for Lucas to negotiate his next move. Although he stated he was open to a rematch with Henneberry, provided the middleweight title was on the line and the bout held at the Sports Ground, the Australian welterweight champion's preferred option was a championship fight with Ross.

On 6 March, Lucas told the Australian newspapers that he had completed negotiations for Barney Ross to travel to Sydney in November and meet Carroll for the welterweight championship of the world. Ross was to be paid a guarantee of £9,000 for the bout, which would take place at the Sydney Sports Ground. Carroll would earn 20% of the takings for the fight, which Lucas estimated to be around £40,000 and, with the amount of money involved, Carroll signed a promotional agreement with Lucas, forgoing the handshake agreement they had in place for the bouts with van Klaveren. Carroll was excited about the chance to prove he was the best welterweight in the world and even more excited that the contest would be held in Australia;

> "Naturally, I'm delighted to have at last secured the chance of fighting for a world's championship, and in Australia. I'm satisfied I'll do well. My two victories over Bep van Klaveren, who was third in the ranking list of the world's best welters, convinces me of that."[11]

Jack Munro disputed Lucas' claims of the agreement, however, and stated that he had been in negotiations with the Ross camp regarding the welterweight championship bout. Munro claimed during the talks that Ross and his managers Sam Pian and Art Winch had told him they had not been in negotiations with Lucas, or, in fact, even heard of Lucas. After agreeing to terms with Ross' managers for the bout, Munro travelled to Melbourne to show the cables he had received from America to Carroll. Lucas shot down these suggestions, stating that Munro and the N.B.C. made the exact same claims after the announcement of the van Klaveren fight. After another meeting with Carroll and O'Brien, in which Lucas assured Carroll that he would make the fight, Lucas set sail for America to finalise the deal and get the signature of Ross and his managers on the contract.

With Lucas' trip expected to take ten weeks, Carroll took the opportunity to have a break from the ring and spend time with his family. Speaking to *The Referee* after signing the promotional contract with Lucas, Carroll said that "until the time comes for me to get ready for the big bout, I'll go on with my job, do a bit of gardening, see the football matches and look after the family." [12] Munro attempted to persuade Carroll to fight at Sydney Stadium while Lucas was out of the country, but Carroll and O'Brien remained loyal to Lucas. Carroll said that he expected to fight before the bout with Ross, but it would be on a card promoted by Lucas, ruling out a return to Sydney Stadium.

In May, Lucas cabled Sydney with the news that he had come to an agreement with Ross and that he was returning home to begin making arrangements to stage the fight. Lucas was required to deposit all of Ross' £12,500 purse, which covered all expenses for the trip, into a Chicago bank account before Ross would set sail. After arriving back in Australia in June, Lucas announced the fight would take place at the Sydney Sports Ground on 8 December. Barney Ross was due to arrive on 31 October, and Lucas began selling tickets for the bout, with the stadium expected to hold 66,000 spectators. Should Carroll dethrone Ross in Australia, he was contracted to fight a rematch with Ross in America. Carroll began training for the bout and announced the first of his two warm-up bouts for the fight with Ross would be against Herb Bishop at the Princess Theatre in Melbourne.

Bishop, the former Australian lightweight champion, was no match for Carroll. Carroll made the welterweight limit for 19 September bout but was still over 3lb heavier than Bishop at the afternoon weigh-in, and it was evident that he had struggled to make the limit. In his first fight in Melbourne since his 1934 win over Billy

Townsend, Carroll beat Bishop in a one-sided contest. The welterweight champion easily outboxed Bishop in the early rounds, completely nullifying Bishop's punches with his footwork and "uncanny anticipation."[13] When Carroll switched his attack to the smaller man's body in the second half of the bout, Bishop began to crumble under the attacks. At the end of round twelve, Bishop surrendered due to a rib fracture caused by Carroll's body assaults.

With Lucas needing to raise the money for Ross' guarantee before he sailed for Australia, tickets for the Ross-Carroll world title fight went on sale in August. There were some early bookings for the bout, but with Ross not in the country and the fight still months away, ticket sales stalled by September. While the world title fight was one of the most talked about upcoming sporting events in Australia, many Australians still suffering the effects of the Great Depression were unable to part with the money for tickets for a match that was still months away. Many ticket sales for the large stadium clashes had been purchased at the door on the evening of the contest, and Lucas had overestimated how many tickets would be booked in advance.

In September, Lucas cabled Pian to advise him he would not be able to raise all of the money required by the deadline. Pian gave Lucas more time but stipulated that he would have to pay a forfeit on top of Ross' purse. Lucas went around to his financial backers with hat in hand but was unable to raise the required money to pay Ross his guarantee before the bout and, after again speaking with Pian, the 8 December date was cancelled. Lucas attempted to come to an agreement for the bout to take place in 1937, but when Ross announced he would fight the number five ranked contender Izzy Jannazzo, Carroll agreed to box in Brisbane.

Although disappointed at not being able to fight for the world title, Carroll was eager to return to the ring and agreed to fight Queensland welterweight Jerry Leonard in Brisbane. Leonard subsequently lost to another Queenslander Sid Powell as Carroll was making his way to Brisbane, and Powell instead got the bout with Carroll. The fight drew a sell-out crowd in Brisbane, with many wanting the chance to see the world ranked Carroll in action. Powell wasn't in Carroll's class, and despite his gameness in taking the fight to the welterweight champion, he was forced to retire after six one-sided rounds due to the effects of Carroll's body blows. Carroll injured his hand during the contest, and the injury would leave him out of the ring until the new year.

During his American trip earlier in the year, Lucas had been able to make a number of contacts with American managers, allowing him to cable offers to other contenders without having to leave Australia. One of those offers was accepted, and Lucas announced that Jimmy Leto, world number ten welterweight, was on his way to face Carroll in the new year. Lucas also announced that he was in negotiations with another ranked contender, with many suspecting it to be the Filipino Ceferino Garcia, to come to Australia after the Leto bout. After his wins over van Klaveren, Carroll was officially recognised as the #1 contender to the world welterweight crown, moving ahead of former champion Jimmy McLarnin, who had retired after defeating world lightweight champion Lou Ambers.

Ross successfully defended his world title against Jannazzo on 27 November, scoring multiple knockdowns on his way to a unanimous decision. Lucas had remained in negotiation with Ross' manager, Sam Pian, in the hopes of making the championship bout in Easter of 1937 and hoped that a Carroll win over Leto would place more pressure on Ross to meet Carroll. Fred Henneberry and Ron Richards were also due to meet for the seventh time, this time with the Australian middleweight title on the line. If Lucas was unable to bring Ross to Australia, a fight between Carroll and the winner of the Henneberry-Richards clash had the potential to earn Carroll the largest payday of his career.

FRED HENNEBERRY VS RON RICHARDS VII

Ron Richards had a break out year in 1935. After opening the year with a pair of knockouts over Alby Roberts and Max Gornik at Brisbane Stadium in early February, Richards rematched Son Tealey at Leichhardt Stadium on 20 February. Giving away three stone in weight to the much larger Tealey, Richards boxed cautiously in the opening four rounds before he began to attack the larger man's body. After scoring knockdowns in rounds five and seven with a left hook to the body, Richards put Tealey down for the count with another left downstairs early in the eighth, proving his first knockout over the larger man was no fluke.

This win qualified Richards to face Ambrose Palmer for the third time. Palmer, who had drawn with Tealey in November before scoring a seventh round stoppage over him one month later, had regularly been fighting at Leichhardt after a dispute with the N.B.C. following his poor showings against Marty Sampson and Tiger Williams. While many regarded Palmer as the Australian heavyweight and light heavyweight champion, the bout with Richards was fought over two-minute rounds with no title on the line. Despite being a non-title fight, and the shorter duration of the contest, the bout drew more than £500.

Palmer had the better of the early rounds, making Richards miss wildly and using his superior in-fighting ability to punish Richards on the inside. Richards, weighing a stone lighter than the heavyweight champion, kept Palmer on the outside in rounds five and six and won the rounds easily. His right counter landed a number of times heavily, once in the fifth staggering Palmer briefly, and when he followed it with a left uppercut, it landed with surprising accuracy. With Richards getting the better of the long-range action, Palmer bulled his way inside in round seven behind a tight guard, and while Richards landed with his jab, any success he had from the outside was offset by Palmer's body punching and uppercuts in close.

Richards landed his best punch of the fight early in the eighth, stunning the heavyweight champion with a long right hand to the chin. Palmer continued to press Richards in the ninth and tenth and seemed to have control of the bout, but the Queenslander showed improved conditioning with a late rally. After opening the eleventh with "a surprising burst of two-handed punching,"[1] Richards continued the aggression for the duration of the round, and when he similarly opened the twelfth, the crowd were on their feet sensing a possible upset. Richards also took the thirteenth with his aggression but Palmer regained control in the final two rounds, and it was enough to earn him a slim margin on referee Jack Haines' scorecard and a third win over Richards.

The reception of the crowd to the decision was mixed, with many thinking that Richards had done enough to take the win. Sydney newspaper *The Referee* also thought that Richards won by a slim margin, but *The Sydney Morning Herald* and Brisbane's *The Telegraph* thought that Palmer's inside work and his ability to make Richards miss was the difference in the fight. Regardless of the decision, the fight showed a marked improvement in Richards' ability in just two years since his last loss to Palmer. The improved fitness and ability to mix in other punches off his long right hand were considerable additions to the game of the 24-year-old and with his popularity thanks to the bouts with Henneberry, Palmer and Carroll, Richards was about to prove himself one of the best boxers in the country.

Over the next five months, Richards fought nine times between Brisbane and Sydney, winning eight contests, five by knockout, and drawing one. The majority of these victories were against larger men and among them were several touring American fighters including Pietro Georgi and Roy De Gans. Richards' good form earned him his first Sydney Stadium date since his loss to Jack Carroll. His opponent would be Tommy King, a middleweight from America who had fought twice in Australia, both matches against Fred Henneberry. King had proved himself as a solid prospect in America before coming to Australia, earning a draw with Ceferino Garcia in 1932 and splitting a pair of fights with Babe Marino.

Before the bout with King, Henneberry had started 1935 quietly, outpointing Jimmie Mitchell and Bob Thornton. Henneberry's next fight, a fifth-round stoppage of Al Schaff, marked his first fight back at Sydney Stadium since his dispute with the N.B.C. Before agreeing to the bouts with Tommy King, Henneberry was making arrangements to tour England for a series of fights, but the N.B.C. convinced him that there were plenty of matches for him in Australia and he agreed to face King after Schaff. After arriving from America just ten days before the bout, King set up his camp at Sammy Hart's gym and his training exhibitions were a hit among Sydney fight fans, who flocked to see him work out in preparation for 24 June debut against Henneberry at Sydney Stadium.

At the 2 pm weigh-in for the bout, King weighed in a pound over the middleweight limit, and Henneberry insisted that the American either pay a forfeit of £50 or re-weigh-in at 8 pm at the same weight he currently was. King happily paid the forfeit if it meant the fight would go on and was overheard telling N.B.C. management that he was "anxious to fight."[2] With a £700 paid attendance at Sydney Stadium, the forfeit was a nice bonus for Henneberry, but with King, he would earn every bit of the purse as the bout was one of the best seen in Sydney for years.

Henneberry took the fight to King, thoroughly outpunching the import in the opening two rounds, hurting him with body blows and bloodying his nose and lips. King seemed to have warmed up by the start of the third, and while Henneberry still outpointed him, King landed counter right uppercuts to the head and body and continued to have success with this punch in the fourth round. King continued to look for the shot and landed it, but not often enough to offset Henneberry's aggression and the Australian outworked King through many of the middle rounds. In the ninth it looked like Henneberry's pace could earn him a knockout as King looked out on his feet as he returned to his corner. King opened round ten with a fast rally which caught Henneberry off guard, cutting the bridge of Henneberry's nose with a right hand.

The American continued his rally in the eleventh and outfought Henneberry for half of the round before he tired, and Henneberry punished him until the bell. Both men were exhausted in round twelve and often sort respite in the clinches and this continued early in the thirteenth until a short right hand opened a cut on Henneberry's left eyelid. King was spurred on by his opponents wound and unloaded on Henneberry, who was handicapped by the blood pouring directly into his eye. The crowd were on their feet in the fourteenth as it looked like King could score a knockout, but Henneberry used all of his ringcraft to see out the round. Henneberry was out on his feet for much of the fifteenth round and was briefly on the canvas but managed to see the final bell. Referee

Joe Wallis, who after the bout said it was one of the best he had ever refereed, ruled the contest a draw.

After the thrills of the first fight, a rematch was scheduled for 29 July, giving Henneberry's eye time to heal. With a potential big-money showdown with Ambrose Palmer on the line, if he won, Henneberry trained hard for the rematch, running in Centennial Park during the early hours of the morning and often sparring more than ten rounds each day in the gym. His hard workouts were in evidence when he weighed more than 2lb lighter than he weighed in the first fight. King comfortably made the middleweight limit for the rematch, entitling him to his full purse. Sydney Stadium was packed for the return contest, and while rematches of great fights are often slower than the first encounter, the rematch between Fred Henneberry and Tommy King would eclipse their first bout.

Henneberry worked well behind his jab in the opening round, using it to close the distance so he could work on the inside. King was once again more than happy to fight Henneberry in the trenches, and while the Australian middleweight champion won the opening round, King worked Henneberry's body well. Early in the second round, the two boxers clashed heads and although neither man suffered a cut, King lost his temper, and he drove Henneberry back with a series of right hands. Henneberry took advantage of the American's aggression and used his jab, bloodying King's nose in the second and outpointing him with his straight left in the third. King found his range in the fourth and worked well early in the round until another clash of heads opened a massive cut on his forehead. The wound bled profusely, and both men were covered in King's blood by the end of the round, but the exchanges that followed the head-clash were savage. The two men stood in the centre and traded punches "faster than the eye could follow"[3] before King finally gave ground towards the end of the round.

King continued to force matters in the fifth, but Henneberry boxed cleverly and used the American's aggression against him, picking him off with the jab as well as landing some solid right hands as King closed the distance. King attempted to disrupt Henneberry's composure by hitting the Australian champion in the back of the head, but Henneberry continued to pick his shots and build a lead on points. With the rough tactics not working, King returned to his jab in round seven and had his best round of the fight, out-jabbing Henneberry and getting the better of the inside work. He had further success in the eighth, landing hard left hooks to Henneberry's jaw on the inside. Henneberry attempted to re-establish control of the fight with a rally, but King outpunched him in a furious exchange to finish round eight.

Confident after his success in the last three rounds, King opened up more in the ninth round, and while Henneberry landed some solid shots of his own, King had clawed back Henneberry's early lead. Sensing Henneberry was tiring, King attacked to start the tenth but Henneberry was still fresh, and he landed his best punch of the fight early in the round, snapping King's head back with a beautiful right cross to the point of the chin. King took the blow and continued marching forward, driving Henneberry back to the ropes with a barrage of punches, winning the round with his aggression. King's punches were harder in the eleventh, and although Henneberry met King on the inside, King forced him to give ground.

The fierce exchanges continued in the next round but the hard work Henneberry put into his training was showing, and King began to show signs of fatigue towards the end of the round. The fight was in the balance in the final three rounds, but the Australian started to take charge in the thirteenth, and while King continued to fight ferociously, Henneberry was able to pick him apart on the inside. Despite his fatigue and the blood loss from his head, King threw everything at Henneberry in the final two rounds but the

Australian champion would not be denied, and his accuracy and cleaner work entitled him to the last two rounds and the referee's decision.

While many in Australia were hoping to see the third clash between Henneberry and Palmer after the bout, Palmer refused to come down to a catch-weight, and the fight could not be made. Tommy King, who stated he felt drained after making the middleweight limit and fought better at 11st-11lb, was groomed as a potential opponent for the Australian light heavyweight champion based off the popularity of his two wars with Henneberry. With Palmer scheduled to fight Deacon Leo Kelly, the latest American to arrive in Australia, in a few weeks, King was scheduled against Ron Richards. With Richards recent strong showing against Palmer, the bout was a good measure for how King would perform against Palmer.

King was a firm favourite leading into the fight, but it would be Ron Richards' break-out performance. King started well and had a slight edge in the early rounds but Richards bloodied his nose in the first, and by the fifth round, the American's left eye was swelling from the harder punches landed by the Queenslander. With his vision impaired, King attempted to take the fight to the inside but this played right into Richards' hands. Using his renowned counter-punching skills, Richards punished the American for the remainder of the contest, swelling his left eye closed before cutting it in the final rounds. King was game, but Richards' improved punch variation and fitness never allowed him back into the fight, and he took an easy decision at the end of fifteen one-sided rounds.

With Richards handling a man who had twice extended the Australian champion, many were calling for a seventh fight between Henneberry and Richards with the Australian title at stake. Leichhardt offered Henneberry a £200 guarantee if he would fight Richards at their stadium, but Henneberry was more interested in facing Palmer. With Richards now established as a drawcard and with many international opponents in Sydney, the N.B.C. didn't want to risk killing off either Henneberry or Richards as a drawcard and made attempts to have Palmer return to Sydney Stadium to face Henneberry. Palmer, however, had accepted an offer to fight in England for a guarantee of £1,000 and a possible shot at the Empire light heavyweight title, so the N.B.C. matched Henneberry with the recently arrived Englishman Moe Moss. Richards' next fight would also not be for the N.B.C, as he had agreed to return to Leichhardt to face Deacon Leo Kelly, who had impressed Australian fans with his punching power.

Ambrose Palmer (left) and 'Deacon' Leo Kelly
(National Library of Australia, nla.obj-148563609)

Deacon Leo Kelly arrived at the end of July at the expense of Leichhardt Stadium, who were after quality opponents for Ambrose Palmer. The 23-year-old Kelly was reported to have scored 27 knockout wins in 42 professional fights and was twice outpointed by the former world champion Maxie Rosenbloom in 1934, but had scored a fourth-round knockout over Pietro Georgi before his arrival in Australia. Kelly would recite the following Psalm of David before stepping into the ring:

"Blessed be the Lord, my strength which leadeth my hand to war and my fingers to fight."[4]

Kelly's Australian debut was against Palmer on 14 August and, despite losing the contest, the bout made him an instant fan favourite in Australia. At the end of the fight, which Palmer won on points, Palmer was spitting blood from cuts inside his mouth and to his lip, had blood flowing from a wound to his cheek and had torn rib cartilage from the power of Kelly's body assault. Palmer's superior jab and defence gave him the edge over the 15x2 minute round contest, but many felt that, with the injuries Palmer sustained, had they fought over three-minute rounds, Palmer would have succumbed to Kelly's power. The bout drew a packed house at Leichhardt Stadium, and Kelly was booked to return against Art Campbell two weeks later. Kelly was keen to fight, however, and travelled to Brisbane for a return with Georgi, which he won again in the fourth round, before returning to Leichhardt, where he knocked out Campbell in six rounds the following week.

The bout between Ron Richards and Leo Kelly fell two days after Henneberry's clash with Moe Moss. With Ambrose Palmer about to leave for the United Kingdom, there were again talks of a seventh clash between Henneberry and Richards for the vacant Australian heavyweight title. Moss had started well against Henneberry and had a slight lead on points before Henneberry dropped him for an eight count with a right hand to the solar plexus in the fifth round. Moss was still weak when he rose, and Henneberry finished him off with a barrage of body punches and a left hook to the head. Despite the quick win, Henneberry was criticised for an unenthusiastic performance. The bout between Leo Kelly and Ron Richards stole the boxing headlines in Sydney that week.

Despite giving away close to a stone in weight to the hard-punching Kelly, Richards' counter punching abilities gave him the edge early in the contest in front of a packed Leichhardt Stadium. The Queenslander showed patience, waiting for Kelly to lead before making him miss and landing a wide variety of punches. Kelly continued to press the smaller man, but throughout the first six rounds, Richards had a clear lead on points. Kelly began his comeback in the seventh, landing heavy uppercuts on Richards, who was being worn down by Kelly's constant aggression. Kelly also took the eighth, staggering Richards with an uppercut early and having more success from the outside due to Richards' fatigue. With seconds remaining in the eighth, however, Richards hurt Kelly with a right hand but the bell sounded before he could follow up.

Using his jab more in the ninth round, which temporarily slowed Kelly's momentum and bloodied his lip, Richards was patient and didn't risk exchanging with the larger man. Kelly was back on top soon after, continuing to walk Richards down in the tenth, driving him back to the ropes with two-handed barrages every time Richards looked to exchange punches. Richards used every defensive trick he knew to survive the eleventh round, and Kelly's seemingly endless gas tank seemed to be emptying as the pace slowed in round twelve finally. The Queenslander's jab gave him the twelfth and the first half of the thirteenth, but Kelly bore his way in, and the boxers exchanged vicious combinations until the bell.

Kelly carried the fight in the fourteenth, punishing Richards with heavy blows along the ropes. With one round remaining, Richards likely had a lead on points, but he was severely tired heading into the final round. The fifteenth started as the fourteenth had ended, with Kelly punishing Richards and when a right cross midway through the round dropped Richards to his knees, it looked like Kelly might have pulled the victory out. Richards rose almost immediately and met Kelly in another savage exchange, punching wildly with the American until the final bell. When referee Jack

Haines crowned Richards, the winner, the crowd erupted into cheers.

Regardless of the Queenslander's new popularity, Henneberry wasn't interested in meeting Richards for the seventh time. With little to gain from beating him again, the Australian middleweight champion turned down offers for the seventh fight, including a £200 guarantee from Brisbane Stadium, and accepted fights with Americans Salvatore Affinito and Vincent Sireci instead to close out 1935. Henneberry stopped both men, Affinito in the final seconds of the 15th round and Sireci in the eleventh, both at Sydney Stadium and both in one-sided fashion. With Charles Lucas' Sydney Sports Ground venture about to begin, N.B.C. boss Jack Munro was after a big domestic fight to rival the open air shows, and he offered an £800 guarantee to Ambrose Palmer to meet Henneberry at Sydney Stadium.

Palmers tour of the United Kingdom had proved disappointing. After arriving, Hugh McIntosh, now living in London, proposed a match with former world light heavyweight champion Tommy Loughran, who now competed as a heavyweight. Palmer, however, wasn't interested in facing another man with over 100 fights who outweighed him by more than a stone. Palmer's first, and only, fight in London was against Canadian Eddie Wenstob at Wembley Arena, and although he won on points and impressed the London fans with his speed and cleverness, he suffered a cut to his left eye and re-injured his thumb, which he jarred in training for the bout. Palmer was struggling in London with homesickness, and after his wife cabled him advising that their daughter had become ill, Palmer abruptly ended his trip before his Empire title fight, arriving back in Australia before Christmas.

Despite making arrangements to return to London with his family, the offer from Munro would be too much money for Palmer to turn down and he agreed to return to Sydney Stadium for a bout with

Henneberry. The fight was initially scheduled for 10 February, just four days after the Carroll-van Klaveren rematch, but when Henneberry's father passed away on 5 February, and then Palmer's mother passed away on 10 February, the bout was rescheduled for 2 March. Despite the repeated postponements, tickets were in high demand and Sydney Stadium announced that all ticket reservations would have to be confirmed before the day of the fight due to the popularity of the contest.

Potentially there was a world title opportunity on the line for both men in their respective weight classes. After Carroll turned down the bout, Henneberry's camp was in talks with promoters in New York to face the middleweight champion 'Babe' Risko, (although Henneberry would only receive the title shot if he signed his contract over to the New York managers if he won). Charles Lucas was also working on bringing new world light heavyweight champion John Henry Lewis to Australia to face Palmer later in 1936. Both men made their respective weight limits, Henneberry comfortably under the middleweight limit at 11st5lb while Palmer had almost a stone weight advantage, weighing 12st-6lb at 2 pm on the day of the fight. The bout was witnessed by 15,000 fans, with another 5,000 outside the stadium unable to get tickets.

Henneberry rushed Palmer in the opening round, but Palmer was happy to meet him at close quarters, where he landed short left hooks to the head and body of the smaller man in the clinches. Palmer was happy to let Henneberry do the leading, and he parried the middleweight champion's blows, scoring with hard counters in a one-sided opening round. Round two saw Henneberry again charging, but he had much more success than in the first. Landing well with his jab and briefly rocking Palmer with a left hook, which bloodied the larger man's mouth. Palmer responded with well-timed body blows and landed his jab effectively, but Henneberry's aggression seemed to give him the edge early.

Continuing to take the fight to the bigger man, Henneberry rushed out again in the third and Palmer continued to pick his shots. Henneberry was throwing more punches, but Palmer was landing the cleaner shots. A body shot that landed low had many thinking the bout was going to end in the same disappointing manner that the second fight had, but Henneberry signalled that he was okay and continued to force the action. Early in round four, Palmer landed a hard left that opened up a massive cut under Henneberry's right eye. Palmer pressed the advantage and rocked Henneberry with a right hand. Henneberry grew desperate and head-butted Palmer repeatedly in the clinches, but Palmer was spurred on by the sight of blood and began to land hard punches from range as well as his shot body shots on the inside.

Henneberry's brother Bill did his best work on the cut between rounds, but Fred was covered in his own blood early in the fifth round. He continued to attack, but Palmer coolly side-stepped his rushes and unloaded with lightning quick combinations. The crowd hooted Henneberry when he again used his head late in the round. At the start of the sixth round, Palmer attacked, and Henneberry could do little to defend himself. The middleweight champion attempted a rally, landing some solid punches, but Palmer quickly reasserted his dominance, snapping Henneberry's head back with his jab and unloading with both hands on the inside. At the end of the sixth round, referee Joe Wallis and the stadium doctor convinced Bill Henneberry to stop the bout.

The receipts for the bout were just under £5,000, earning each man a career-high purse of £1,200. Henneberry dismissed Palmer's victory over him and claimed that it was a head-clash, rather than a Palmer left, that opened the cut that stopped the bout. Writing for *The Labor Daily* after the fight, Fred wrote that "it was Palmer's head in the fourth round that did the real damage," and that he was after a rematch with Palmer for the heavyweight title.[5] The injuries he suffered in the bout would keep Henneberry out of training until

April, and by that time a fight with Palmer was off the table as Palmer had announced his retirement.

The Australian light heavyweight and heavyweight champion had returned just two weeks after his win over Henneberry, stopping Johnny Miler in eight rounds in front of 10,000 fans at Sydney Stadium. Three weeks later, Palmer fought Deacon Leo Kelly in a rematch from their August thriller. Kelly had signed with the N.B.C. after his loss to Richards and won eight straight fights by way of knockout. A win for Palmer was likely to lead to a match with former world light heavyweight champion Maxie Rosenbloom, who was due in Australia at the end of April. Expecting another sell-out, the N.B.C. almost doubled ticket prices to maximise their profits. When Palmer and Kelly were introduced to the crowd at Rushcutters Bay at the fights a week before, the crowd booed the two men as a protest to the increased admission.

The second fight was similar to the first, with Palmer using his speed to outpoint Kelly early while Kelly continued to come forward and land the harder blows. Palmer was in complete control of the bout until round seven when he came out of a clinch with blood flowing from a cut above his right eye after a head clash. Kelly was spurred on by Palmer's blood and attacked ferociously, rocking Palmer numerous times in rounds eight and nine, and opening a second cut above his left eye. A right hand in the tenth round put Palmer on the canvas, but he beat the count and fought back valiantly in the eleventh. Referee Joe Wallis tried to stop the bout after the eleventh round, but Palmer wanted to continue. After just a few seconds of the twelfth round, Palmer's manager Jack Warner threw in the towel, giving Leo Kelly a twelfth round technical knockout.

Despite the initial reports of the injuries to his eye not being serious, after a couple of weeks, Palmer announced his retirement from the ring. Palmer spoke to doctors, who said that the frequent cuts to his eyes could damage his eyesight later in life and with a young family and financial stability, Palmer took their advice and hung up the gloves. It was a massive blow for the N.B.C. with Maxie Rosenbloom arriving just days after Palmer's retirement. Despite his claims that he "shall never attempt to make a return to boxing, "[6] the bout with Leo Kelly wouldn't be the last in Palmer's boxing career.

With Palmer's retirement, there was an opportunity for both Ron Richard and Fred Henneberry to establish themselves as the N.B.C's leading drawcard. Richards had signed a four-fight contract in November, guaranteeing him £825. The first of those matches came against the New York boxer Mark Hough, who had won the New York Golden Gloves tournament in 1932 and 1934. Despite just two years of professional experience, Hough shocked Richards with his boxing ability and was able to avoid Richards right hand while fighting evenly with the former Australian champion both at long-range and on the inside. Hough was more aggressive, but Richards had success with his left hook to the head and seemed to land the harder blows. Referee Joe Wallis ruled Hough the winner after fifteen rounds, favouring the American's aggression over Richards' harder punching.

Richards wanted an immediate rematch, but Hough turned it down as he was offered a fight with Deacon Leo Kelly two weeks later. Kelly had knocked Tommy King out in nine rounds in his Sydney Stadium debut on 28 October and was proving to be one of the best importations by the N.B.C. The Kelly-Hough bout drew 7,000 spectators at Rushcutters Bay, a huge number for two American boxers, and they witnessed an early slugfest. Both men were hurt in an exciting first round before Hough sent Kelly to the canvas at the bell. Kelly was up at the count of three and took the fight to Hough in the second and third rounds before dropping Hough in the fourth with a right hand. Hough boxed more cautiously after tasting the canvas and Kelly's aggression had worn him down by the eighth. Kelly battered Hough for the next four rounds before a pair of knockdowns forced the stoppage in the eleventh.

Hough and Richards fought again on 2 December, just two weeks after Hough's knockout loss to Kelly. The effects of the Kelly bout had taken their toll on the New Yorker and, after giving a good account of himself in the first half of the contest, Hough slowed down, and Richards was able to pick him apart. Hough won the appreciation of the Sydney fans when he fought the last six rounds of the bout with a badly broken nose, courtesy of a Richards left-hook in the ninth. Richards won referee Joe Wallis' decision, giving him his 14th win of 1935 against two losses and a draw. It was Richards' last bout of the year, and he capped off a memorable year by getting married on 15 December. Richards and his new wife, Dorothy, were married in Brisbane with Richards' brother Max acting as the best man at the service.

After taking some time off to enjoy married life, Richards first bout in 1936 wasn't until 10 February, when he faced Tommy Jones, who had only lost once in eight fights since the defeat to Carroll in July. The smaller Jones, who weighed in half a stone lighter than Richards, retreated throughout the contest and looked to counter-punch the counter-punching Richards. The tactic resulted in a slow fight but Jones had the better of the little action in the early rounds, and his blows caused Richards' left eye to swell. In the sixth round, referee Joe Wallis warned both men for not trying their best and Richards took the fight to Jones for the remainder of the bout. Richards seemed to have the better of the contest, and when he battered Jones in the final three rounds, the decision seemed to be his, but Wallis disagreed with the crowd and crowned Jones the winner.

It was a blow for Richards, who was looking for a win to put pressure on Henneberry and force him to defend his middleweight title. Despite both men coming off a loss, the N.B.C. matched

Henneberry and Richards for the Australia title on Easter Monday. Richards took up residency in Sydney to concentrate on his training and stated that he planned to defeat Henneberry for the middleweight title and then win Palmer's heavyweight title before he returned to Brisbane. The bout was postponed until May when Henneberry's cut that he suffered in the Palmer fight re-opened in training and Richards was matched with the American middleweight Marty Simmons on 20 February.

The short and stocky Simmons, who regularly fought as a middleweight in America, came in over the middleweight limit, outweighing Richards by 4lb, almost causing the bout to be cancelled, but Richards elected to fight regardless of the weight difference. Simmons, who was quicker than his height and body-type suggested, was able to beat Richards to the punch and tie him up before the Queenslander could counter. The bout was slow and messy, and Richards' performance was lacklustre. After fifteen rounds, Simmons took the decision, giving Richards his second loss in a row. The N.B.C. still re-scheduled his shot at Henneberry's middleweight title, this time for 11 May but Henneberry's bad luck continued, and the bout was cancelled after he fractured his thumb in training. With Henneberry out injured and Palmer now retired, Richards returned to Brisbane to spend more time with his new wife.

With Richards back in Queensland and Maxie Rosenbloom in Australia, Brisbane Stadium management saw the opportunity for a huge gate by matching the pair. Rosenbloom had agreed to make his Australian debut in Sydney on 18 May against Deacon Leo Kelly, but Jack Munro had permitted him to travel to Brisbane for a contest in between his Sydney fights. The proposed match between Rosenbloom and Richards was abandoned, however, when Kelly was cut during training, which delayed his fight with Rosenbloom. Jack Munro wanted the former world's light heavyweight champion to debut in Sydney rather than Brisbane or Melbourne, so

Rosenbloom's Brisbane bout was put on hold until he had fought in Sydney. Brisbane Stadium did secure Richards' services for a number of matches, and the N.B.C. were willing to lend their other importations.

Brisbane Stadium's first match for Richards was with Filipino born heavyweight 'Young' Aguinaldo, who was no match for the Queenslander. Aguinaldo rushed Richards throughout the contest but was knocked down seven times in the second round before being counted out early in the third. Aguinaldo attempted to continue fighting after referee Pat Hill stopped the bout, sparking a wild brawl between boxers and seconds after the bout. With better opposition needed to test the improved Richards, his next fight would be a third with Mark Hough on 4 July. Hough had only managed one win from three matches since his two bouts with Richards, with both of his losses coming against Marty Simmons.

Hough was no match for Richards after the first round, in which he momentarily stung Richards with an overhand right. Richards kept the fight at a distance, bloodying Hough's mouth in the second round and punishing him with right hands to the body at range and uppercuts in close. Hough rallied in round seven, and a right hand caused swelling around Richards left eye, but Richards was soon back on top, hurting Hough with a right to the body in the eighth before scoring two knockdowns in the ninth. Richards was wild after the knockdowns and unable to finish the American off until the thirteenth when, after two more knockdowns, referee Pat Hill waved off the contest.

After Maxie Rosenbloom easily accounted for Deacon Leo Kelly with an easy points decision, Brisbane Stadium manager Jack Hoult announced that Rosenbloom would meet Richards at Brisbane Stadium on the Wednesday of Exhibition Week. Rosenbloom, however, withdrew from the bout after telling Hoult that he would not fight Richards unless Joe Wallis was the referee. Rosenbloom would fight once more in Australia, travelling to Melbourne where he again met Leo Kelly. Joe Wallis also travelled to Melbourne to act as referee, and his presence robbed Rosenbloom of a win. His choice of referee repeatedly penalised 'Slapsie Maxie' for not hitting with a closed fist, and after fifteen "dreary" rounds, Wallis ruled the bout a draw.[7] Rosenbloom returned to the United States after attempts to bring Ambrose Palmer out of retirement failed.

After the Rosenbloom bout fell through, Richards' next bout was against Sydney's Les Brander on 1 August at Brisbane Stadium. Brander had worked his way up through preliminary bouts in Newcastle and Leichhardt Stadium and surprised many with his game showing against Richards. He frequently made Richards miss through the first eight rounds before Richards' experience in the later rounds gave him the edge and, after being hurt numerous times, the referee saved Brander from further punishment in the twelfth. With Palmer's heavyweight title vacant, Brisbane Stadium announced that the Exhibition Week main attraction would be between Ron Richards and Art Campbell for the Australian heavyweight title.

The bout was a rematch of their March 1935, Brisbane Stadium slug-fest, where Richards had stopped the Newcastle based southpaw in twelve. Campbell's corner had stopped the bout after Richards dropped him in the final seconds of round twelve with a huge right uppercut. Before the knockout, Campbell had Richards on the canvas in the fourth, more the result of a head-clash than the left hook that followed it, but was on the floor himself later in the round and again in the ninth. Campbell had fought Deacon Leo Kelly twice since the Richards bout and was ahead on points in the second bout before Kelly ended matters with a right hand in the seventh.

The bout was a disappointing affair for both Brisbane Stadium and Campbell. Despite being outweighed by almost two stone, Richards made light work of Campbell in front of fewer than 1,000 spectators. The bout was one-sided, with Campbell unable to get himself into a position where his weight advantage could be a factor. Richards hurt the larger man twice in the sixth round before ending matters in the seventh with a left hook to the jaw. With the victory, Richards became the first Aboriginal to win the Australian heavyweight title and only the fourth man to have held both the Australian middleweight and heavyweight titles, joining Palmer, Les Darcy and Dave Smith.

After winning the heavyweight title, Richards set his sights back on Henneberry's middleweight title. Henneberry had returned to the ring just days before the Richards-Campbell heavyweight title bout, winning a controversial fight over Mexican Olympian Al Romero at Sydney Stadium. Romero, who had outpointed Tommy Jones in a 15 round slug-fest in his first fight in Australia, demanded a purse of £500 before he would even step in the ring, delaying the start of the bout for close to an hour. Henneberry used his jab to control the first ten rounds before Romero rallied in round eleven and the two men traded punches in a furious rally. The exchanges continued into round twelve before Romero landed a right to Henneberry's body after referee Joe Wallis had called a break. The blow dropped Henneberry, and Joe Wallis disqualified Romero. Later that night, the N.B.C. overruled Wallis' call, changing the result to a no contest before reverting to the original result, giving Henneberry the win by disqualification.

Rather than defend his title against Richards, Henneberry signed for a title defence against Tommy Jones on 14 September. Jones, who had been in Australia for more than twelve months and qualified for a title shot, had a win over Richards and, despite few agreeing with Joe Wallis' decision in that bout, it was a chance for Henneberry to demonstrate his superiority to his rival without risking his title against him. Richards responded similarly, agreeing to return to Sydney and fight Henneberry's last opponent, Al

Romero, two weeks after the Henneberry-Jones clash. The N.B.C. had promised Richards that they would force Henneberry to defend his title against him should he defeat Romero.

Tommy Jones, weighing half a stone lighter, was no match for the Australian middleweight champion. Although Jones boxed well in the opening two rounds, Henneberry began to inflict heavy punishment on the American in the third and any chance that Jones had of winning vanished when he broke his right hand in round four. Henneberry slowed his pace in round five and Jones rallied in the sixth, throwing a wide variety of left-handed punches to take the round, but when Henneberry came out strong in the seventh, it was a matter of time before the knockout. After taking heavy punishment in the eighth, Jones' corner asked referee Wallis to have their boxer's hand examined. Wallis refused and ordered Jones to keep fighting. Henneberry ended matters early in the ninth round with a barrage of blows in the corner.

Two weeks later, Richards pounded out a fifteen round decision over Romero to secure his shot at Henneberry. Romero had been warned by many of Richards' ability to counter punch, and he boxed cautiously. Rather than wait for Romero to lead, Richards set an uncharacteristic pace and maintained it for the 15x3 minute round fight. Despite displaying a wide variety of defensive manoeuvres, Romero was unable to mount any attack, even when he switched to southpaw during the middle rounds. The decision was never in doubt, and with both Henneberry and Richards victorious in their recent bouts, it seemed a fight for the Australian title made the most sense for both men. Henneberry, however, turned the bout down as he wanted more time to prepare for a fight with Richards.

Richards returned to Brisbane but told Jack Munro that he would return as soon as Henneberry was ready, or if he could arrange for a fight with Deacon Leo Kelly, provided Kelly could make a catch-weight of 11st-11lb. Kelly's manager, Billy Newman, turned the offer down, stating that his boxer is a natural light heavyweight and he refused to allow him to fight under that weight class and offered 12st.[8] After a conference involving the managers of both men, Richards and Kelly agreed to box at a catch-weight of 11st-12lb with the weigh-in taking place at noon, rather than 2 pm. A forfeit of £100 was set in place if Kelly came in over the weight limit. Henneberry, meanwhile, signed to face Al Romero but the bout was at first postponed due to a boil on Henneberry's nose, and then cancelled after Romero married a North Sydney woman and had to leave for America to secure her visa.

Arriving back in Sydney three weeks before the bout, Richards trained hard at Jack Fennell's gym in the Sydney suburb of Lewisham. Fennell told reporters that Richards was undergoing "systematic training" for the three-minute rounds and that it was this conditioning program that lead to his improved conditioning against Romero. Richards had also travelled with his wife this time as the newly married man felt more at home with her by his side. There was much talking between Richards and Kelly leading up to the bout with Kelly offering to wager his entire purse that Richards couldn't knock him out. The Richards' camp was so confident in victory that they wagered £200 that he would defeat the American[9] and Richards told reporters that he would be so fast that Kelly will never hit him with his right hand.[10] Kelly had trained hard for the contest and made the weight limit with surprising ease, hitting the scales at 11st-9.5lb.

The bout drew a crowd of more than 10,000 spectators at Sydney Stadium. Both men began cautiously in the opening round, but Richards took the initiative late in the opener, landing a hard right to Kelly's jaw. Richards worked his jab well in the second round, setting up a wide variety of attacks that kept Kelly's hands protecting his head and body rather than throwing punches. Kelly opened up in the third round, landing a left that opened a small cut over Richards' right eye, but Richards again won the round with a series of clean left jabs. The American tried to establish his jab more in the fourth and fifth rounds, but Richards stepped back to make the blow fall short and scored with combinations to the head and body.

'The Deacon' took more chances in the sixth and forced Richards to the ropes, but even with his smaller opponent trapped, Kelly was still being outpunched and had no match for the Queenslander's speed. The crowd cheered as Richards went to work in round seven, landing several hard right hands and left hooks while evading Kelly's retaliation. Kelly had his best moments of the fight in the eighth round, landing a hard overhand right and then a right uppercut moments later but Richards took the blows well and flurried with both hands. Richards added to his lead in rounds nine and ten, continuing to land with the jab and outpunching Kelly when the American closed the distance and exchanged.

It took eleven rounds before Richards showed any signs of tiring and Kelly attempted to rally and score the knockout that he now required for victory. A hard left hook and a right to the body gave Kelly round eleven, but Richards' clever boxing had most of Kelly's blows falling short. Richards used his feet well to evade Kelly in the next two rounds and, apart from one hard left hook in round thirteen; Kelly was unable to land anything of significance. The American charged out in the fourteenth but still couldn't find Richards with anything to turn the tide, and the crowd were cheering as Richards traded with Kelly in the closing moments of the round. With the fight in the bag, Richards exchanged with Kelly in the early parts of the final round, landing many hard right hands as Kelly tried desperately for the knockout. It wouldn't come, and Richards scored the biggest win of his career. The Sydney fans gave Richards a standing ovation for several minutes after the final bell.

Despite all the talk between the two men leading up to the bout,

Kelly praised Richards' performance after the fight. "It was a hard fight, and I was beaten fairly. Richards is a good boy," Kelly said after the bout.[11] It would be Kelly's last bout in Australia in 1936 as he had accepted an offer to tour New Zealand after the contest. In his 16 fights in Australia, Kelly had won eleven, all by knockout, against four losses with one draw. In those bouts Kelly had made over £15,000, proving to be one of the biggest international drawcards ever brought to Australia. While his manager had suggested he would return to America after his fights in New Zealand, the purses he had earned in Australia would bring Kelly back early in 1937.

Richards' win had established him as the new star at Sydney Stadium and, after beating Kelly, the talk was all about the Richards-Henneberry title bout. The bout was scheduled for 14 December but delayed one week until 21 December after Richards injured his hand in training. Before the delay, Richards had accepted a fight at Brisbane Stadium on 5 December, knocking out unheralded American Al Norwood in three one-sided rounds. This fight would be one of the more controversial moments in Australian boxing history, when it was later revealed that Norwood was, in fact, a Sydney preliminary fighter Lance May, who had served as a sparring partner for Richards for the second bout with Kelly. The scheme was uncovered when a Sydney reporter spotted "Norwood" working as a "bowser boy" at a Sydney petrol station days before the seventh fight with Henneberry. Richards, however, denied any involvement in the scheme.

After much talking between the two men through reporters, both Henneberry and Richards agreed on a £200 side wager for the bout and deposited the money with Sydney newspaper *The Daily Telegraph*. Both men were looking in tremendous shape for the fight, and huge crowds flocked to see both boxers during their training exhibitions. The early bookings for the contest were exceeding the Henneberry-Palmer clash from March and Sydney Stadium was worried about congestion outside the stadium that they kept their offices open after hours and told anyone after tickets to get them as soon as possible in order not to miss out. Both boxers comfortably made the middleweight limit, with Henneberry surprisingly heavier at 11st-4.5lb compared to Richards at 11st-1.5lb.

There are stories that Henneberry and Richards almost came to blows either at the weigh-in or backstage before their seventh bout however these stories are not backed up by any newspaper articles at the time. In a series of interviews about their rivalry years later, neither Henneberry or Richards mentions an altercation occurring pre-fight. The story is that Richards overheard Henneberry refer to him as "the black," as he had during their previous fights, prompting an argument, followed by the two men almost coming to blows with their handlers separating them. Richards mentions in his 1947 interviews that Henneberry referred to him as "the black" many times throughout the years they fought each other, listing separate incidents when this happened, but does not mention it occurring before their 1936 meeting. While Henneberry's resentment of Richards came from the Richards' popularity, despite having scored more wins over Richards, Richards hatred of Henneberry came from the racist slur that Henneberry repeatedly used to address him.

The seventh fight saw both men meeting at the height of their abilities and popularity, and 13,000 fans were in attendance to see Australia's two best middleweights square off for the Australian title. Members of the Australian and England cricket team, including Australian captain Don Bradman, were in the crowd between days of their test match at the Sydney Cricket Ground. Henneberry took the fight to Richards as the opening bell sounded but was unable to avoid being tied up by Richards. The first round was messy, both men feinted for openings and then fell into clinches as they got in close. Richards took the honours in the first when he landed a short right hand, the only significant punch of the round.

The fight exploded in the second round. Henneberry continued attacking, but Richards timed one of his rushes and wobbled him with a right hand to the champion's jaw that "lifted Fred off his toes and swept him sideways through the air." Henneberry "recovered in a flash," [12] and drove Richards back in the clinch and the two men exchanged on the inside while the crowd roared. Richards was landing the better shots in the round, but Henneberry continued to push him back, and the bell ended as Richards was backed into his own corner. Henneberry ignored the bell, and kept fighting and, as Joe Wallis came between the two men, Henneberry landed a right on Richards jaw. Richards retaliated by sidestepping the referee and firing his right hand, and the two men tore into one another between rounds as Wallis, and the corner-men of both boxers, attempted to separate the fighters.

Henneberry used his jab more effectively in the third round, but the pace had slowed after the wild second round as both men looked to pace themselves. The champion's left worked well again in the fourth round, and Richards waited for his opening, which came in the fifth when another hard right landed on Henneberry's jaw. Henneberry still forced matters, but Richards was pulling away on the cards and picking the champion off with his jab. A right uppercut and a left hook gave Richards round six but Henneberry landed a series of hard jabs to Richards' mouth as the round came to a close and he was having more success with his jab as the fight went on.

The champion trapped Richards against the ropes in the seventh round and while Richards had success with his uppercut, Henneberry began to claw his way back into the fight and was moving "as swiftly as a mongoose attacking a cobra."[13] Richards' blows were becoming wilder as Henneberry was beating him to the punch with his jab and working well on the inside. Richards landed a hard right hand to Henneberry's jaw early in the ninth, but Henneberry dominated the final two minutes of the round on the inside, scoring with short left hands to the head and body and looked to have pulled in front as the tenth round began.

Henneberry continued to attack in round ten and was pushing Richards around the ring. Richards landed a hard right uppercut to the champion's jaw early, but Henneberry was relentless. The end, however, came suddenly and against the tide of the fight. According to Richards, he landed a short right hand to Henneberry's jaw as Henneberry pushed him towards the corner. As referee Joe Wallis broke the two men, Henneberry collapsed to the floor, where he was counted out. The reporters ringside did not see a punch from Richards, and reported that Henneberry collapsed due to some sort of "epileptic fit."[14] Whether a punch or some other illness caused it, Henneberry could not continue, and Ron Richards was once again the Australian middleweight champion.

Henneberry was down for several minutes after the incident while the Stadium medical team examined him, but he was able to leave the ring. The crowd booed him as he left the ring, with some under the impression that he had taken a dive but while reporters ringside weren't sure how he ended up on the floor, all accounts state his head hit the canvas with a thud, and he was unconscious. Henneberry was also clueless as to what happened. After the fight, he told *The Sydney Sportsman* that "Richards didn't hurt me, and I had him well beaten. I might have tripped, but I don't know."[15] While Henneberry sought a return with Richards, he ended up taking his doctor's advice and took a few months off training.

Despite the manner of the victory, Richards was now the Australian middleweight and heavyweight champion and Sydney Stadium's leading star. Both men were paid approximately £1,000 with the live gate totalling over £4,000 and, with Richards also winning the side wager, it was a career-high payday for the Queenslander. With rumours circulating that Ambrose Palmer would return to the ring and that Deacon Leo Kelly was on his way back to Australia, there were many options for big money fights for Richards. With Jack Carroll again in training, Australian reporters were already talking of a second bout between Richards, now the middleweight and heavyweight champion, and the welterweight king, Carroll.

#1 CONTENDER

Jack Carroll's hand injury had recovered by Christmas, and he was back in training before the new year, chopping down trees as a part of his regime to help rehabilitate his hand. There were a number of options for fights for Carroll. Ron Richards had issued a challenge for Carroll to meet him at catch weights in the days after he beat Henneberry, but Charles Lucas was still looking at a world title fight for Carroll. If Lucas could get Richards under contract, he was more interested in matching him with Ambrose Palmer, who had returned to the ring in New Zealand and was talking about fighting once again in Australia. The chance at a world title shot for Carroll got its second wind when news from New York that Barney Ross' manager, Sam Pian, was suspended by the New York Boxing Commission for refusing to make a title fight between Ross and Ceferino Garcia.

Lucas and Pian again opened communications for the title bout but Lucas was adamant that he would not be able to raise the money before Ross set sail. He asked that Pian send a representative to Australia to iron out the final details and then he would cable them travel and training expenses before paying them their purse after the bout. The proposed date was again Easter Monday, with Lucas hoping to match Carroll with either Izzy Jannazzo, Cleto Locatelli or Jimmy Leto in the meantime. A few weeks later Lucas announced that he would hold three bouts at the Sydney Sports Ground in 1937, with Carroll appearing on two of them.

Barney Ross
(Acme, Press Wire Photo 19 December, 1934)

While the negotiations for the title fight again proved slow, Carroll told reporters that he would go to America for the right offer. If he was to leave Australia, however, he wanted similar conditions to those Ross wanted if he were to leave America:

> "You remember, of course, that Barney Ross asked for a big guarantee before he would come to Australia and wanted the money lodged in America. Well, I'm asking for a guarantee, too. Nothing like what Ross demanded, but enough to make the trip

a payable one for me and I want the money to be lodged in Australia before I set foot on the steamer. Otherwise, nothing doing. I don't have to go to America and I don't intend to risk the money I've had to work hard to earn in Australia. If America wants me it can make it worthwhile for me to travel. Incidentally, that goes as well for anybody in Australia who has a proposition to make that means a visit to the United States for me. Money down or I don't leave Australia."[1]

Jimmy Leto
(Photo courtesy Harry Otty)

Jimmy Leto was the first to respond to the offers made by Charles Lucas and, after Lucas was able to transfer the money to Leto that he had cabled for Ross to travel, it was announced that Leto would meet Carroll at the Sydney Sports Ground. Leto, born in Bayonne, New Jersey, in 1911, had been fighting as a professional since he was 13 and had over 100 wins as a professional including wins over Jannazzo, Locatelli, Wesley Ramey, Cocoa Kid, Benny Bass and Fritzie Zivic.

The contest was scheduled for 30 March, and Carroll commenced serious training in late February, with plans to travel to Sydney two weeks before the bout. Leto, arriving on 1 March, impressed the Sydney fans with his first workout, displaying both speed and power. Leto, who stood just over 5'5" tall, dismissed the height advantage that Carroll held, arguing that he had defeated Phil Furr in one of his last bouts and Furr was reportedly over 6'0" tall. While Carroll was hoping to use a win over Leto to pressure welterweight champion Ross into the ring with him, Leto was confident that it would be him fighting Ross, but after he returned to America with a win over Carroll.

Leto's style of punching in the gym had many comparing him to Tod Morgan, but not many gave him a chance due to the size difference between the two men. Still, Carroll was in his 15th year as a professional, and his age and ability to make the welterweight limit were the most significant questions around his form. In the gym, Carroll looked as sharp as he ever had, with his trainer Bill O'Brien telling the media that he had never seen him "in such devastating form" in the ten years that he had trained him.[2] Whether he would look as sharp on fight night, after dropping the necessary weight to make the welterweight limit, was a different matter.

The weather had finally been more favourable for Lucas' open air venture, and the bout would be fought under clear skies with a "pale moon watching over Carroll's corner."[3] While the attendance numbers differ according to various sources, the clear skies and the intrigue of the bout proved popular with the Sydney fans. *The Sydney Morning Herald* reported that as many as 25,000 were in attendance, but *The Daily Telegraph* and *The Referee* report the number as between 18,000 and 20,000. One of those spectators was

Carroll's wife, Doreen, who had also travelled to Sydney and the bout with Leto would be the first time she had seen her husband fight. Both men made the welterweight limit, with Carroll, who weighed 10st-6.5lb, having a weight advantage of 3.5lb.

The Australian champion was in his first serious contest in well over 12 months, but he started much more confidently than Leto, immediately establishing his jab in the early moments of the fight. Leto attempted to fight at close range, but he was met with an uppercut and easily tied up by Carroll on the inside. Leto fought better in the second and third rounds, trapping Carroll along the ropes but he was unable to score with more than one punch at a time as Carroll proved too elusive. Outside of his consistent jab, Carroll's work was sporadic in the first three rounds, and he rarely let his hands go until the fourth, when he unloaded a series of body shots with his back to the ropes, driving Leto back across the ring. Leto fought back well but was now hesitant to let his hands go, and Carroll had no trouble picking off his single leads and scoring with his jab.

Carroll fought with his old form early in round five, snapping Leto's head back with his jab from the outside, and unloading punches at close range with blistering hand speed. Leto handled the assault well and landed a hard right hand in return. Despite Carroll's early lead, Leto was not discouraged. Sensing he couldn't match Carroll's speed on the outside, Leto took the fight into close quarters in rounds six, seven and eight. Despite opening a cut on Carroll's cheek with a left hand in the clinch, Carroll had the edge on the inside as well, landing short uppercuts to the head and hard blows to Leto's body with both hands. While Carroll wasn't fighting with his usual speed and vigour, he had a clear lead on points as the bout entered the second half.

The American continued looking for a way to get to Carroll, and he retreated to start round nine. As Carroll pursued, Leto countered a lazy left lead with a hard right hand to Carroll's jaw, his best punch of the fight. The shot momentarily stunned Carroll, but Carroll responded immediately, driving Leto across the ring with a barrage of punches. Carroll continued to unload with punches for the remainder of the round and Leto looked dejected as round ten began. He continued to retreat in the tenth round, but Carroll was careful and would position himself before he unloaded his combinations. The American's earlier aggression was gone, and Carroll won rounds eleven and twelve, easily defending against Leto's infrequent attacks and scoring with both hands.

Leto's manager, Lou Viscusi, screamed at his fighter before the start of the 13th round. "Jimmy, you've got to go to town. You've got to get all hot. There are three rounds to go. You must win these three rounds to win the fight."[4] The speech seemed to wake Leto from his slump, and he took the fight to Carroll in the thirteenth. Although he was mostly ineffective against Carroll's jab and brilliant defence, he caused more damage to the cut on Carroll's cheek. The American opened round fourteen with a hard left hook on Carroll's jaw and continued to apply pressure and back Carroll up. As Carroll was retreating towards his own corner, Leto delivered a huge right hand that landed flush on the Australian champion's jaw and dropped him to the seat of his pants.

Carroll looked stunned, but he rose at the count of three before stumbling into the ropes. Leto tried to find the blows to send him down again, but despite Carroll's grogginess, he defended himself intelligently and tied up the American. Leto landed more heavy punches at the end of the round, but Carroll absorbed them, although he was hurt as the bell sounded to end the round. After being revived by Bill O'Brien between rounds, Carroll continued to spoil and tie Leto up early in the final round. When Leto argued with referee Baker about a Carroll body shot in the clinch that he felt was low, Carroll used the respite to clear his head. Leto fought wildly but found his mark with a few of his shots as Carroll continued to run down the clock. In the final seconds, Leto landed a left hook that again wobbled Carroll and moments later, Carroll slipped to the floor. The referee ruled another knockdown, but Carroll was up immediately just before the bell sounded to end the contest.

Referee Baker crowned Carroll as he rose and the crowd applauded the decision and the tremendous action they had witnessed in the closing rounds of the fight. Leto disagreed with the decision but received a standing ovation from the Australian crowd as he left the ring. Viscusi thought that Leto had done enough to win the decision. "I think Leto won," he told *The Daily Telegraph* "he was fouled in the fourth round, and he won the last two rounds with his knock-downs. Carroll is certainly a good fighter, and I think both he and Leto would defeat Barney Ross, the welterweight champion of the world."[5]

Jimmy Leto (2nd from left) with manager Lou Viscusi (far right) and sparring partner Tommy Jones (far left)
(National Library of Australia, nla.obj-148564756)

Leto later described Carroll as a "freak" and said that he would be a sensation if he fought in America. "That habit of his of coming in side-ways and throwing an unexpected punch for any angle makes him hard to handle,"[6] he told reporters. Both Leto and Viscusi were keen for a rematch, but talks from the Carroll camp were back to Ross, and Bill O'Brien sat down with Charles Lucas in the days after the fight to begin negotiations for Carroll to travel to America and fight for the title. Lucas cabled New York after the bout, asking for terms for a title fight. Carroll, however, had other ideas and was more interested in a rematch with Leto. Reporters from *The Daily Telegraph* caught Carroll on the balcony of his hotel and managed to get a quick interview with the Australian champion. As well as blaming his poor performance on a combination of ring rust and over-training, Carroll talked about fighting Leto and his retirement plans:

> "I'll take on anyone at my weight. I'm not frightened of any of them. I've been at the game for 14 years, but I'm as good as I ever was. Leto's a good man. I don't deny that, but I can improve 50 per cent on the form I should last night. The trouble is I don't get enough fights. It's the same with a race-horse, he's no good unless they race him. They've only given me two fights in the past 14 months. I trained too much for the fight with Leto. I was in pretty good nick at the start. I want to fight Jimmy Leto again. I'm going to see Charles Lucas tomorrow to see if he can arrange it. The thing is I want to show people that I'm good for a few years yet. Then I'll retire when I've got together a bit of money. I want to leave the slaughtering trade and become a boxing instructor. I can't do it unless I get more fights. When they are a long time apart, the money from one goes all before the next one comes along."[7]

With the gate receipts totalling £3,750, it was another payday of over £900 for Carroll to put towards his retirement plan. Carroll gave his wishes, which were for two return contests with Leto (one in Sydney then one in Melbourne) before leaving for Melbourne by car with his wife and children. Carroll was disappointed with the gate for the Leto bout as he had hoped to make more than he did in the matches with van Klaveren. Leto wasn't interested in a return fight at the Sports Ground as he was worried that the rain could affect the gate. Dick Lean, manager of Stadiums Ltd, had travelled to Sydney in February. After meeting with the N.B.C., who were rumoured to be out of money, Sydney Stadium was once again under Stadiums Ltd control, and the N.B.C. dissolved. Lean had also approached Charles Lucas about becoming Sydney Stadium manager, although Lucas denied these rumours while he was in business with Sydney Sports Ground.

Leto's refusal to fight in the open air brought Sydney Stadium back into the picture. Lou Viscusi also offered Carroll a guarantee of £2,500 if he would fight Leto in New York. After negotiations with Stadiums Ltd, Lucas agreed to stage the rematch at Sydney Stadium, and the date of 22 April was agreed to for the Carroll-Leto rematch. Both men returned to the gym in early April, with Carroll training in Melbourne before returning to Sydney. Carroll showed his old form in public spars with Jack McNamee, making him the favourite. Leto's manager had booked passage for the pair to return to New York one week after the bout, regardless of the result. The American was also showing improved form in the gym, but few in the Australian press thought he would handle Carroll if the Victorian were at his best.

Just days before the fight, Carroll was examined by a doctor after he had felt run-down for a few days. The doctor determined that Carroll had not recovered from his first bout with Leto and instructed Carroll not to go through with the rematch and that he should, instead, rest for two months. Carroll was replaced by Australian lightweight champion Alf Blatch, who was to tour America with Carroll after the bout and was hoping a win over a high ranking American would propel him into big fights upon his arrival in the United States. Promoters offered refunds for any ticket holder who did not wish to see Blatch in against Leto, and the attendance for the bout dropped from the expected figure of 15,000 down to 8,000. Blatch gave a good account of himself in the first three rounds before Leto hurt him in the fourth round and dropped him twice in the fifth with left hooks to the body. On the second knockdown, referee Harald Baker disqualified Leto for a kidney punch, giving the Australian lightweight champion an unlikely victory.

Before leaving Australia, Leto and his manager Lou Viscusi complained about the referee's decision, arguing that if the bout were in New York, such a foul would have only entitled Blatch to win the round, not the fight. Leto also stated that he would return to Australia to fight Carroll in a rematch as soon as he was fit for one. Carroll rested for just under a week before returning to Melbourne. He dismissed any talk that his boxing career was over, saying that he would take his doctor's advice and return to training after a rest of a few months:

> "My plan is to rest at home for a couple of weeks, and then go to the country, probably to Daylesford, and I shall not look at a gym for a couple of months. After that, I intend to move along quietly into real condition and then put the gloves on again."[8]

While on his doctor-ordered break from training, Carroll was challenged by a number of local fighters who were keen for a shot at the Australian welterweight champion. Among those was Ron Richards, who had sought the rematch since his victory over Henneberry for the Australian middleweight title. Richards had lost a decision to Deacon Leo Kelly in his first fight in 1937, although his training was interrupted when he had to return to Brisbane after his wife fell ill. The two men then fought a draw in their fourth fight, held at Brisbane Stadium. Tragically, Richards' wife passed away from her illness in June, and Richards took a break from boxing to mourn her loss.

The other man who repeatedly challenged Carroll was Dick Humphries, the welterweight champion of New South Wales. Humphries was 21 years old and had been fighting professionally since 1934. He had lost twice in 1935, to touring Americans Willard Brown and Tommy Jones, but had scored wins over Herb Bishop, Cyril Pluto, Jack McNamee and Max Raynor. He had outpointed McNamee, a regular training partner of Carroll, at the Sydney Sports Ground on a Charles Lucas promoted show in February. While Humphries continually called out the welterweight champion, Carroll's manager Bill O'Brien told him there was "no use" as Carroll would not rush his return, instead offering a side wager for a rematch with McNamee.[9]

By June, Carroll had returned from the country with his family but was still not ready to resume working in the gym. He occasionally worked as a referee at West Melbourne Stadium but was soon forced to return to the abattoir to earn a living. Charles Lucas had continued with his trip to America without Carroll, taking the lightweight champion Alf Blatch with him. Lucas matched Blatch with Henry Armstrong, the number one contender for the world featherweight title, at Madison Square Garden in New York, hoping that a win for Blatch would secure him a title shot with world lightweight champion Lou Ambers. Blatch was no match for Armstrong, who had only lost once in his last 23 bouts. Armstrong dropped Blatch eight times in three rounds before the referee mercifully halted the contest.

Although heavily criticised by both the Australian and American press for overmatching his fighter on his American debut,[10] matches for Blatch wasn't Lucas' only reason for his trip to the United States. After witnessing Madison Square Garden, Lucas saw an opportunity in Australia:

> "The more I look at Madison Square Garden, the more I realise what Australians are missing. The Sydney Sports Ground has everything that is needed to make the finest sporting arena in the world for summer and winter sport."[11]

Lucas announced another summer of boxing at the Sydney Sports Ground, with his hopes to open the season with a rematch between Carroll and Leto at the end of November followed by bouts involving Alf Blatch.

His new season would bring Australian boxing rules in line with those in America. The main change was the removal of fifteen round main events, with the main event of his Sports Ground bouts now being fought over 10x3 minute rounds. He also removed two-minute rounds in preliminaries, which Lucas said made Australia the "laughing stock" of the boxing world. While Lucas was in New York, Barney Ross had signed to defend his welterweight title against Ceferino Garcia in September. Lucas had negotiated with Garcia and had an agreement with the Filipino to come to Australian and defend his title against Carroll, should he defeat Ross. Alf Blatch fought once more at Madison Square Garden, dropping a narrow decision to Carl Guggino over eight rounds before he and Lucas returned to Australia.

Dick Humphries, meanwhile, had claimed the welterweight championship of Australia in Carroll's absence. He declined Bill O'Brien's proposal of meeting McNamee in a return contest, stating that he wanted to move forward, not backwards, in his career. Carroll finally felt fit enough to return to the gym in September and began light training to prepare himself for Lucas' summer of boxing. After arriving back in Australia, Lucas announced that the first American to come to Australia would be Izzy Jannazzo, who challenged Ross for the welterweight championship in 1936. After a month of training, Carroll wrote to Lucas to inform him he wished to fight twice before he met Jannazzo. Lucas permitted him to fight for another promoter in the interim, and Carroll agreed to fight for Dick Lean at West Melbourne Stadium, with his first opponent to be Dick Humphries on 6 November.

After the National Boxing Club had disbanded, Charles Lucas decided to use Jack Munro and his connections. He made Munro a partner of his venture at the Sports Ground, now called Olympia Sports Ltd. Lucas dreamed of an Australian version of Madison Square Garden and, with Munro's financial backers also at his disposal it would allow for more significant guarantees to lure the likes of Barney Ross to Australia for world title bouts. Lucas and Munro were to stage six cards in the Australian summer, beginning with a December fight between Carroll and Jannazzo, and then promote other bouts using Australian boxers in England during the Australian winter. The winner of the Carroll-Jannazzo bout would fight Jimmy Leto, who was due to arrive in December. Lucas was hopeful of matching the winner of that bout with Ceferino Garcia, who had lost a lost decision to Barney Ross in his September title challenge, although he didn't yet have Garcia under contract. Lucas hoped that the winner of this series of welterweight bouts would entice Ross to defend his world title either in Australia or England on one of his shows.

With the opportunity to fight three of the top ten welterweights in the world in the space of a few months, Carroll began training for Humphries. A loss to the brash Sydney welterweight would derail his chance to secure his fight with Ross. The bout was postponed on Humphries request, first to 13 November, then to 20 November, as Humphries wanted a warm-up fight on 6 November, which upset Carroll, as any further postponement could interfere with his 21 December engagement with Jannazzo.

> "The Humphries party have been free enough with their challenges in recent months, yet when a fight is arranged, they want it postponed. That's no way to help boxing. I'm not going

to be fooled about by people who have been so free with challenges when they probably thought there was little chance of acceptance."[12]

After Carroll threatened to withdraw entirely, Dick Lean assured Carroll there would be no further delays. Humphries warm-up opponent was Jerry Leonard, and although Humphries dominated the contest, he did not look to be in Carroll's league. Leonard was cut above both eyes early in the bout, which blinded him in the late rounds and, in the tenth round, after his lack of vision caused him to deliver a low blow, he was disqualified.

Carroll had worked his way into condition slowly, but by mid-November, he was reportedly in tremendous shape and not far off the welterweight limit. Bill O'Brien said that Carroll, despite his age and inactivity, was still good enough to beat the Americans on their way to fight him. "Do you think we would be taking on these young Americans if we were at all doubtful about the prospects? You think we're content to risk a beating for one big purse?" O'Brien asked a reporter when questioned about Carroll's condition.[13] A crowd of 11,000 fans flocked to West Melbourne Stadium to see if Carroll could regain his old form or if Humphries was the best welterweight in the country, as he claimed. Both men weighed slightly over the welterweight limit, with Humphries having a slight advantage in weight.

While Carroll looked in excellent condition, his timing was slightly off, and he lacked the speed that he had shown just under two years ago when he outpointed van Klaveren twice. Despite his noticeable drop in speed, Carroll won six of the first seven rounds at ease as his speed was still too much for the 21-year-old challenger. Humphries nearly caused the upset in the eighth round when he hurt Carroll briefly with a left hook to the chin, but Carroll used all of his experience to weather the storm and was back in control in the ninth round. The Australian champion slowed down in the final rounds, but Humphries was unable to take advantage, and Carroll did not lose a round after the eighth, easily winning the decision rendered by former world heavyweight title challenger Bill Lang, who served as referee.

Many Australian reporters questioned whether Carroll, with his weakened condition, would be able to hold off Jannazzo or Leto. Carroll dismissed that he was past his best and stated that he had no intention of knocking Humphries out d that he wanted 15 rounds under his belt before he took on the fighters imported by Olympia Sports Ltd:

> "I fight my own fights and I'm not worried by adverse criticism. I know more about myself than anyone else does.
>
> Against Dick Humphries, I fought according to circumstances. I summed Dick up early in the piece as a one-handed fighter, and one against whom I could take no risks. I wasn't out to punish Humphries or to try and stop him. It suited me to have the fight go 15 rounds. I wanted to try myself out over the distance. Well, you saw me finish. I was a bit tired, but not so much as I thought I would be. As a matter of fact, Humphries seemed to be more done up than I was. What I can't understand is why people should have thought I was going to fight at the top of my form. I know I wasn't. I don't kid myself about that at all. You can't be out of the game for nearly 12 months, then come back and shape like a champion right away.
>
> Wait til December 21 when I fight Izzy Jannazzo in Sydney. Some of the critics will have to back down after that. I know that he won't be in any better condition that I am, and I'm confident I will be boxing as well as ever by then."[14]

Jannazzo had arrived days before Carroll's bout with Humphries and began training for his fight with Carroll in a month. Izzy Jannazzo was just 21 years old but had already fought more than 50 bouts in his career. Before challenging Ross, Jannazzo had outpointed the European champion Gustav Eder, who had previously knocked out Jimmy Leto. Jannazzo wowed Australian media members when he walked into the gym for his first training session smoking a pipe, which he told reporters he found "soothing."[15] Izzy impressed in his first public sparring session on 25 November, boxing three rounds with his sparring partner 'Hockey' Bennell, where he displayed "a brilliant display of straight punching."[16]

The bout would be fought under the New York rules, with 10x3 minute round distance and a "minor foul" such as a low blow or a kidney punch only costing a boxer the round, rather than a disqualification. Carroll arrived in Sydney two weeks before the bout, his first trip back since the fight with Leto, and he told reporters he planned to continue boxing until he was beaten. The Australian champion reportedly looked in much better shape than he did before his fights with Leto. Alf Blatch served as his chief sparring partner in the early days of training before he headed to Melbourne to fight the Hawaiian 'Clever' Henry. Carroll's recent opponent, Dick Humphries, took over as Carroll's chief sparring partner and the pair engaged in many hard sparring sessions in the lead-up to the Jannazzo bout.

Jannazzo looked to be in excellent condition as the bout drew closer. Unlike the shorter Jimmy Leto, Jannazzo had the size to go with his skills, standing only 2" shorter than Carroll and weighing at the limit of the welterweight class. Many were predicting that Jannazzo's size, combined with Carroll's decline in skill, would allow the 21-year-old American to overpower the Australian champion. Carroll was confident in his condition and determined to prove that he was still one of the best welterweights in the world. "I am feeling very fit and am quietly confident of doing well," he told reporters after one of his last training sessions. "You know I have been tipped as the loser many times before but showed the tipsters were wrong."[17]

For Lucas and Munro, their new joint venture was looking to be a success and, with the number of early bookings, they were expecting a gate of £6,000.[18] Jimmy Leto arrived days before the fight and was expected to face the winner of the bout in a month. The contracted weight for the fight was one pound over the welterweight limit, which both men were under on the morning of the fight when they checked their weight. Jannazzo came in slightly over the agreed weight limit while Carroll was over even more. After O'Brien conferred with Jannazzo's manager, Guy Anselmi, they were both convinced that the scales weren't accurate and neither manager insisted on a penalty.

The civility between the managers ended on the evening of the fight when O'Brien complained about how the laces were tied on Jannazzo's gloves, worried that they could be used to cut Carroll. Anselmi was enraged when referee Baker ordered him to re-tie his fighter's gloves. While the managers were arguing over the tying of the gloves, a record crowd was entering the Sydney Sports Ground during the preliminary contests. When the time came for the main event, there was over 30,000 in attendance. Jannazzo was first into the ring and was cheered by the Sydney fans as he entered, seemingly anxious for the bout to begin. Carroll, on the other hand, was relaxed, smiling at ringsiders as he entered the ring with Bill O'Brien.

At the opening bell, Carroll surprised many when he immediately tore into Jannazzo. Izzy was taken aback by the aggression and retreated as Carroll attacked, but while Carroll was aggressive, he wasn't accurate, and he missed wildly. Jannazzo began to time Carroll's rushes by the halfway mark of the round and scored with a long jab while slipping Carroll's leads and scoring to the body and seemed to be in control as the round ended. Carroll's accuracy improved, and he landed a series of left hooks in the first half of the second round. The American tried to respond on the inside with short punches to Carroll's body but Carroll's defence was tight, and his superior hand-speed gave him a clear edge in the round. Jannazzo landed the best punch of the second in the form of a right cross to Carroll's jaw, but Carroll took the blow well and responded with a volley of lefts to Izzy's head and body.

Carroll kept up the pace in the third and fourth rounds, and Jannazzo looked bewildered by the speed of the Australian's attacks. Jannazzo grew hesitant to lead as Carroll punished him with left hands in every exchange. Jannazzo came out strong for round five and had success at long range, but once Carroll brought the fight to close quarters, Izzy was no match for Carroll's speed. Izzy's jab landed flush in the fifth, and it seemed to renew his confidence in the sixth, where he scored with a hard right to Carroll's jaw and a left to the midsection. Carroll responded with "a hail of leather thrown from all angles"[19] that backed Jannazzo into the ropes.

The long-range punches from Izzy were becoming less effective in the second half of the fight as Carroll took fewer chances to protect his lead. Jannazzo would attack periodically in an attempt to try and turn the tide, but the speed and volume of Carroll's work gave him rounds seven and eight. The American had a glimmer of hope after Carroll emerged from a clinch with blood flowing from a cut to his left eye, but Carroll stifled the follow-up attack and backed Jannazzo up with a barrage of left hooks and right uppercuts. Carroll's corner was unable to stop the flow of blood, but it did not affect the bout as Carroll continued to dominate. Jannazzo was aggressive in rounds nine and ten but Carroll was still in excellent condition, and he defended Izzy's blows with ease while outpunching him on the inside. At the end of the tenth and final round, Harald Baker declared Carroll, the winner on points.

Guy Anselmi complained after the bout that the referee had favoured Carroll throughout the contest and that Baker had allowed Carroll to get away with holding and hitting on the break. While Anselmi agreed with the decision, he was confident that Jannazzo would emerge the winner if the two fought a rematch over fifteen rounds and he also told reporters that Carroll would never defeat Barney Ross. Lou Viscusi, manager of Jimmy Leto, disagreed, however, on both counts. "I did not see anything wrong with Carroll's tactics," he told *The Daily Telegraph*. "On his present form Carroll would beat Ross." In the aftermath of the Jannazzo fight, fans were talking about the Carroll-Leto rematch, and Charles Lucas proposed the date of 11 January, potentially with Ambrose Palmer fighting for the first time in Australia since his loss to Deacon Leo Kelly on the undercard.

While everyone was talking about Carroll's next move the day after his win over Jannazzo, Carroll was busy shopping for Christmas presents for his children. Armed with the £935 he earned for his victory, Carroll was spotted in the Sydney suburb of Paddington where he was more keen to talk about what he had purchased for his children than the fight. "Hundreds of people have asked me the same question all day in town," he answered when the talk eventually went to his injured eye and whether he would be fit to face Leto in early January. "Oh, I'm alright. If you give, you must expect to cop." [20] Carroll's eye received two stitches, and he left for Melbourne the day after the bout so he could spend Christmas with his family. Carroll had also been battling the flu in the days leading up to the fight but chose to fight through it rather than delay the bout.

Jimmy Leto started training for the Carroll fight after Christmas and had Ambrose Palmer to work with as a sparring partner. Palmer's retirement had lasted less than 12 months before he fought in New Zealand, knocking out Roy De Gans in five rounds. He had also played 15 games for the Footscray Bulldogs in the Victorian

Football League in the 1937 season. The 11 January date was delayed for one week to allow Carroll's cut eye to head fully. Izzy Jannazzo, who offered a £500 side bet for an immediate rematch with Carroll, was matched with Dick Humphries a week later with both bouts to be held at the Sydney Sports Ground.

Charles Lucas had once again been in communication with Sam Pian about Barney Ross defending his title against Carroll in Australia. Pian made the same demands; $50,000 US (or £13,5000) paid in advance, plus travel expenses, before they would leave for Australia. With Lucas unable to raise the money, he contacted New York promoter Mike Jacobs about staging a Ross-Carroll fight being held in New York. Carroll and Lucas spoke after the Australian champion arrived back in Sydney for his bout with Leto, but Carroll was still against leaving Australia:

> "If I defeat Leto and the victory brings me a concrete offer from Mike Jacobs for a title fight, Bill O'Brien and I will give it serious consideration. But if it necessitates my journeying to the USA, I'm telling you it will have to be the richest prize ever offered an Australian champion. Right now I have not, and never have had, any idea of leaving Australia."[21]

Carroll again sparred Dick Humphries in preparation for the bout and was focused entirely on Leto. Bill O'Brien reported that Carroll's bouts with Humphries and Jannazzo had brought Carroll back to the old form that he was showing before the first bout with Leto close to twelve months ago. Leto, meanwhile, finished his preparations with a public sparring exhibition with Ambrose Palmer, who described him as the "most awkwardly clever fighter I have ever seen."[22]

Leto was well under the weight limit on the morning of the bout and was fed a large breakfast to bring his weight up closer to the weight limit. Carroll, on the other hand, spent the morning of the bout in a Turkish bath to bring his weight down to the limit. The effort was futile as Carroll missed the agreed 10st-7lb limit, weighing in 10st-8.5lb. Viscusi was confident that his fighter would win, despite weighing in 2lb less, and didn't enforce any penalty. With both Ambrose Palmer and Jack Carroll featuring on the same bill, the popularity of the contest was immense.

After Palmer had warmed the large crowd up with an easy eight-round decision over the Perth heavyweight Claude Nichol, the world ranked welterweights entered the ring for their rematch. Carroll was out fast at the opening bell, and while he landed more punches and took the round, he was over-eager, and Leto was able to time him and score with his hard counter punches in a close opening round. The action heated up in the second round as Leto took the fight to Carroll, who was happy to exchange blows with the American. The large crowd roared as the two men traded, with Leto's power carrying the round. After a hard-fought second round, the pace slowed in the third and both men took respite in frequent clinches. During the final seconds of the third, Leto surprised Carroll with his speed, stealing the round with a fast volley of shots.

Leto was growing with confidence, and he took the fight to Carroll more in the fourth round, cleverly evading the Australian champion's leads and driving him to the ropes where his shorter arms gave him the advantage. Carroll coolly defended but was having trouble keeping Leto on the end of his punches, and the American was building a small lead over the ten-round contest. Rather than keeping Leto on the end of his punches in the fifth, Carroll tied up the smaller man as he advanced and the round was messy. Carroll began to work in punches on the inside, and the strength of his blows was keeping Leto wary of trading in close. With the American hesitant about coming forward, Carroll returned to his jab and found the target with more consistency, which began to frustrate Leto.

The second half of the fight was one-sided. Carroll, in his typical fashion, used his speed and a wide assortment of blows from both the outside and at close quarters, to keep Leto confused. Carroll fought with "the confidence of a seasoned veteran,"[23] outboxing and outpunching the experienced American. Leto rallied in the seventh round but his success was short-lived, and he was resigned to his fate as he had no way of evading Carroll's left or finding the mark with a punch that would end the fight. With Leto needing a knockout in the final two rounds, Carroll took no chances, although he continued to score often enough to win both rounds. Referee Harald Baker's decision was never in doubt, and the crowd cheered as he placed his hand on Carroll's head after round ten.

Jimmy Leto (right) lands on Jack Carroll during their second fight - Sydney Sports Ground: 18 January, 1938
(Photo courtesy Harry Otty)

The official attendance was reported at 25,000. However, the ticket prices were more expensive, with the gate receipts totalling just under £6,000, with both Carroll and Leto earning £1,300 each (around $5,800 US), which was the largest purse paid to an Australian boxer for a boxing match in Australia. With the size of the crowd, Charles Lucas grew more optimistic about his chances of bringing Ross to Australia, restarting negotiations with Sam Pian in New York. Lou Viscusi was upset about Carroll's weight advantage after the fight. "This was supposed to be a welterweight elimination tournament, yet he was a middleweight when he fought Izzy and again tonight," he complained to reporters. "I'm satisfied Jimmy was beaten, but he was not beaten by a welterweight, and that is what Carroll claims to be."[24]

The negotiations with Barney Ross once again stalled after Sam Pian demanded that Ross' purse had to be sent out of Australia before Ross would set sail from America. Lucas looked for another way to place pressure on Ross to defend his title and began negotiations with Ceferino Garcia and his team for him to come to Australia. Behind Ross and Carroll, Garcia was the next highest ranked contender and he had extended the champion fifteen rounds in his most recent title defence. Lucas figured that a one-sided win over the next logical challenger would only add to Carroll's claim for a title shot. Carroll, however, did not want to stay idle, and with Leto's management upset about the weight for their second fight and with neither man badly hurt in the ten round contest, an offer for a third fight between Carroll and Leto came from Melbourne.

The offer had come from an independent Melbourne syndicate which ran The Melbourne Exhibition Grounds. They had approached Carroll directly with the offer, but when Lucas insisted that Carroll would be given a guarantee £750 or 25% of the gate, Olympia Sports Ltd became co-promoters of the bout. The final hurdle for the third fight was the duration of the contest. Leto demanded fifteen rounds while Carroll wanted ten, but the two men reached a compromise of twelve rounds, and the bout was set. Carroll gave an uncharacteristic outburst when asked about the dispute over the length of the fight:

"I'll have a crack at Leto over any distance I don't care if the fight is over 50 rounds. Leto has made me bear the brunt of all this squabbling, but he seems to have forgotten that he suggested ten rounds for his fights in Australia. Leto got his way for our recent fight in Sydney, and I didn't feel disposed toward making a change for the Melbourne fight. Leto seems to have the idea that I tired over ten rounds, but I'll give him all the bother he's looking for - and I don't mean maybe!"[25]

Charles Lucas, meanwhile, had completed negotiations for Ceferino Garcia to travel to Australia and meet Carroll. Garcia would sail for Australia on 1 March and would be guaranteed either £1,875 or 30% of the takings for the fight. Garcia had scored three knockout wins since his decision loss to Barney Ross, all three bouts taking place in California. Barney Ross still hadn't announced his next title defence as he was freshly married and still recovering from a broken hand that he suffered during training, and then fought through, for the bout with Garcia.

Leto had completed most of his training for the bout in Sydney before arriving by train one week before the bout. He was hoping that a win over Carroll would give him, rather than Carroll, first shot at Ceferino Garcia when the Filipino-born fighter arrived in Australia. The American's chief sparring partner was Cyril Pluto, who would fight Tommy Jones on the undercard, as well as the occasional rounds with Ambrose Palmer. Lou Viscusi told reporters that his fighter was on weight when he arrived in Melbourne and he was confident that he would knock Carroll out if the Australian champion made the welterweight limit.

For Carroll, the Melbourne bout with Leto was a fresh change as he wouldn't have to spend weeks away from his young family leading up to the bout. The Australian champion had spent his 32nd birthday with his family at their home in Moonee Ponds before he began serious training for the third fight with Leto. Carroll told reporters that he had no thoughts of retirement, despite his age, and that as long as he could match it with the best in the world, he would continue to fight. Carroll's struggle to make the welterweight limit, however, had begun to take a toll on his physical and mental health in the days before the fight. He began to suffer symptoms similar to those that forced his layoff after the first bout with Leto and visited his doctor on the day before the bout.

After a physical examination, his doctor advised him that he should retire and not go through with the bout. Carroll considered the advice, but with as many as 16,000 expected at the Melbourne Exhibition Grounds, he did not want to let down his hometown fans or miss out on another potential four-figure purse. He decided to go through with the fight, but he knew that the third fight with Leto would probably be his last, although he kept this fact a secret from everyone but his family and trainer. Without telling them the extent of his health, Carroll told Benny Bear, who was looking after Charles Lucas' interests for the Melbourne fight, not to cable Ceferino Garcia any expenses until he had seen his doctor after the fight. Although he was lighter for the third fight with Leto than he was for the second, Carroll once again weighed in over the welterweight limit, coming in at 10st-8.5lb, 4.5lb more than Leto.

A crowd of 16,000 fans filled the Exhibition Grounds, a stadium normally used for cycling, to see Carroll's first international bout in his home city since he had thrashed Billy Townsend almost four years ago. Leto was determined to get the victory over Carroll and, despite the weight disadvantage, he pressed forward at the opening bell. Carroll was sharp with his jab early, but Leto defended well, and his aggression gave him the opening round. A right hand early in the second round was the American's only success as Carroll established his jab and repeatedly scored with the punch before punctuating it with flurries to the head and body on the inside. Carroll's jab continued to give him the edge in a slow third round, and he made Leto miss easily while outscoring him on the inside. At the end of the third round, Lou Viscusi complained to the referee, Bud Jennings, about Carroll's holding and hitting.

After eating a hard uppercut, Leto came back in the fourth round and drew Carroll into an exchange at close quarters that had the crowd on their feet. Carroll opened a cut on Leto's cheek early in the fifth round but Leto's aggression was keeping the rounds close, and after five rounds, the bout was still up in the air. The American won the sixth round easily, opening a nasty cut on the bridge of Carroll's nose that bled profusely. The blood seemed to spur Carroll on, and the Australian champion had his best round of the fight in the seventh, scoring with blazing combinations to the head and body on the inside. Leto welcomed the exchanges and landed a series of hard punches in the eighth but Carroll's superior speed and his jab, which continued to land with authority, gave him the round.

After Leto landed a hard right early in the ninth round, opening a cut over Carroll's left eye, Carroll evened up the round with a series of sharp counter punches before again outpunching the American on the inside. As the tenth round began, Carroll's face was covered in blood, and the pace of the fight was starting to take its toll as Leto out-muscled him in the clinches and scored with hard body rips. The fight was still in the balance going into the final two rounds, but Carroll showed that he had plenty in reserve and attacked at the start of the eleventh. The Australian champion repeatedly scored with his left hand, both at long-range and on the inside, and while Leto couldn't match him for speed, he stood and traded, looking for a punch to end matters. The final round was vintage Carroll; he jabbed and hooked Leto with the left while circling and tying him up on the inside. The crowd erupted when referee Bud Jennings crowned Carroll, the winner.

The bout was considered one of the best seen in Melbourne's boxing history and many, including Ambrose Palmer, who was ringside, thought that Leto deserved at least a draw. Leto was disappointed with the loss and repeated his wish for another crack at Carroll, but over fifteen rounds. Lou Viscusi also expressed these wishes, but only if Carroll made the welterweight limit. While the talk among the fans and managers after the fight revolved around how Carroll would fare with Garcia or Ross or whether Leto deserved a fourth chance with the top ranking welterweight, Carroll was about to drop a bombshell on Australian boxing.

The large crowd produced a gate of over £4,000, giving Carroll his second payday of £1,000 in as many fights. After the bout, Carroll's eyes and nose were stitched up by stadium medics before he saw his doctor three days later to have the cuts checked over. After another examination, his doctor reiterated that, despite being in perfect physical health, if he didn't stop boxing, he would suffer a nervous breakdown. After leaving the doctor's office, Carroll telegrammed Charles Lucas, informing him that he had retired from the ring. Reporters interviewed Carroll as he returned home from a wedding the following night, and Jack answered a few of their questions about his retirement.

> "I don't want to hang up my gloves just when the game is booming, but my doctor, who is also my friend, assures me that I would be heading for a nervous breakdown to continue fighting."[26]

Unlike many boxers, Carroll had managed to set himself up financially, with a house and a car and savings in the bank. Also, unlike many boxers, Carroll never had the urge to return to the ring, and he retired on top and never fought again. As he often did after many of his big fights, Carroll took his family for a holiday in the country at the end of his 14-year boxing career.

AFTERMATH

Jimmy Leto would never get his shot at Barney Ross. Ross chose to defend his welterweight title against the world featherweight champion, Henry Armstrong. 'Hammerin Hank' had continued on his undefeated streak since knocking out Alf Blatch, winning his first world title against Petey Sarron in October with a sixth-round knockout. Ross was no match for Armstrong, who was in the midst of one of the greatest runs in boxing history, and the welterweight champion suffered a frightful beating, but managed to last the 15 rounds, surrendering his title by wide points decision. It was Armstrong's 37th win in a row, and Ross was only the third man to see the final bell against him during this time. Armstrong added the lightweight title to his collection in August and would continue to hold the welterweight title until 1940.

Leto would continue boxing for another five years. He won three more fights in Australia before returning to America. Perhaps his most significant win came the following year, when he outpointed a Pittsburgh fighter named Charley Burley and, although he lost the rematch, Leto would be one of only nine men to defeat Burley

AFTERMATH

in his 15-year career. Leto also knocked out Cocoa Kid in 1940, which lead to a fight with Izzy Jannazzo, who narrowly outpointed him over fifteen rounds in 1941, ending Leto's days as a top contender.

Tod Morgan returned to Australia in 1936 where fought until 1942. He won the Australian lightweight title from Joe Hall in 1940 but lost it on a controversial decision to up and comer Vic Patrick the following year. Morgan, who had defeated Patrick earlier that year, fought Sydney southpaw two more times and Patrick would become the only Australian to ever score a stoppage win Morgan in their fourth fight. The former world junior lightweight champion returned to America after serving in the Australian army in Africa during World War II. He died in 1953 after a period of illness.

Barney Ross retired from the ring after losing his title to Armstrong, but his incredible life story didn't end with his boxing career. He enlisted in the US Marines at the outbreak of World War II where he was deployed to the Pacific. After his four-man platoon was ambushed on Guadalcanal Island, Ross fought off the attacking Japanese troops single-handedly until back-up arrived hours later. He was awarded the Purple Heart and Silver Star for his heroics, but contracted malaria and became addicted to the morphine that was used to treat him. He became an addict and blew his career earnings on heroin before he kicked the addiction. He lived a quieter life after his recovery but later appeared as a character witness for his childhood friend, Jack Ruby, after Ruby murdered Lee Harvey Oswald, who was under arrest for killing a police officer and was being questioned for his involvement in the assassination of United States President John F. Kennedy.

After the retirement of Jack Carroll, Charles Lucas praised Jack Carroll as Australia's greatest ever welterweight and said that he and O'Brien were always a pleasure to deal with. Olympia Sports Ltd continued to promote fights at Sydney Sports Ground, but

AFTERMATH

Lucas was not involved after the company fired him for allegedly importing fighters for Stadiums Ltd. Lucas unsuccessfully sued the company before he was eventually employed by Stadiums Ltd, using his contacts in America to import fighters to oppose Australia's top boxers. Lucas also continued to manage boxers and promote the occasional show until his death in 1944 after a period of illness.

Ambrose Palmer continued his comeback, knocking out Frank Rowsey at Sydney Sports Ground in February before outpointing Tom Chester at West Melbourne Stadium on 12 March. A £1,000 guarantee to face Deacon Leo Kelly on 29 March at Melbourne Exhibitions Grounds would prove too tempting to turn down, however, it would be Palmer's finest moment in the ring. In front of his hometown fans, Palmer whipped the man who had beaten him into retirement almost two years ago, dominating the fight from the opening bell until the end of the eighth round when Kelly could not continue.

Ron Richards became Australia's top drawcard after Carroll's retirement, and although he recorded some of his best wins after the seventh bout with Henneberry, his skills began to decline after the passing of his wife. Richards added the Australian light-heavyweight title to his collection in 1937, knocking out Melbourne fighter Jack Wilson in the first round and he headlined a Sydney Sports Ground show one week before Jack Carroll's final fight with Leto, outpointing the Puerto Rican Atilio Sabatino over ten rounds, earning £750 in the process. It was announced shortly afterwards that Richards and Palmer would battle for a fourth time on 12 April at Sydney Sports Ground for the Australian heavyweight title, presenting both an opportunity to earn a career-high pay-day as well as avenge three earlier losses to Palmer.

For the first twelve rounds of the fifteen round affair, Richards looked like he would finally get his victory over Palmer. In front of

AFTERMATH

10,000 fans, the Queenslander was too good for Palmer, despite being 9lb lighter, opening cuts above both of Palmer's eyes and bloodying his nose early in the contest. The fight grew more one-sided as the rounds progressed until Palmer turned the tide suddenly in the 13th round, dropping Richards with a left hook to the jaw. Richards beat the count, but Palmer was all over him, dropping him for an eight count with a right hand before knocking him out with another left hook. With the victory, Palmer had regained his Australian heavyweight title.

Palmer subsequently vacated the title to play Australian Rules Football again but would fight one more time, losing a points decision for the first time in his career to American Gus Lesnevich, who was ranked in the top ten in the world at light heavyweight. Palmer suffered another cut to his troublesome eyes, and the decision loss was enough to convince him to retire from the ring for good. He continued playing Australian Rules Football for Footscray, totalling 83 games for the club before retiring in 1943. In 1939, Palmer had his jaw fractured in three places during his first game of the season, an injury far more severe than any he suffered in the boxing ring. After his football career finished, Palmer began training young fighters in Melbourne, opening a gym shortly after the conclusion of World War II. He briefly trained future world title challenger Paul Ferreri early in his career, but his greatest charge was Johnny Famechon, who won the world featherweight title in 1969.

Richards bounced back from the loss to Palmer with eleven straight wins. Among those victories were two stoppage wins over Claude Nichol, which earned him the Australian heavyweight title that was vacated by Palmer, as well as a knockout win over Tommy Jones and points wins over Sabbatino and 'Alabama Kid.' His finest victory, however, would come over Gus Lesnevich at Sydney Sports Ground on 27 October, 1938. Richards dominated Lesnevich, who would hold the world light heavyweight title from 1941 until 1948, dropping him in the third round and swelling his left eye closed on his way to a wide points victory. This series of wins moved Richards into the top five in the world at both middleweight and light heavyweight. He continued his winning ways in 1939, winning six and losing only once to American Ossie Stewart, a loss he twice avenged.

Fred Henneberry's comeback from the loss of his middleweight title to Richards was slow but, after a loss and a draw to Sabatino in 1938, Henneberry scored one of the biggest wins of his career with a decision win over world ranked Ken Overlin. Overlin, who won the world middleweight title in 1940 by outpointing Ceferino Garcia, built up an early lead but Henneberry finished strongly, winning the final six rounds to take a narrow decision and re-establish himself as a contender in the middleweight division. His career would be on hold again temporarily, after a series of run-ins with Joe Wallis at Sydney Stadium lead to back to back disqualifications. Henneberry, however, would do something that neither Carroll, Palmer or Richards would ever do, and he spent the second half of 1939 touring the United Kingdom before fighting at Madison Square Garden in New York.

After beating the world ranked middleweight 'Ginger' Sadd in Liverpool, Henneberry travelled to New York where he headlined against Georgie Abrams. He had gone to New York chasing Ceferino Garcia and the world middleweight title and was promised an eliminator if he could get past Abrams in his New York debut. Despite dominating the fight, Henneberry was penalised three rounds for low blows, and the eight round contest was ruled a draw. After receiving a massive offer to meet Ron Richards back in Australia for the British Empire middleweight title, Henneberry returned home to face his old rival.

Richards and Henneberry would fight three more times in their careers, and Henneberry would lose all three by disqualification. The first of these fights, in front of 14,000 fans at Sydney Stadium

AFTERMATH

on 26 February, saw Henneberry build an early lead before Richards took over in the eighth round and hurt Henneberry with a right to the jaw in the ninth. After Richards punished him in the tenth round, Henneberry was disqualified for intentionally head-butting the Queenslander in the eleventh. Their next encounter, fought on 16 December, was more one-sided and after Henneberry's face had been severely cut and his eyes swollen shut, he repeatedly butted Richards in the twelfth round to earn his disqualification. They met for the last time on 27 November, 1941, and Henneberry, who had not fought since the ninth battle almost a year ago, was badly punished until repeated infringements culminating with a deliberate head-butt ended the ten bout series.

Both Henneberry and Richards shared another common opponent in the final years of their respective careers. Charles Lucas had imported a young middleweight from San Diego named Archie Moore, who debuted in Melbourne with a 4th round knockout over Jack McNamee. Richards would get the first crack at the newest American challenger, and almost ended the American's reputation in the first round of their Sydney Stadium bout when a counter right hand put Moore down for the count of nine. Moore rallied back, cutting Richards' right eye badly with his jab in the middle rounds and built a lead on points as the bout headed into the late rounds. After a one-sided tenth round, referee Joe Wallis halted the bout at the end of the round and crowned Moore the winner after examining Richards' eye.

After three more wins, including a fifth-round stoppage over Atilio Sabatino, Moore was matched with Henneberry. Henneberry built up an early lead by swarming the American, but Moore adjusted and began to slow Henneberry down with body blows as the rounds progressed. A left hook, either on the belt line or slightly below the belt, dropped Henneberry badly early in the seventh round and, after five minutes had passed, Henneberry was deemed unable to continue and Moore declared the winner. Henneberry was disgruntled by the ending of the fight and demanded a rematch, but it would have to wait.

Richards earned himself a rematch with Moore by outpointing the Olympic champion Carmen Barth in May and the second fight with Moore, which was held on 11 July, drew 12,000 fans at Sydney Stadium. The Australian champion was better prepared for Moore in the rematch, and he took the opening two rounds before Moore came back with his jab in the third and fourth, bloodying Richards' nose. Richards targeted Moore's body in an attempt to slow him down and then shook Moore with a right hand in the eighth round. Sensing Moore was tiring, Richards attacked in the next two rounds, but Moore weathered the storm and threw everything at the Australian champion in the final two rounds, winning both and doing enough to take a narrow decision on referee Wallis' card.

It was revealed after the fight that Moore had broken his hand in the second round, ending his tour of Australia. Moore returned to America, where he was a top ranking middleweight and light heavyweight for the next eleven years before he finally received a shot at the world light heavyweight title, which he won and subsequently held for the next ten years as well as twice challenged for the world heavyweight title. Both Richards and Henneberry had shown their class by giving one of the all-time greats a hard fight.

Henneberry's disqualifications against Richards and his loss to Moore were the last bouts of his career. With a disqualification result cancelling all bets on any boxing match in Australia at the time, and Henneberry also being a licensed bookmaker who was known to bet large amounts of money on himself, the disqualifications against Richards in their last three fights were likely a way for him to keep the money he otherwise would have lost if he had not fouled out. Ironically, Henneberry worked as a referee sporadically throughout the 1940s, 50s and 60s but later made his career as a publican. He married in 1943 and moved to the country town of

AFTERMATH

Dungog with his wife Molly, where he lived until his death at the age of 86. Although there was bad blood between Richards and Henneberry during their careers, Henneberry had "the greatest respect for Richards as a fighter," saying that Richards hit him harder than anyone he ever fought and that he "never gave him a thought" outside the ring, dismissing the hatred between the two men.[1]

Ron Richards continued fighting until 1945, but his days as a contender ended after the second loss to Archie Moore. He had begun to drink heavily, which diminished his abilities in the ring and went through the money he had made during his career. After earning an estimated £20,000 (around $90,000 US) in his career, Richards was broke one year after his final fight. He continued to drink heavily, which resulted in him being beaten senseless by patrons of the bars that he frequented who wanted nothing more than to say they had beaten a champion. Sydney Police officers sent him to the Palm Island Aboriginal Settlement after he was arrested for vagrancy in 1947 and he worked there as a carpenter for 17 years. Richards died in 1967 from a heart attack, and although there was an element of tragedy to his career, his crossover appeal to fans in Australian boxing paved the way for future generations of Aboriginal boxers such as the Sands brothers, Elley Bennett, Lionel Rose, Hector Thompson and Tony Mundine.

Jack Carroll returned to work in the abattoirs after his retirement from the ring. While he spent much of his time with his children, his youngest son, Donald, was involved in an accident where he was hit by a truck in 1940. After being rushed to the hospital where he had his spleen removed, doctors at the children's hospital in Melbourne saved his life. Jack frequently helped out with fundraisers for the Children's Hospital for the rest of his life:

> "I am one of the thousands of fathers who owe the lives of their children to the grand people of the Children's Hospital, and, if I

can help make the general public realise what a worthy institution it is, it will repay in some small way the debt that I owe to them."[2]

Carroll's involvement in the sport continued as he refereed bouts until 1945 but gave that away to focus on training and managing boxers after Bill O'Brien passed away in 1946 at the age of 65. While Carroll's talents as a trainer did not match his abilities as a boxer, Carroll remained active as a trainer and manager well into the 1950s and his involvement in the sport dwindled coincidentally as his children reached adulthood. He died suddenly in 1976 at the age of 70 from heart disease.

The popularity of Dave Sands and Vic Patrick in the 1940s and the success of Jimmy Carruthers, who became Australia's first universally recognised world champion in 1952, led to many forgetting Carroll's achievements and his place among Australia's greatest boxers is often disregarded. While Carroll's achievements in the ring are often overlooked, he achieved a level of financial security that few boxers do. He continued to live at the house at Moonee Ponds that he bought with the money he made from the van Klaveren fights.

At a time when the welterweight division, one of the historically competitive divisions in the rich history of boxing, was arguably at its peak, Carroll was a highly ranked contender for many years. On top of this, Carroll was unmatched as a welterweight in Australia for more than ten years and also defeated world-rated men in the middleweight division. Nat Fleischer, founder and editor of the American boxing publication 'Ring Magazine' believed, after seeing footage of Carroll, that he would have defeated Barney Ross had he been given a chance.

ACKNOWLEDGEMENTS

This book would not have been possible without the available resources of the National Library of Australia. Also thanks to my friends James Kernodle, for being the first person to read through my work and offer some much-needed feedback, and Tony Hood, whose knowledge of Australian boxing has helped me fill in some of the other missing pieces over the years.

The release of this book would not have been possible without the help of Harry Otty. I feel like I had to learn an entirely new language in my attempts to publish the book and Harry helped me make sense of everything that needed to be done and his advice was invaluable. On top of this, Harry helped me out with everything I wasn't able to do myself, such as the layout of the book and I am forever indebted for your help in helping me "be a part of boxing history."

Last, but definitely not least, my wife Amiee, who has been by my side for the last few years while I have battled through this project. From refilling my coffee during my writing binges to putting up with me when I had computer trouble, none of this would have been possible without your love and patience.

BIBLIOGRAPHY

Books

Lords of the Ring: A History of Prize Fighting in Australia; Peter Corris (1980) Cassell Australia Limited

Fighters by Trade; Robert Drane (2008) ABC Books

Unforgivable Blackness: The Rise and Fall of Jack Johnson; Geoffrey C. Ward

Newspapers

The Age (Melbourne)

Argus (Melbourne)

Arrow (Sydney)

The Australian Worker (Sydney)

Brisbane Courier

Daily News (Perth)

BIBLIOGRAPHY

Daily Pictorial (Sydney)

Daily Standard (Brisbane)

The Daily Telegraph (Sydney)

Evening News (Sydney)

Evening News (Rockhampton)

The Herald (Melbourne)

The Labor Daily (Sydney)

The Mercury (Hobart)

Referee (Sydney)

Sporting Globe (Melbourne)

The Sun (Sydney)

Sunday Mail (Brisbane)

Sunday Times (Sydney)

The Sydney Morning Herald

Sydney Sportsman

The Telegraph (Brisbane)

Townsville Bulletin

Truth (Sydney)

Truth (Brisbane)

Worker (Brisbane)

Barrier Miner (Broken Hill)

Geelong Advertiser

BIBLIOGRAPHY

Morning Bulletin (Rockhampton)

National Advocate (Bathurst)

The Northern Herald (Cairns)

Northern Miner (Queensland)

Queensland Times (Ipswich)

Evening Post (New Zealand)

Press (New Zealand)

New Zealand Truth (New Zealand)

New Zealand Herald (New Zealand)

Photographs

p7- Bill O'Brien, trainer of Jack Carroll (National Library of Australia, nla.obj-148582450)

p20- Jack Carroll (National Library of Australia, nla.obj-148582356)"

p40- Ambrose Palmer (National Library of Australia, nla.obj-162673690)

p62- Jack Haines (left) poses with Ambrose Palmer (right) (National Library of Australia, nla.obj-148564454)

p83- Wally Hancock (National Library of Australia, nla.obj-148607703)

p128- Young Stribling (1929 Agency Maurice - Bibliotheque de France. Retrieved from Wikimedia.org)

p140- Fred Henneberry and Jack Carroll (National Library of Australia, nla.obj-148562750)

p144- Ron Richards (National Library of Australia, nla.obj-148606605)

p189- Tod Morgan, ex-world junior lightweight champion (National Library of Australia, nla.obj-148612108)

BIBLIOGRAPHY

p241- *Jack Carroll and Jack Portney before their April 1935 bout (National Library of Australia, nla.obj-148615407)*

p259- *Jack Carroll and Bep van Klaveren posing for an advertisement in 1935 (National Library of Australia, nla.obj-148524292)*

p280- *Ambrose Palmer (left) with Deacon Leo Kelly (right) (National Library of Australia, nla.obj-148563609)*

P302- *Barney Ross - Lightweight Champion (1934 Press Wire Photo-Acme. Retrieved from Wikimedia.org)*

p303- *Jimmy Leto - undated, autographed photo (from collection of Harry Otty)*

p307- *Jimmy Leto (2nd from left) with manager Lou Viscusi (far right) and sparring partner Tommy Jones (far left) (National Library of Australia, nla.obj-148564756)*

P322- *Jack Carroll versus Jimmy Leto (press photo - The Sun, Elizabeth St., Sydney - from collection of Harry Otty)*

Television

That's Boxing: The Greatest Hits of Australian Boxing (1996)

Websites

www.boxrec.com

www.cyberboxingzone.com

www.ancestory.com

NOTES

INTRODUCTION

1. Referee (Sydney) Thursday 13 February 1936

1. EARLY CAREER

1. Sporting Globe (Melbourne) Saturday 6 June 1936
2. Sporting Globe (Melbourne) Saturday 6,13 June 1936
3. Referee (Sydney) Wednesday 28 March 1923
4. Sporting Globe (Melbourne) May 23 1923
5. Sporting Globe (Melbourne) Saturday 13 June 1936
6. Referee Wednesday 19 December 1923
7. Argus (Melbourne) Thursday 6 November 1924
8. Sporting Globe (Melbourne) Wednesday 19 November 1924
9. Sporting Globe (Melbourne) Wednesday 13 May 1925
10. The Age (Melbourne) Thursday 4 March 1926
11. Sporting Globe (Melbourne) Wednesday 11 April 1928
12. The Argus (Melbourne) Tuesday 1 February 1927
13. Sporting Globe (Melbourne) Wednesday 2 March 1927

2. SYDNEY

1. Sporting Globe (Melbourne) Wednesday 11 May 1927
2. Sporting Globe (Melbourne) Saturday 10 September 1927
3. The Telegraph (Brisbane) Saturday 3 December 1927

3. AUSTRALIAN CHAMPION

1. Sporting Globe (Melbourne) Wednesday 9 May 1928
2. Sporting Globe (Melbourne) Saturday 4 August 1934
3. Evening Post (New Zealand) Tuesday 24 July 1928
4. Sunday Times (Sydney) Sunday 21 October 1928
5. Sporting Globe (Melbourne) Wednesday 23 January 1929
6. Sporting Glove (Melbourne) Wednesday 22 May 1929

NOTES

4. AMBROSE PALMER

1. Daily News (Perth) Monday 1 July 1929
2. Sporting Globe (Melbourne) Wednesday 28 August 1929

5. JACK HAINES

1. Sporting Globe (Melbourne) Wednesday 16 May 1928
2. Sydney Sportsman Tuesday 15 May 1928
3. Referee (Sydney) Wednesday 12 December 1928
4. Referee (Sydney) Wednesday 17 July 1929
5. Referee (Sydney) Wednesday 23 October 1929
6. Arrow (Sydney) Friday 15 November 1929
7. Referee (Sydney) Wednesday 20 November 1929
8. Sydney Sportsman Tuesday 3 December 1929
9. Referee (Sydney) Wednesday 11 December 1929
10. Brisbane Courier Saturday 23 November 1929
11. Brisbane Courier Saturday 18 January 1930
12. Referee (Sydney) Wednesday 22 January 1930
13. Brisbane Courier Wednesday 22 January 1930
14. Evening News (Sydney) Saturday 25 January 1930
15. Referee (Sydney) Wdnesday 19 January 1930
16. The Australian Worker (Sydney) Wednesday 18 June 1930
17. Sun (Sydney) Sunday 10 August 1930

6. JACK HAINES VS AMBROSE PALMER

1. Evening News (Sydney) Saturday 4 October 1930
2. Sporting Globe (Melbourne) Wednesday 8 October 1930
3. Labor Daily (Sydney) Saturday 1 November 1930
4. Labor Daily (Sydney) Monday 3 November 1930
5. Truth (Sydney) Sunday 2 November 1930
6. Sydney Sportsman Tuesday 4 November 1930

7. THE TITLE CLAIMANTS

1. Sydney Sportsman Tuesday 6 August 1929
2. The Telegraph (Brisbane) Saturday 27 July 1929
3. Sporting Globe (Melbourne) Wednesday 14 August 1929
4. Sporting Globe (Melbourne) Wednesday 14 August 1929
5. Sydney Sportsman Tuesday 18 February 1930

NOTES

6. Daily Pictorial (Sydney) Wednesday 19 February 1930
7. The Herald (Melbourne) Thursday 19 June 1930
8. Daily Standard (Brisbane) Monday 11 August 1930
9. Telegraph (Brisbane) Thursday 14 August 1930
10. Truth (Brisbane) Sunday 24 August 1930
11. Daily Pictorial (Sydney) Saturday 30 August 1930
12. Labor Daily (Sydney) Monday 1 September 1930
13. Referee (Sydney) Wednesday 17 September 1930
14. Sporting Globe (Melbourne) Wednesday 25 February 1931
15. The Sun (Sydney) Sunday 26 April 1931
16. Referee (Sydney) Wednesday May 6 1931

8. FRED HENNEBERRY

1. Sydney Sportsman Tuesday 1 March 1931
2. Sydney Sportsman, Tuesday 12 May 1931
3. Referee (Sydney) Wednesday 3 June 1931
4. The Maitland Mercury Saturday 30 May 1931
5. Referee (Sydney) Wednesday 15 July 1931
6. Sydney Sportsman Tuesday 28 July 1931

9. AMBROSE PALMER VS FRED HENNEBERRY

1. The Telegraph (Brisbane) Saturday 11 July 1931
2. The Daily Telegraph (Sydney) Monday 27 July 1931
3. Daily Standard (Brisbane) Thursday 13 August 1931
4. The Labor Daily (Sydney) Tuesday 18 August 1931
5. Daily Standard (Brisbane) Saturday 22 August 1931
6. The Daily Telegraph (Sydney) Friday 28 August 1931
7. Referee (Sydney) Wednesday 30 September 1931
8. Referee (Sydney) Wednesday 7 October 1931
9. The Sydney Sportsman Tuesday 6 October 1931

10. JACK CARROLL VS FRED HENNEBERRY

1. Sydney Sportsman Tuesday 22 December 1931
2. Daily Telegraph (Sydney) Monday 29 February 1932
3. Referee (Sydney) Wednesday March 2 1932
4. Sporting Globe (Melbourne) Wednesday March 2 1932

NOTES

11. AMBROSE PALMER VS FRED HENNEBERRY II

1. Referee (Sydney) Wednesday 9 December 1931
2. Daily Standard (Brisbane) Saturday 6 February 1932
3. The Australian Worker Wednesday March 9 1932
4. Truth (Sydney) Sunday 20 March 1932

12. AMBROSE PALMER VS YOUNG STRIBLING

1. Referee (Sydney) Wednesday 15 June 1932
2. Referee (Sydney) Wednesday 22 June 1932.
3. National Advocate (Bathurst) Wednesday 22 June 1932
4. Referee (Sydney) Wednesday 29 June 1932
5. Sydney Sportsman Saturday 9 July 1932

13. FRED HENNEBERRY VS JACK CARROLL II

1. Sun (Sydney) Tuesday 10 May 1932
2. Sydney Morning Herald Thursday 12 May 1932
3. Arrow (Sydney) Friday 12 August 1932
4. Brisbane Courier Tuesday 10 January 1933

14. RON RICHARDS

1. Queensland Times (Ipswich), Saturday 5 May 1928
2. Referee (Sydney) Wednesday 22 June 1932
3. The Queensland Times Thursday 30 June 1932
4. The Brisbane Courier Thursday 7 July 1932
5. The Brisbane Courier Friday 12 August 1932
6. The Brisbane Courier Friday 19 August 1932
7. The Brisbane Courier Monday 26 September 1932
8. Referee (Sydney) Wednesday 2 November 1932
9. Daily Standard (Brisbane) Wednesday 9 November 1932
10. Referee (Sydney) Wednesday 26 October 1932
11. Referee (Sydney) Wednesday 7 December 1932

15. FRED HENNEBERRY VS RON RICHARDS

1. Referee (Sydney) Wednesday 12 October 1932
2. Referee (Sydney) Wednesday 18 January 1933

NOTES

3. Telegraph (Brisbane) Tuesday 17 January 1933
4. Sydney Sportsman Saturday 21 January 1933
5. Referee (Sydney) Wednesday 7 September 1932
6. Referee (Sydney) Wednesday 23 November 1932
7. Australian Worker (Sydney) Wednesday 15 March 1933
8. The Sun (Sydney) Monday 20 March 1933
9. Truth (Brisbane) Sunday 3 August 1937
10. Daily Standard (Brisbane) Wednesday 3 May 1933
11. Sydney Sportsman Saturday 3 June 1933
12. Smith's Weekly (Sydney) Saturday 10 June 1933

16. JACK CARROLL VS FRED HENNEBERRY III

1. The Australian Worker (Sydney) Wednesday 28 September 1932
2. Sydney Morning Herald Saturday 1st October 1932
3. Sydney Sportsman Saturday 20 May 1933
4. The Australian Worker (Sydney) Wednesday 20 September 1933
5. Referee (Sydney) Thursday 21 September 1933
6. Labor Daily (Sydney) Thursday 21 September 1933

17. THE AMERICAN INVASION

1. Daily Telegraph (Sydney) Tuesday 5 September 1933
2. Referee (Sydney) Thursday 12 October 1933
3. Sydney Morning Herald Thursday 10 August 1933
4. Referee (Sydney) Thursday 21 September 1933
5. Referee (Sydney) Thursday 30 November 1933
6. Sydney Sportsman Saturday 2 December 1933
7. New Call (Perth) Thursday 4 January 1934
8. Daily Telegraph (Sydney) Wednesday 10 January 1934
9. Referee (Sydney) Thursday 1 February
10. Labor Daily (Sydney) Thursday 4 January 1934
11. Labor Daily (Sydney) Wednesday 14 March 1934
12. Referee (Sydney) Thursday 15 March 1934
13. Referee (Sydney) Thursday 26 April 1934

18. JACK CARROLL VS RON RICHARDS

1. Daily Standard (Brisbane) Tuesday 30 January 1934
2. Courier-Mail (Brisbane) Tuesday 8 May 1934
3. Daily Mercury (Mackay) Tuesday 8 May 1934
4. The Courier Mail (Brisbane) Tuesday 29 May 1934

NOTES

5. Sydney Sportsman Saturday 21 July 1934
6. Courier Mail (Brisbane) Friday 7 December 1934

19. CLIMBING THE WORLD RANKINGS

1. Labor Daily (Sydney) Tuesday 28 April 1934
2. Referee (Sydney) Thursday 27 September 1934
3. Referee (Sydney) Thursday 4 October 1934
4. Sydney Sportsman Saturday 24 November 1934
5. Sydney Sportsman Saturday 1 December 1934
6. Daily Telegraph (Sydney) Tuesday 5 February 1935
7. Daily Telegraph (Sydney) Wednesday 6 February 1935
8. Sydney Sportsman Saturday 9 March 1935
9. Sporting Globe (Melbourne) Wednesday 6 March 1935
10. Argus (Melbourne) Friday 8 March 1935
11. Daily Telegraph (Sydney) Wednesday 13 March 1935
12. Daily Telegraph (Sydney) Thursday 14 March 1935
13. Daily Telegraph (Sydney) Wednesday 3 April 1935
14. Referee (Sydney) Thursday 11 April 1935
15. Sporting Globe (Melbourne) Wednesday 17 April 1935
16. Daily Telegraph (Sydney) Tuesday 18 June 1935
17. Sydney Morning Herald Tuesday 18 June 1935
18. Labor Daily (Sydney) Tuesday 18 June 1935
19. Referee (Sydney) Thursday 20 June 1935
20. Labor Daily (Sydney) Tuesday 9 July 1935
21. The Age (Melbourne) Wednesday 176 July 1935
22. Labor Daily (Sydney) Wednesday 11 September 1935
23. Daily Telegraph (Sydney) Tuesday 17 September 1935
24. Labor Daily (Sydney) Wednesday 18 September 1935

20. JACK CARROLL VS BEP VAN KLAVEREN

1. Evening Post (Los Angeles) Saturday 8 December 1934
2. Sydney Sportsman Saturday 2 November 1935
3. The Sun (Sydney) Sunday 6 October 1935
4. Sun (Sydney) Sunday 24 November 1935
5. Argus (Melbourne) Friday 27 December 1927
6. Sporting Globe (Melbourne) Wednesday 1 January 1936
7. Sporting Globe (Melbourne) Wednesday 1 January 1936
8. Sporting Globe (Melbourne) Saturday 11 January 1936
9. Sporting Globe (Melbourne) Saturday 8 February 1936
10. The Herald (Melbourne) Friday 7 February 1936
11. Referee(Sydney) Thursday 12 March 1936
12. Referee (Sydney) Thursday 21 May 1936

13. Sporting Globe (Melbourne) Wednesday 23 September 1936

21. FRED HENNEBERRY VS RON RICHARDS VII

1. Referee (Sydney) Thursday 14 March 1935
2. Daily Telegraph (Sydney) Tuesday 25 June 1935
3. Referee (Sydney) Thursday 1 August 1935
4. Daily Telegraph (Sydney) Monday 29 July 1935
5. Labor Daily (Sydney) Tuesday 3 March 1936
6. The Argus (Melbourne) Friday 17 April 1936
7. Referee (Sydney) Thursday 20 August 1936
8. Sydney Sportsman Saturday 10 October 1936
9. Labor Daily (Sydney) Thursday 12 November 1936
10. Referee (Sydney) Thursday 12 November 1936
11. Referee (Sydney) Thursday 19 November 1936
12. Truth (Sydney) Sunday 3 August 1947
13. Referee (Sydney) Thursday 24 December 1936
14. Daily Telegraph (Sydney) Tuesday 22 December 1936
15. Sydney Sportsman Saturday 26 December 1936

22. #1 CONTENDER

1. Referee (Sydney) Thursday 28 January 1937
2. Labor Daily (Sydney) Tuesday 23 March 1937
3. Sporting Globe (Melbourne) Wednesday 31 March 1937
4. Daily Telegraph (Sydney) Wednesday 31 March 1937
5. Daily Telegraph (Sydney) Wednesday 31 March 1937
6. Sydney Sportsman Thursday 1 April 1937
7. The Daily Telegraph (Sydney) Thursday 1 April 1937
8. Sporting Globe (Melbourne) Wednesday 28 April 1937
9. Referee (Sydney) Thursday 20 May 1937
10. Sydney Morning Herald Monday 12 July 1937
11. The Sun (Sydney) Thursday 15 July 1937
12. The Herald (Melbourne) Tuesday 26 October 1937
13. Referee (Sydney) Thursday 11 November 1937
14. Referee (Sydney) Thursday 2 December 1937
15. Daily Telegraph (Sydney) Wednesday 24 November 1937
16. Daily Telegraph (Sydney) Friday 26 November 1937
17. Sporting Globe (Melbourne) Wednesday 15 December 1937
18. Labor Daily (Sydney) Saturday 18 December 1937
19. Referee (Sydney) Thursday 23 December 1937
20. Daily Telegraph (Sydney) Thursday 23 December 1937
21. Referee (Sydney) Thursday 13 January 1938
22. Daily Telegraph (Sydney) Thursday 13 January 1938

NOTES

23. Daily Telegraph (Sydney) Wednesday 19 January 1938
24. Referee (Sydney) Thursday 20 January 1938
25. The Herald (Melbourne) Tuesday 8 February 1938
26. The Sun (Sydney) Sunday 27 February 1938

AFTERMATH

1. Truth (Brisbane) Sunday 30 April 1950
2. Sporting Globe (Melbourne) Saturday 28 March 1942

www.ingramcontent.com/pod-product-compliance
Lightning Source LLC
Chambersburg PA
CBHW032025290426
44110CB00012B/674